50

REAL ESTATE INVESTING CALCULATIONS

CASH FLOW, IRR, VALUE, PROFIT, EQUITY, INCOME, ROI, DEPRECIATION, AND MORE

WITH LINKS TO THE 24 BEST CALCULATORS

MICHAEL LANTRIP

ATTORNEY | ACCOUNTANT | INVESTOR

THE AUTHOR

Michael Lantrip, Attorney at Law, is licensed to practice law in Texas, North Carolina, Virginia, and the District of Columbia.

He has a B.B.A. in Finance from the University of Houston School of Business, and he has a Juris Doctor (J.D.) in Law from the University of Texas School of Law.

He is admitted to practice in all Courts in Texas, North Carolina, Virginia, and the District of Columbia, as well as the U.S. Tax Court, the U.S. Federal District Court, Eastern District of Texas, and the D.C. Court of Appeals.

He practices in the fields of Tax Law, Real Estate Law, Corporate and Business Law, and Wills, Trusts and Estates.

As a Criminal Defense Attorney, he has taken three cases to the Texas Court of Criminal Appeals, winning two of them.

As a County Attorney, he handled almost 2,000 misdemeanor criminal cases.

Formerly a Tax Examiner for the IRS, and a Tax Accountant for a Big 8 Accounting Firm, he has also been a Newspaper Reporter, Radio Announcer,

Radio News Director, Television Reporter and Anchorman, Television Executive News Producer, and Military Intelligence Analyst.

In addition to 35 years of practicing law, he built and operated his own Title Insurance Company, and has been an Approved Title Attorney for seven national Title Insurance Underwriters.

He has handled more than 2,000 real estate closings.

Prior to his law career, he was a Radio Announcer at WQTE in Detroit during the "Motown" era, and he was a DJ at KIKK in Houston when it was named "Country Music Station of the Year" by Billboard Magazine.

He has written and produced mjore than 1,000 half-hour Television Newscasts.

He has written more than 700 stories as a daily Newspaper Reporter.

He has logged over 8,000 hours on the radio.

His Amazon Author Page is:

amazon.com/Michael-Lantrip/e/B01N2ZRGUY

His personal website is MichaelLantrip.com.

INTRODUCTION

This book is not a promise that you will make money investing in real estate, nor is it an explanation of how to do it.

There are other books for that.

This book is a presentation of all of the Calculations that you must understand in order to realize the dynamics that are controlling Real Estate Investing, and controlling whether or not you will make a profit.

That idea might not get you excited right now.

But when you use one of these Calculations to find another $30,000 of profit in the deal, I promise you will get excited.

These Calculations are essentially the Set Of Rules in the world of Real Estate Investing.

And whether or not you know the Calculations, they are still silently at work behind the scenes determining whether you will be profitable and successful.

I have selected 50 of them, and I will provide a separate Section for each Calculation. I believe that about 15 of them you have not seen before.

Many of them that you *have* seen elsewhere are usually over-explained to the point of confusion, and some explanations are just incorrect.

Most of the Calculations are very simple to do. Some are complex. A few are complicated.

But if you can add, subtract, multiply and divide, you can do these Calculations.

I will also provide free online Calculators.

The important thing is to understand:

* the origin of the numbers you are putting into the Calculation, and

* the meaning of the number produced by the Calculation.

I will explain both in detail.

You do not have to read the book start to finish. You can read the Sections in any order that is convenient for you.

As you gain an understanding of the Real Estate Investing Calculations, it will be like looking behind the walls of a Model Home and seeing how the model is built.

You will see the foundation, framing, wiring, plumbing, and everything else that causes Real

Estate Investing to behave the way it does, and how all of the parts are related and connected.

You will become the Master Builder of your investment portfolio.

I will provide you with links to a total of 24 Free Calculators that I think you will find useful for doing quick Calculations.

And then when you understand them better, I think you will find them even more useful for trying other combinations to see how you might find a better ratio, or a different path.

I will also show you how to create your own Calculations that will answer questions for your personal investment strategy that are not answered by the standard Calculations.

You will come to realize that Real Estate Investing Calculations are the way that you manage each of the elements of your investments.

And you will see that in order to manage them, you must first measure them.

Good Luck!

COPYRIGHT PAGE

specifically disclaim any liability resulting from the use or application of the information contained in this book, and the information is not intended to serve as legal, tax, accounting, or other financial advice related to individual situations.

DISCLAIMER

Although I am a lawyer, I am not your lawyer. I would be honored if I were, but I am not.

Reading this book does not create an attorney-client relationship between us. This book should not be used as a substitute for the advice of a competent attorney admitted or authorized to practice law in your jurisdiction.

CONTENTS

1. APPRECIATION

2. BALANCE SHEET

3. BASIS

4. BASIS: ADJUSTED

5. BASIS: CARRYOVER

6. BASIS: STEPPED-UP

7. BASIS: TRANSFERRED

8. CAPITAL EXPENDITURES

9. CAPITAL GAINS

10. CAPITALIZATION RATE

11. CASH FLOW

12. CASH FLOW: DISCOUNTED

13. DEBT SERVICE RATIO

14. DEPRECIATION

15. DEPRECIATION: ACCELERATED

16. DEPRECIATION: COMMERCIAL PROPERTY

17. DEPRECIATION: DOUBLE DECLINING BALANCE

18. DEPRECIATION: RESIDENTIAL REAL ESTATE

19. DEPRECIATION: SECTION 1245 PROPERTY

20. DEPRECIATION: SECTION 1250 PROPERTY

21. DEPRECIATION: STRAIGHT LINE

22. DEPRECIATION: 150% DECLINING BALANCE

23. DEPRECIATION RECAPTURE

24. EQUITY

25. FAIR MARKET VALUE

26. FUTURE VALUE

27. INCOME STATEMENT

28. INCOME: BREAK-EVEN RATIO

29. INCOME: GROSS OPERATING

30. INCOME: GROSS POTENTIAL

31. INCOME: GROSS RENTAL MULTIPLIER

32. INCOME: NET INCOME MULTIPLIER

33. INCOME: NET OPERATING

34. INTEREST: COMPOUND

35. INTEREST: SIMPLE

36. LATE FEES

37. OPERATING EXPENSES

38. OPERATING EXPENSE RATIO

39. PAYBACK PERIOD

40. PRESENT VALUE

41. PROFIT

42. RETURN: INTERNAL RATE OF RETURN

43. RETURN ON CASH

44. RETURN ON EQUITY

45. RETURN ON INVESTMENT

46. RULE OF 72, 69 AND 113

47. TIME VALUE OF MONEY

48. TRUE PURCHASE PRICE

49. VACANCY AND CREDIT LOSS

50. VALUE

SECTION 1.

APPRECIATION

"Appreciation" is the term applied to the increase in value of your investment property.

Of course, if you've owned the investment property for a period of time, you can determine the increase in value by subtracting the Original Value from the Present Value.

But you will usually be more interested in the appreciation that you expect to take place in the future, the "what if."

To determine the *percentage* of Appreciation, you divide the Appreciation by the Original Value.

**A = (PV – OV) ÷ OV, WHERE
A IS THE APPRECIATION PERCENTAGE,
PV IS THE PRESENT VALUE, AND
OV IS THE ORIGINAL VALUE**

For Example, you bought a Fourplex for $400,000 a year ago and now you have determined by using the market Capitalization Rate for this type of property that it now has a value of $426,800.

$$A = (PV - OV) \div OV$$

$$A = (426{,}800 - 400{,}000) \div 400{,}000$$

$$A = 26{,}800 \div 400{,}000$$

$$A = 6.7$$

The investment property has appreciated in value 6.7% in one year.

FUTURE VALUE

But we are usually interested in determining the Appreciation that will occur in investment property that we are considering purchasing.

For this, we use the Future Value Calculation.

**FV = PV x (1+ I), WHERE
FV IS THE FUTURE VALUE,
PV IS THE PRESENT VALUE,
1 IS 1, AND
I IS THE PERCENTAGE INCREASE FACTOR.**

For Example, we buy a $400,000 Fourplex and expect it to increase in value 6.7% each year, or we want to know what will happen if it does increase 6.7% in value each year.

FV = PV x (1 + I)

FV = 400,000 x (1 + .067)

FV = 400,000 x 1.067

FV = 426,800

At the end of Year 1, your Fourplex will have appreciated in value to $426,800.

Now, for the Calculation of the appreciation for the second and subsequent years, you use a new PV figure for the ending of the prior year, which is the same as the beginning of the year of calculation.

In this Example for the second year we would use a PV of $426,800 because that is what it was at the end of the first year.

FV = PV x (1 + I)

FV = 426,800 x 1.067

FV = 455,396

At the end of your second year of ownership, your Fourplex will have appreciated to a value of $455,396.

Alternatively, you could multiply 1.067 times 1.067 and get 1.1385, and multiply 1.1385 times 400,000 and get the same number, 455,396.

See SECTION 26. FUTURE VALUE (P. 109) for more information, and a Free Calculator to use:

https://www.calculatorsoup.com/calculators/ financial/future-value-calculator-basic.php

EQUITY

The above Calculation will serve you well if you pay cash for the investment property, but few of us do. We usually have debt on the property.

If you have debt on the property, then what you actually have that is appreciating in value is more than just the Fair Market Value (FMV) of the property, although that is going up.

What you have that is actually appreciating in value is your Equity in the property.

There is a Calculation for Equity.

E = FMV – MPO – L – OD, WHERE
E IS YOUR EQUITY IN THE PROPERTY,
FMV IS THE FAIR MARKET VALUE OF THE PROPERTY,
MPO IS THE MORTGAGE PAYOFF AMOUNT,
L IS LIENS ON THE PROPERTY, AND
OD IS OTHER DEBTS ON THE PROPERTY

A month after you purchase the property, the FMV will already have gone up, because that is what property does, and the Mortgage Payoff amount (MPO) will go down, because each of your mortgage payments will be a combination of interest and reduction of principal. The reduction of principal amount will reduce your MPO. The reduction will be small at the beginning, and huge in the final years of the mortgage.

To Calculate your probable Equity in the future, you would use the Future Value Calculation to determine the new amount of the FMV, and then use your Amortization Schedule for you mortgage payments that you received from your lender to get your Mortgage Payoff amount for the specific date you are calculating for.

Then plug the two numbers into the above Equity Calculation to determine your Equity at any point.

For more information, see SECTION 24. EQUITY.

VALUE AND CAPITALIZATION RATE

In using all of these Calculations, it is very important that you have an accurate number to use for the "value" factor in the Calculations. Without a correct FMV input, your output will not be as correct as it shoud be.

The best number to use is the actual selling price of comparable properties in your market.

But if you do not know what these are, or do not have enough comparable sales, or your property is unique and there are no comps, then you can still Calculate a figure for Value.

See SECTION 50. VALUE (P. 205).

That Calculation will require you to also Calculate a Capitalization Rate, referred to as the Cap Rate.

See SECTION 10. CAPITALIZATION RATE (P. 40).

SECTION 2.

BALANCE SHEET

A Balance Sheet is normally prepared for a company, showing the company Assets, the company Liabilities, and the company Net Worth.

It can also be done for a business activity that is part of everything else, so that you can track it to see if it is viable as a separate business.

And it can also be done for a single real estate project, or a real estate investment.

You can even do it for your own personal finances.

A Balance Sheet is a snapshot of the specific entity or activity at a specific point in time, and covering everything up to that time.

The next day or the next month after it is prepared, the numbers will be, or could be, different.

Therefore, the most important item on your Balance Sheet is the date that you put at the top.

The time chosen is usually the end of the year, or the end of one of the quarters.

This is what a Balance Sheet looks like:

ABC COMPANY

Anytown, USA

March 31, 2018

ASSETS

CURRENT ASSETS

Cash	9,000	
Accounts Receivable	3,140	
Tax Deposits	8,000	
Prepaid Expenses	1,270	
TOTAL		21,410

LONG-TERM ASSETS

Land		45,000
Building	360,000	
Accum. Dep.	(71,280)	
Book Value		288,720
Fix. & Equip.	38,000	
Accum. Dep.	(9,441)	
Book Value		28,559
TOTAL		362,279

OTHER ASSETS

Security Deposits	1,400	
Notes Receivable	1,160	

TOTAL	2,560

TOTAL ASSETS	386,249

LIABILITIES

CURRENT LIABILITIES

Accounts Payable	7,250	
Credit Card	2,500	
Sales Taxes Accrued	1,450	
TOTAL		11,200

LONG-TERM LIABILITIES

Mortgages	272,544	
Notes Payable	1,750	
TOTAL		274,294

TOTAL LIABILITIES	285,494

NET WORTH	100,755

Often, an Income Statement is prepared at the same time to accompany the Balance Sheet.

See SECTION 27. INCOME STATEMENT (P. 113).

The Calculation for a Balance Sheet is:

A = L + N, OR (MORE HELPFULLY)
N = A − L, WHERE
N IS NET WORTH,
A IS TOTAL ASSETS, AND
L IS TOTAL LIABILITIES

Look at the Balance Sheet above and you will see how these elements are related to each other.

Net Worth is sometimes also called "Equity," but this is not correct.

The Calculation for Equity is:

E = FMV − MPO − L − OD, WHERE
E IS YOUR EQUITY IN THE PROPERTY,
FMV IS THE FAIR MARKET VALUE OF THE PROPERTY,
MPO IS THE TOTAL AMOUNT OF YOUR MORTGAGE PAYOFF,
L IS THE LIENS ON THE PROPERTY, AND
OD IS OTHER DEBT ON THE PROPERTY

Notice that the Value of the property in the Equity Calculation is the Fair Market Value (FMV). That is the amount that the property will sell for on the open market today.

In the Balance Sheet, the FMV is not used. The Value that is used on the Balance Sheet to determine your Net Worth is the Depreciated Book Value. That number is much lower, and will not tell you what your Equity is.

The terms "Equity" or "Owner's Equity" that are often used in reference to a Balance Sheet should be avoided in favor of using the term "Net Worth."

However, like "Equity," the term "Net Worth" also does not accurately describe what it is.

Net Worth is just the difference between the Book Value of the company assets, and the total amount of your Liabilities. It's just a number. It does not tell you the total value of the company.

SECTION 3.

BASIS

If you own real estate, you have a "Basis" in that property.

There are three ways that your Basis (B) in property comes into existence.

1.) You bought the property.

2.) You received the property as a gift, or

3.) You inherited the property.

PURCHASED PROPERTY

If you bought the property, your Basis is what you paid for the property.

If you've made any capital improvements to the property, this amount is added to your Basis, unless you identify the improvements separately and depreciate them on your Depreciation Schedule.

Internal Revenue Code (IRC) Section 1012, entitled "Basis of Property – Cost," says simply that "The basis of property shall be the cost of such property..."

Of course, it goes on to cover specific and unusual situations, but "Cost Basis" is the general rule for purchased property.

If you purchased a Duplex for $265,000 today, your Basis in that property is what you paid for it, plus any costs of acquisition, usually just your closing costs.

If you incurred $5,000 in acquisition costs, then your Basis in the property is $270,000.

If you spend $30,000 improving the property, then your Basis in the property becomes $300,000.

If you sell at this point, your Capital Gains will be the differences between your $300,000 Basis and your Net Sales Proceeds.

If you rent out the property, you will be allowed to claim an annual depreciation allowance, and deduct that amount from your rental income, and this Depreciation will lower your Basis in the property.

See Sections 14 through 23 on Depreciation for complete explanations of the Calculations involved in the process of doing Depreciation.

But let's assume that you assign a value of $25,000 to the land on which the Duplex is sitting, and subtract that out because land is not subject to depreciation.

That leaves a Depreciable Basis in the property of $275,000 which can be depreciated over a period of 27.5 years, resulting in an annual depreciation allowance of $10,000.

After you have rented the Duplex for five years and claimed $50,000 in depreciation allowance, your Basis in the property is $250,000 because you must deduct Depreciation from your Basis.

So, for property that you purchased, your Basis is the purchase price, plus cost of improvements, and minus depreciation allowed.

B = PP + CI − D, WHERE:
B IS THE BASIS IN THE PROPERTY,
PP IS THE PURCHASE PRICE,
CI IS THE COST OF IMPROVEMENTS, AND
D IS THE DEPRECIATION ALLOWED.

For our Example above:

B = 270,000 + 30,000 − 50,000

B = 250,000

GIFTED PROPERTY

If you received property as a gift, your Basis in the property will be the same as the Basis of the individual who gifted the property to you.

See SECTION 7. BASIS: TRANSFERRED (P. 29) for more details.

INHERITED PROPERTY

If you inherited property, you might or might not receive a Step-up in Basis.

See SECTION 6. BASIS: STEPPED-UP (P. 23) for an explanation.

SECTION 4.
BASIS: ADJUSTED

Your "Basis" in your property is what you paid for it, plus any capital improvements you have made.

Your "Adjusted Basis" in your property is the basis adjusted for the Depreciation that you have taken. In other words, the book value less the depreciation deduction.

Adjusted Basis is also referred to as "Depreciated Basis."

In fact, the Balance Sheet for your investment, if you have one, will be divided by Assets and Liabilities.

Under Assets, you will see your major assets listed separately, with the price that you paid, or the price allocated for each.

Then you will see an entry underneath called "Accumulated Depreciation," and a number, and then you will see another figure.

This other figure is your Adjusted Basis. It is the amount paid for the property less any depreciation taken.

For Example, let's assume that you purchase a Duplex for $240,000 and have $10,000 closing costs. You then spend $25,000 on improvements, and you hold the investment for three years and consider selling it. What is your Capital Gains?

The first thing you need to know in order to answer this question will be the number for your Adjusted Basis.

Your total cost to start with is $275,000.

This is the total of your Purchase Price, your Closing Costs, and your Capital Improvements.

During the three years, you have claimed $9,091 in Depreciation each year, for a total of $27,273.

You subtract the $27,273 from the $275,000 and you have your Adjusted Basis. That number is $247,727.

There are other situations which might result in adjusting the Basis of your asset, such as a casualty loss (fire) for which you were reimbursed by insurance.

In this case, you deduct the amount of your insurance check from your Basis, and this is your new Adjusted Basis.

But in most cases, your Adjusted Basis will only be the result of the amount of your depreciation taken.

CALCULATOR

Now that you understand how this works, let's run it through a Free Calculator and see what we get.

https://www.ajdesigner.com/php_ab/adjusted_basis.php

1.) For "original basis (OB)" enter 250000 (no comma).

2.) For "Capital additions (CA)" enter 25000.

3.) For "sales costs (SC)" enter 0.

4.) For "cumulative real estate depreciation (CRED)" enter 27273.

5.) For "cumulative capital improvements depreciation (CCAD)" enter 2727.

6.) Click "Calculate."

Your Adjusted Basis is $245,000.

This is a different number from the one we got above because we did not account for the value of the land.

This Calculator also allows you to calculate for any of the elements when you know all of the others.

Just click on one of the choices in the "Change Equation" box and the screen will give you a different Calculation page.

SECTION 5.

BASIS: CARRYOVER

Carryover Basis (CB) is often mistakenly referred to as Transferred Basis (TB).

The two are not the same, and the differences are very important to understand.

See SECTION 7. BASIS: TRANSFERRED (P. 29) for a *full explanation* of Transferred Basis and how it is created.

But in general terms, when property is gifted from one person, called the donor, to another person, called the donee, the Basis that the donor has in the property is transferred to the donee, becoming the Transferred Basis.

But Carryover Basis is when there is a business transaction involving two pieces of property, one being sold and one being purchased, by a single investor, and the Basis of the sold property actually carries over into the Basis of the purchased property.

An Example of this would be when you engage in a Section 1031 Like Kind Exchange.

You bought a Duplex ten years ago for $200,000 and have operated it as an investment property. You have claimed $65,000 in Depreciation during that time.

Now you are selling the Duplex for $400,000 and you are buying a Replacement Property of equal or greater value, engaging in a Section 1031 Like Kind Exchange in order to avoid paying taxes on the Capital Gains and the Depreciation Recapture.

You paid $200,000 for the Duplex and you claimed $65,000 in Depreciation, which is deducted from the beginning Basis of $200,000, leaving you with a Basis of $135,000.

Under Section 1031, when you sell, you are allowed to take the $135,000 of Basis that you have left in the Duplex that you have not yet depreciated, and carry it over into the Replacement Property, and continue to claim Depreciation on it, even though you no longer own it.

And this Basis is called Carryover Basis.

All in all, a pretty great deal.

By the way, if you are interested in learning more about the Section 1031 Like Kind Exchange, I can highly recommend an excellent book on the subject.

"How To Do A Section 1031 Like Kind Exchange" is available on Amazon, and you can do a "Look Inside" at:

www.amazon.com/Michael-Lantrip/e/B01N2ZRGUY

SECTION 6.

BASIS: STEPPED-UP

FOR INDIVIDUAL TAXPAYERS

A step-up in Basis happens when the property owner dies, and the property is inherited either through the probate of a Will or the administration of an intestate estate, or the property goes into a trust.

Internal Revenue Code Section 1014, entitled "Basis Of Property Acquired From A Decedent," provides that the Basis of a Decedent's property will be changed (usually increased) to its Fair Market Value (FMV) as of the Date of Death (DOD).

IRC Section 1014(a) says "... the basis of property in the hands of a person acquiring the property from a decedent or to whom the property passed from a decedent shall, if not sold, exchanged, or otherwise disposed of before the decedent's death by such person, be (1) the fair market value of the property at the date of decedent's death, ..."

It can be confusing, but it just means that there is a step-up in Basis when a person dies and leaves property to an heir.

The step-up in Basis will usually mean that the person inheriting the property can sell it without having to pay any Capital Gains Tax because the sale will usually be for the FMV, and the seller's Basis in the property is also the FMV, because that is what the step-up in Basis does, raise the Basis to the FMV.

The real benefit of the Stepped-up Basis is when you use Section 1031 Exchanges for your entire lifetime to defer the Capital Gains taxes, and then pass your property to your heirs tax-free.

You might have started with an investment in a property with a Basis of $50,000 and, through a series of Section 1031 Exchanges, now have property worth $1,000,000 but with a Basis of less than $100,000.

With a Capital Gains rate of 20%, the step-up in Basis will avoid a tax bill of about $180,000.

After deferring taxes on Capital Gains and Depreciation Recapture for your entire life, the "pot of gold at the end of the rainbow" is to pass the property to your heirs, and eliminate all of your tax liability and create none for them.

Stepped-up Basis turns the "tax-deferred" taxes from all of your past sales into "tax-free" for your heirs.

However, it is critical whether you are holding title to the property in your own name, or you own the property through a business entity.

You might still be entitled to claim a Stepped-up Basis if you hold the property through a business entity, but it will depend on the business entity in which you are holding the property.

FOR BUSINESS ENTITIES

If you are not holding real property in your own name, then Partnerships and LLCs are the best business entities to use.

The LLC can elect to be treated as either a disregarded entity, a partnership, or as an S Corp for tax purposes. But it should not be treated as a C Corp.

By taking an Internal Revenue Code Section 754 election upon the death of a shareholder, the Partnership or LLC gets a step-up in Basis for the property in the hands of the beneficiary.

For Example, let's assume that you and your brother set up a corporation and each of you put in $50,000 and each of you own 50% of the stock. The corporation buys a warehouse for $100,000.

Ten years later, you die and leave everything to your son, and the warehouse is worth $1,000,000.

Your son will receive a Stepped-up Basis *in the value of the corporate stock.*

But the corporation will not receive a Stepped-up Basis in the value of the warehouse. The warehouse is owned by the corporation, and the corporation did not die. If the warehouse is sold, the corporation will owe taxes on $900,000 of Capital Gains. (Including an undeterminable amount for Depreciation Recapture Tax). In effect, your son will pay half of the taxes because it will come out of his half of the corporation's funds.

Now, let's assume that you and your brother set up an LLC instead of a corporation, and that everything else is the same. The LLC will be treated for tax purposes as a Partnership because there is more than one owner.

When you die, the LLC makes a Section 754 election, and the son's share of the LLC assets receives a Stepped-up Basis to $500,000.

If the LLC sells the warehouse, the son will have no Capital Gains taxes to pay. If the LLC does not sell the warehouse, the son has a Basis of $500,000 inside the LLC which he can depreciate.

FOR HUSBANDS AND WIVES

If a Husband and Wife own the real estate together, the survivor will receive a Stepped-up Basis in the share owned by the deceased spouse, but may not receive a Stepped-up Basis in their own share upon the death of the spouse.

It will depend on the state in which they live, and how they are holding title to the property.

If the real estate is held in Joint Tenancy, and one spouse dies, the surviving spouse will received a Stepped-up Basis in the share of the property inherited from the deceased spouse, but will not receive a Stepped-up Basis in the share of the property that was already owned. This share retains its Cost Basis.

But in Community Property states, the opposite is true.

If the surviving spouse inherits the property, all of the property receives a Stepped-up Basis.

In our Example of a $300,000 property, if the Community Property surviving spouse sold it shortly after the death of her spouse for $500,000, there would be no Capital Gains tax because the Sales Price would be the same as the Stepped-up Basis.

But if the Joint Tenancy surviving spouse did the same, her Basis in the property would be $150,000, half of the Cost Basis of $300,000, plus $250,000, the Stepped-up Basis of the share of the deceased spouse, for a total Basis of $400,000.

The Joint Tenancy surviving spouse would have a $100,000 Capital Gains, and a tax liability.

(These Examples ignore allowable depreciation.)

Community Property states are Arizona, California, Idaho, Louisiana, Nevada, New Mexico, Texas, Washington, and Wisconsin.

Alaska allows spouses to opt-in to a Community Property arrangement.

SECTION 7.
BASIS: TRANSFERRED

If you receive property as a gift, your Basis (B) in the property will be the same as the Basis of the individual who gifted the property to you.

The Basis is "transferred" to you and is called Transferred Basis (TB).

Internal Revenue Code Section 1015, entitled "Basis of Property Acquired By Gifts And Transfers In Trust," says "If the property was acquired by gift ... the basis shall be the same as it would be in the hands of a donor or the last preceding owner by whom it was not acquired by gift, except that if such basis ... is greater than the fair market value of the property at the time of the gift, then for the purpose of determining loss the basis shall be such fair market value."

For Example, a mistake often made by elderly parents regarding their real property is that they want to gift it to their children before they die so that it will not have to go through Probate, having heard horrible things about the Probate process.

Here's the problem with that.

They might have property worth $400,000 that they have owned all of their lives and in which they might have a very low Basis, or no Basis at all due to Depreciation taken.

If it is gifted to the children, when the children sell it, they will have a Capital Gains tax on the entire $400,000, possibly as high as 20%, because they have no Basis in the property, or very low Basis, to deduct from the Sales Price because their Basis is the same as the Basis of the parents who gifted the property.

This is Transferred Basis.

For an explanation of what would happen if the situation were handled differently, perhaps putting the property into a Revocable Living Trust that becomes Irrevocable upon death, see SECTION 6. BASIS: STEPPED-UP (P. 23).

Also, note that Transferred Basis is often also referred to as Carryover Basis, but the two are not the same.

See the SECTION 5. BASIS: CARRYOVER (P. 20) for a full explanation.

SECTION 8.
CAPITAL EXPENDITURES

Capital Expenditures (Cap Ex) is a category of expenses that includes those major repairs such as a roof, furnace, HVAC system, or foundation that are bound to happen if you own the investment property long enough.

However, a roof replacement is not a monthly expenditure to be deducted from cash income to determine Cash Flow (CF), until it happens.

When it does happen, you are faced with trying to deduct a $25,000 expense from $1,000 of available income that month to calculate CF.

Of course, that Calculation of minus $24,000 is worthless for management and analytical purposes, and renders all of the previous Cash Flows worthless, because Cap Ex is supposed to be part of your CF calculations, and you have not been deducting an allowance for Cap Ex.

The Cap Ex is really an expenditure that should be deducted over the life of the asset that failed, and if you acquire that asset late in its life, you must start with lumping the past amounts.

Or you can deduct a larger amount each month for the remaining life.

Spreading it out this way gives you a true Calculation of what your Cash Flow actually is, or will be, if you are doing a CF projection.

But how do you do this?

Well, you can do it the easy way, or you can do it the hard way.

The easy way is to look at your Depreciation Schedule and see what assets you are depreciating.

You will have a building, called Section 1250 Property, that you are depreciating in a straight-line method over a period of 27.5 years if it is Residential Real Estate, and 39 years if it is Commercial Real Estate.

(The depreciation periods for Residential Real Estate and for Commercial Real Estate were not changed in the new tax act.)

For Example, you have a Duplex with a Fair Market Value (FMV) of $185,000. You assign $20,000 to the value of the land, leaving $165,000 value in the building available for depreciation.

Divide that by 27.5 years and you can claim $6,000 per year in Depreciation, or $500 per month.

Let's say you are also depreciating personal property as part of the package, called Section 1245 Property, and using one of the Accelerated Depreciation methods such as Double Declining Balance (DDB).

Your initial monthly depreciation amounts will be large, and decline over the life of the asset.

But you can smooth that out by just taking the total value of the Section 1245 Property and divide it by the life of the assets.

If you have $15,000 of such property with a depreciable life of 60 months, then use $250 as the average of monthly claimed Depreciation.

Your total claimed Depreciation, both Section 1250 Property and Section 1245 Property, is $750 per month.

You might choose to use this amount as your monthly estimate for Cap Ex.

Doing it this way will give you two advantages.

The first is that it saves a lot of time, because the number already exists.

The second is that it will also allow you to track your Taxable Income (TI) at the same time.

Taxable Income is just your CF with Cap

Ex added back to it, and then Depreciation and Mortgage Interest (MI) subtracted.

Using the same numbers for Cap Ex and Depreciation make them a wash.

You can take your monthly Cash Flow number and subtract Mortgage Interest, and you have a good estimate of your Taxable Income.

The other way, the hard way, involves actually listing all of the components that could cause a major expense to occur, like the roof, the HVAC system, the furnace, the foundation, etc.

You identify how much it would cost to replace each one, the Replacement Cost (RC).

Then you look at the charts that show how long each one would last, and estimate how much of that life is left remaining for each of your items.

Divide the remaining life into the Replacement Cost and you have a yearly Cap Ex amount for that item, the eventual cost of replacing the item spread over its remaining life.

For Example, a 25-year roof that would cost $25,000 to replace, and which you estimate has a remaining life of 18 years would create a Cap Ex figure of $104.16 per month.

When you have done this for all of the major components, you will have a Cap Ex figure to use in your Cash Flow estimate that will help you avoid the disaster of losing you entire investment because of one large repair.

If you do not suffer any large repairs while you own the property, you have that Cap Ex fund as a bonus when you sell.

SECTION 9.

CAPITAL GAINS

Let's start simple.

Capital Gain, basically, is the profit that you make when you sell your investment property.

From there, it becomes more complex.

Your Capital Gains is the difference between what you paid for your property and what you sold the property for.

Except that there are some adjustments to be made.

First, you can deduct from the selling price all or most of the costs of the transaction. Usually, you will have these charges listed on your HUD-1 Settlement Statement. Also, there might be some expenses that were paid outside of closing that were also expenses of the sale.

That takes care of the amount that you received for the property, your Net Sales Proceeds.

Now, what you deduct from your Net Sales Proceeds is called your Adjusted Basis in the property.

See SECTION 3. BASIS (P. 12) and SECTION 4. BASIS: ADJUSTED (P.16) for a full explanation.

But for now, a quick description of your Adjusted Basis in the property is the amount that you paid for the property, plus any capital improvements made to the property, and minus any depreciation claimed on the property.

CG = NSP – (OPP + CI – D), WHERE CG IS CAPITAL GAINS, NSP IS YOUR NET SALES PRICE, OPP IS YOUR ORIGINAL PURCHASE PRICE, CI IS CAPITAL IMPROVEMENTS, AND D IS DEPRECIATION TAKEN

For Example, you purchased a Duplex ten years ago for $200,000. You added two garages for $30,000 and replaced the furniture and fixtures for $20,000.

You have taken $65,000 Depreciation on the Duplex and you have taken $8,000 Depreciation on the garages, and you have taken $15,000 Depreciation on the furniture and fixtures.

Now you sell the Duplex for $400,000 and have $10,000 in transaction costs.

CG = NSP – OPP + CI – D

CG = (400,000 – 10,000) – [200,000 + (30,000 + 20,000) – (65,000 + 8,000 + 15,000)]

CG = 390,000 – (200,000 + 50,000 – 88,000)

CG = 390,000 – 162,000

CG = 228,000

Your Capital Gains on that transaction is $228,000.

If you had held the property for one year or less, the Capital Gains would be classified as Short-Term Capital Gains.

Short-Term Capital Gains is taxed at the same rate as your personal ordinary income tax rate for the tax year in which the transaction took place.

But you held the property for at least a year and a day, so the Capital Gains is classified as Long-Term Capital Gains.

Long-Term Capital Gains is taxed at different rates for different taxpayers, depending on the amount of their other income, ranging from 0% to 20%.

But part of your Capital Gains will be taxed at the Capital Gains tax rate, and part of it will be taxed as Depreciation Recapture, and at what will probably be a higher rate.

See SECTION 23. DEPRECIATION RECAPTURE (P. 97) for a full explanation.

SECTION 10.
CAPITALIZATION RATE

The Capitalization Rate (CR), referred to as the Cap Rate, is the ratio of the Net Operating Income (NOI) to the Fair Market Value (FMV) of the property.

The Capitalization Rate is your overall rate of return on the value of the asset.

**CR = NOI ÷ FMV, WHERE
CR IS THE CAP RATE,
NOI IS THE NET OPERATING INCOME, AND
FMV IS THE FAIR MARKET VALUE OF THE
PROPERTY.**

For Example, if you have a $500,000 multi-family property that has a Net Operating Income of $65,000 the Calculation is:

CR = NOI ÷ FMV

CR = 65,000 ÷ 500,000

CR = 0.13

The Cap Rate for this property is 13%.

Investors in a particular market, or for a particular type of real estate investment, don't actually declare what their Cap Rate is.

But they establish the Cap Rate by their decisions on how much to pay for an investment property that has a specific Net Operating Income.

In the above Example, investors in that market are willing to pay $500,000 for an investment property that has Net Operating Income of $65,000. That consensus among them creates the 13% factor as the market Cap Rate for property of that specific type in that specific price range in that specific market.

The Law of Supply And Demand will create the consensus.

So, you will hear references that say the Cap Rate is such-and-such for this type of property in this market.

One of the values of using the Cap Rate to compare different properties is that the NOI does not include debt service, an expense which will be different for every potential buyer, and using the Cap Rate allows for across-the-board comparisons of just the properties, with the same assumptions applied to each one.

You can use the Cap Rate alone to compare potential investment properties, and you can also use it in association with Cash Flow analysis.

A calculation based on Cap Rate and Discounted Cash Flow might give you even more valuable information.

CALCULATOR

You can quickly Calculate your Cap Rate with the following Free Calculator.

https://www.ajdesigner.com/php_ capitalization_rate/capitalization_rate.php

1.) For "net operating income (NOI)" enter 65000 (no comma).

2.) For "value or cost (V)" enter 500000.

3.) Click "Calculate."

Your Cap Rate is 13%.

This is the same number that we got when doing it by hand.

You can use one of the other calculations on the page to determine NOI or Value if you already know your Cap Rate.

SECTION 11.

CASH FLOW

Cash Flow is easy to Calculate for property you already own, and almost impossible to Calculate for property that you are thinking about buying.

Cash Flow is the cash left over after you take the monthly income from the property and pay all of the monthly expenses of the property.

In other words, it is cash in, less cash out.

CF = I – E, WHERE
CF IS CASH FLOW,
I IS ALL OF THE CASH INCOME, AND
E IS ALL OF THE CASH EXPENSES.

Although you will read otherwise, "Expenses" as used in Cash Flow analysis does not include Debt Service (DS) because that is not one of the characteristics of the property that you are analyzing.

After all, the purpose of calculating Cash Flow in the first place is to determine if there will be enough to make the monthly payments on the loan to purchase it.

Your Lender wants to see the Cash Flow from the operation of the property to see if you will be able to make the note payments, and cover other contingencies (See Cap Ex reference below).

Also, how could you compare the Cash Flow of two properties if you include the Debt Service as an expense, when the Debt Service is all about the credit worthiness of the person who got the loan, and has nothing to do with the particular characteristics of the property?

The expenses also don't include Depreciation, since it is not a cash expense, but is an "expense allowance" that allows you to deduct over a period of time what you paid for the property.

However, you do include an expense called Capital Expenditure, referred to as Cap Ex, even if that expense does not actually occur that month. It is a "set-aside" to build up a fund to pay for the Cap Ex when it does occur.

Although most discussions of Cash Flow leave out Cap Ex, you should include it because your Lender will want to see it, and because it is an actual expense that will definitely happen at some point. This is the Cap Ex that I referred to above.

See SECTION 8. CAPITAL EXPENDITURES (P. 31) for an explanation of this.

The key to getting a valuable Calculation of the Cash Flow lies in what you decide to include in the category of "expenses."

See more on that below.

But first, let's clear up a fallacy.

LOAN PROCEEDS AND INTEREST INCOME

Some investors using this Calculation include loan proceeds and interest income in Total Income, in addition to the rents.

If that serves your needs, then do it. But it is not what the Calculation is designed for, and it distorts the results.

I never include loan proceeds, and I have never had an investment property loaning out money and receiving interest payments.

The Cash Flow calculation is all about the property, and only income from the operation of the property should be considered, and loan proceeds are not income.

And an interest-bearing account is not part of the property; it is where past income from the property, like Cap Ex funds, are being held in an account in the owner's name.

So, the interest is not income from the property.

For example, what if someone has a Fourplex for sale, and he told you that the Fourplex had a monthly CF of $3,000 last year, and when you look at the income you see four units renting for $1,000 per month, and a 10% VACL, resulting in $43,200 annual Gross Income. And when you look at expenses you see a total of $31,200. Subtract that, and it leaves a CF of $12,000 and a monthly Cash Flow of $1,000 instead of the $3,000 claimed.

When you ask about the discrepancy, they say, "Oh yeah, I got a loan for $24,000 and that adds $2,000 a month to the Cash Flow."

That's why I don't see any place for loan proceeds in your CF calculation.

Loan proceeds are not Cash Flow from the property; worse, they represent debt which must be repaid from income.

EXPENSES

To repeat, "expenses" as used in Cash Flow analysis, does not include Depreciation and it does not include Debt Service.

It does include an expense called Capital Expenditures, referred to as Cap Ex, which is deducted every month whether there is an actual Cap Ex that month or not.

See SECTION 8. CAPITAL EXPENDITURES (P. 31) for a full explanation.

Basically, Cap Ex is the amount that you have estimated should be set aside each month to cover the occasional major repair, such as a roof, HVAC system, furnace, foundation, or other item. It is treated as an actual cash expense each month and accumulated for this purpose.

When you do have an event requiring this major expense, you use the money accumulated for that purpose. You have already been taking it out of the Cash Flow calculations, and now you don't have to. This gives you an even cash flow Calculation over time instead of one that cruises along at a high level and then one day it goes seriously negative and stays that way.

If the fund you have is not adequate to cover the expense, you get a second lien improvement loan.

The remainder of your expenses for Cash Flow analysis are these.

TAXES. This is Property Taxes. It is a good number to track. Property Taxes are increasing so rapidly across the country that they are turning some positive Cash Flows negative. That could make your property very difficult to sell.

INSURANCE. This is Hazard Insurance, Flood Insurance, and Liability Insurance. If you are owning your investment property through a business entity such as an LLC, which you should, you might consider keeping your Liability insurance coverage as low as possible. Large policies just attract lawsuits. And as for other policies, you might want to go with the minimum. Insurance companies usually refuse to pay a claim anyway, and end up settling for an amount that is probably less than what you have already paid them in premiums.

UTILITIES: WATER. Your local government entity might include water, sewer and garbage together in one bill.

UTILITIES: GAS/ELECTRIC.

UTILITIES: SEWER. Your local government entity might include water, sewer, and garbage together in one bill.

UTILITIES: GARBAGE. Your local government entity might include water, sewer, and garbage together in one bill.

REPAIRS.

MANAGEMENT. Whether you include this as an expense will depend on your situation. Property management companies typically charge a fee of 10-12% of the monthly rent, plus 50% of the first month's rent when a unit turns over.

VACANCY AND CREDIT LOSS (VACL). If you are projecting expenses on a potential purchase you will use the Gross Potential Income as your cash income number. This number should be 10% of the Gross Potential Income (GPI) from rents. If you are compiling a current Cash Flow Accounting, you should discount the GPI by 5% to arrive at Gross Operating Income (GOI) because the 5% will represent your actual loss over time because a unit is empty, and use a 5% factor here to reflect the loss or expense that you will incur because of hot checks or reversed bank transfers, or other scams.

BEFORE-TAX AND AFTER-TAX CASH FLOW

Many discussions of Cash Flow will tell you that what you should do is first calculate the Cash Flow before taxes and then determine the amount of taxes and calculate another Cash Flow figure for after taxes.

This is not only a waste of your time, but it is impossible to do.

I have been a Tax Attorney and a Tax Accountant for over 35 years and I can promise you that this function is too complicated to be put into a Calculation with any hope of arriving at a usable number.

And the explanation of why it cannot be done with any accuracy is also too complicated to be attempted here.

Accountants for Corporations can calculate "before-tax" and "after-tax." Individuals cannot.

CALCULATOR

Once you know your Cash Flow, it is a good idea to Calculate some ratios that will tell you how healthy your investment is in terms of liquidity.

One of those Calculations is the Cash Flow To Total Debt ratio, and here is a Free Calculator to do that.

http://www.danielsoper.com/fincalc/calc. aspx?id=67

1.) For "Cash flow" enter 37250 (no comma).

2.) For "Total debt" enter 300000.

3.) Click "Calculate."

Your Cash Flow To Total Debt Ratio is 12.42%.

Of course, your ratio will improve as you hold the property, because the level of your debt will decrease, and, assuming that you are able to raise rents, you Cash Flow will increase.

SECTION 12.

CASH FLOW: DISCOUNTED

Discounted Cash Flow (DCF) is a Calculation of the Present Value (PV) of future streams of cash flow, based on an interest rate used as a discount factor.

It is similar to the Section on Present Value that determines the present value of real estate assets with a known value in the future, but the Discounted Cash Flow Calculation deals with a stream of periodic payments in the future, and determines what they are worth today.

It is really the inverse of the Compound Interest concept. Instead of adding interest and interest-on-interest to a present value going into the future, we are pulling out an interest factor and an interest-on-interest factor from a future amount as we bring it back to the present.

Once you set up your Calculations on this, keep a copy and use the same numbers the next time you do a workup.

Let's assume that you have projected a stream of payments that you expect will result from an investment property, like Cash Flow.

You have a multi-family property that is creating monthly Cash Flow of $2,400 and you want to know the present value of twenty-four months, two years, of such payments.

You have placed a time value on the use of money in your set of circumstances at 12%. In other words, you are willing to pay 12% for the use of other people's money because you know you can make a profit using that money in your business activities. Therefore, the Time Value of Money *for you* is 12%.

The monthly Interest rate factor of 12% annual interest is 1%.

First, let's discount the value of the first twelve months of Cash Flow.

For the first month, the value is $2,400 because you have the money in your hand now, assuming that you collect rents on the first day of the month.

But to determine the value today, the Present Value, of that $2,400 that you will not receive until a month from now, you discount it by the 1% interest rate that you have assigned as your time value of money.

Here is the Calculation:

**PV = CF ÷ (1 + I), WHERE
PV IS THE PRESENT VALUE,
CF IS THE CASH FLOW AMOUNT, AND
I IS THE INTEREST RATE FACTOR YOU HAVE
ASSIGNED TO THE TIME PERIOD.**

For our discount of next month's rent:

PV = 2,400 ÷ (1 + .01)

PV = 2,400 ÷ 1.01

PV = 2,376.24

So, the Discounted Cash Flow value of the $2,400 that you will receive at the beginning of next month is $2,376.24 today.

To discount the Cash Flow for the third month, the Calculation is slightly different.

**PV = CF ÷ (1 + I)^n, WHERE
PV IS THE PRESENT VALUE,
CF IS THE CASH FLOW AMOUNT,
I IS THE INTEREST RATE FACTOR YOU HAVE
ASSIGNED, AND
^{n} IS THE NUMBER OF PERIODS YOU ARE
DISCOUNTING FOR.**

The Calculation is the same as above, except that you are receiving the CF at the beginning of the third month and discounting it back for two months instead of one.

PV = 2,400 ÷ [(1 + .01) (1 + .01)]

PV = 2,400 ÷ (1.01 x 1.01)

PV = 2,400 ÷ 1.0201

PV = 2,352.71

So, your third month Cash Flow of $2,400 has a value today of $2,352.71.

You see the pattern here, so I'll run quickly through the rest.

Fourth: 2,400 ÷ 1.0303 = 2,329.42

Fifth: 2,400 ÷ 1.0406 = 2,306.36

Sixth: 2,400 ÷ 1.051 = 2,283.54

Seventh: 2,400 ÷ 1.0615 = 2,260.95

Eighth: 2,400 ÷ 1.0714 = 2,240.06

Ninth: 2,400 ÷ 1.0828567 = 2,216.36

Tenth: 2,400 ÷ 1.093685 = 2,194.42

Eleventh: 2,400 ÷ 1.104622 = 2,172.69

Twelfth: 2,400 ÷ 1.115668 = 2,151.18

The total amount of the twelve *Discounted Cash Flows* is $27,583.93.

The *undiscounted amount* would be 12 x 2,400 = $28,800.

The difference is $1,216.07, which is 4.22% less.

The difference between the stated amount and the discounted amount for the second year of payments would be even less.

If you just look at the 13th Cash Flow amount, you will see.

$$PV = CF \div (1 + I)^n$$

$$PV = 2{,}400 \div [(1 + .01)(1 + .01)(1 + .01)(1 + .01)(1 + .01)(1 + .01)(1 + .01)(1 + .01)(1 + .01)(1 + .01)(1 + .01)(1 + .01)]$$

$$PV = 2{,}400 \div (1.01 \times 1.01 \times 1.01 \times 1.01 \times 1.01 \times 1.01 \times 1.01 \times 1.01 \times 1.01 \times 1.01 \times 1.01 \times 1.01)$$

$$PV = 2{,}400 \div 1.126825$$

$$PV = 2{,}129.77$$

The Present Value of that $2,400 monthly Cash Flow a year from now would be $2,129.77, and that would be a difference of $270.23, which is 12.69%.

Discounted Cash Flow becomes important when you are looking at your Cash on Cash Return (COCR) on your investment.

For more information on this, see SECTION 43. RETURN ON CASH (P. 173).

COCR = CF ÷ ICI, WHERE COCR IS YOUR CASH ON CASH RETURN, CF IS YOUR CASH FLOW FOR THE PERIOD, AND ICI IS YOUR INITIAL CASH INVESTMENT.

If your ICI was $160,000 for this multi-family property that is producing $28,800 in annual CF:

COCR = CF ÷ ICI

COCR = 28,800 ÷ 160,000

COCR = 18.0

So, your Cash on Cash Return for the first year would be 18.0%.

But since you put all of the $160,000 into the investment up front, and received the Cash Flow over a 12-month period, a more accurate calculation would be to use the Discounted Cash Flow method.

$COCR = CF \div ICI$

$COCR = 27,583.93 \div 160,000$

$COCR = 17.24\%$

This is for the first year. The amount would be lower for the second, and the third, and so forth.

The Discounted Cash Flow method will also give you a more accurate estimate of your Payback Period.

For more information, see SECTION 39. PAYBACK PERIOD (P. 158).

$PP = ICI \div CF$

$PP = 160,000 \div 2,400$

$PP = 66.67$

The Payback Period is 66.67 months using the undiscounted Cash Flow method. That's five years, six months and 20 days.

To do the same Calculation for Discounted Cash Flow, we would need to know the amount for each month for the same period, add them together, and divide by the total number to get the average, and use that number.

Instead, we'll just use that 13th payment that we calculated above.

PP = ICI ÷ CF

PP = 160,000 ÷ 2,129.77

PP = 75.125

So, just using a single one-year-old Discounted Cash Flow, the Payback Period is pushed out to 6 years, 3 months and 4 days.

There are many reasons for using Discounted Cash Flow when comparing numbers in the present time with numbers in the future. You will always get a more accurate Calculation.

CALCULATOR

Now that you understand how to use Discounted Cash Flow, here is a Free Calculator that will do it for you.

https://www.calculatorsoup.com/calculators/ financial/present-value-cash-flows-calculator.php

1.) For "Interest Rate" enter 1 to indicate the monthly rate of 1% that reflects our 12% annual discount rate.

2.) For "Compounding" enter 1 to indicate that we only want the discount to be applied monthly instead of yearly.

3.) For "Cash Flow at" select "Beginning" to indicate when in the month the payment is received.

4.) For "Number of Line" select 10 just for this Example.

5.) For "Periods" enter 1 for each line.

6.) For "Cash Flow" enter 2,400 for each line.

7.) Click "Calculate."

You will get a chart showing the Discounted Cash Flow for each of the monthly amounts of $2,400 and a total for all.

Look at Period #10, which represents the tenth month of payments that we are discounting, and you will see that the Discounted Cash Flow is $2,194.42.

This is exactly the same amount that we got in the above Calculation that we did by hand.

So, we did OK.

However, this Calculator can do Calculations that, while I might be able to do them, I would never be able to explain them to you.

For instance, you can use this Calculator to discount future monthly payments that are uneven, or are even, but include something else occasionally such as a principal payment, or a late payment.

You just plug in whatever that amount will be in the appropriate "Period" line.

For this Calculator you only have to make sure that the payments are all at the same interval, and the same discount rate is applied throughout.

You could probably spend an hour on this page if you are in the process of analyzing one or more properties.

SECTION 13.

DEBT SERVICE RATIO

The Debt Service Ratio (DSR) tells you the relationship between the Net Operating Income (NOI) and the amount necessary to service the debt on the property.

DSR = NOI ÷ DS, WHERE DSR IS THE DEBT SERVICE RATIO, NOI IS THE NET OPERATING INCOME, AND DS IS THE DEBT SERVICE.

You have a 10-unit Apartment Building and your NOI is $47,500.

You have a $525,000 Mortgage with monthly payments of $3,150, which is an annual total of $37,800.

DSR = NOI ÷ DS

DSR = 47,500 ÷ 37,800

DSR = 1.2566

Your Debt Service Ratio is 1.2566, or 125.66%.

Also, this means that after payment of the Mortgage from the Net Operating Income, there will be $9,700 left.

CALCULATOR

The Debt Service Ratio is a fairly simple two-factor Calculation that you can probably do yourself, but if you would like to use a Calculator to do it, here's one:

https://www.ajdesigner.com/php_dcr/debt_ coverage_ratio.php

1.) For "annual net operating income" enter 47500 (no comma).

2.) For "annual debt service" enter 37800 (no comma).

3.) Click "Calculate."

Your Debt Service Ratio is 1.2566.

This is the same Calculation that we got above doing it by hand.

This is a good page. Look at the "Change Equation" box and solve for another unknown.

SECTION 14.

DEPRECIATION

When a taxpayer buys an investment property such as a Duplex, the money he pays for it is not an expense that can be deducted from the income produced by the property before the taxable income amount is determined.

This rule applies whether he pays cash for the property, or finances the entire amount, or any combination of the two.

Only the interest paid on the loan, if there is a loan, is deductible, because interest is a deductible business expense.

It seems unfair, and maybe it is, but the way the IRS make this unfair situation into a fair situation, and encourages investors to put their money into such projects, is through what is called "Depreciation Allowance," which is usually just referred to as Depreciation.

Depreciation is not an actual out-of-pocket expense, but the taxpayer can deduct it like any other business expense as though it were actually paid, because it is what the IRS considers an "expense allocation."

The IRS claims to have a rational explanation for this. Their position is that during the life of the asset, as the asset is producing income, it will be wearing out. Therefore, the deduction of the amount paid should be taken over the life of the asset, as it wears out, at the same time that the asset is producing income.

It sounds good, but it is difficult to reconcile with another IRS creation, the Section 179 Bonus Depreciation, in which the taxpayer can take an immediate 100% Depreciation Deduction in the first year for certain new or used personal assets purchased for the business.

But let's just take it as it is.

The assets that you purchase and depreciate will have a "life," the period of time over which the asset can be depreciated.

It is not the actual life of the asset, but a number assigned by the IRS, just because they are the IRS and they can do whatever they want.

The Depreciation will either be Straight-line Depreciation, or Accelerated Depreciation.

For more , see SECTION 21. DEPRECIATION: STRAIGHT LINE (P. 89) and SECTION 15. DEPRECIATION: ACCELERATED (P. 68).

Accelerated Depreciation comes in different forms.

For more information, see SECTION 17. DEPRECIATION: DOUBLE DECLINING BALANCE (P. 75) and SECTION 22. DEPRECIATION: 150% DECLINING BALANCE (P. 93).

Whether your Depreciation is Straight-line or Accelerated will depend on whether your investment is Section 1250 Property or Section 1245 Property.

For more information, see SECTION 20. DEPRECIATION: SECTION 1250 PROPERTY (P. 87) and SECTION 19. DEPRECIATION: SECTION 1245 PROPERTY (P. 84).

And finally, when you sell the property, the IRS wants the money back.

For more information on this, see SECTION 23. DEPRECIATION RECAPTURE (P. 97).

This is an overview of Depreciation.

I have a Section on each type of Depreciation, with an explanation, and an Example worked through. For five of them I also have a Free Calculator for you to try out.

Now that you understand what Depreciation is, go to each of those Sections for the details.

I have made more money by using Depreciation wisely than I have by trying to negotiate the lowest possible prices.

I strongly recommend that you learn everything you can about Depreciation. There is a lot of room for flexibility here that can have a major effect on your taxes.

SECTION 15.

DEPRECIATION: ACCELERATED

Depreciation is the annual "expense allocation" that the IRS allows you to deduct from the operating income of your investment real estate, even though it is not a cash, out-of-pocket expense.

There are different categories of property that can be depreciated, such as real property and personal property.

The real property is usually referred to as Section 1250 Property.

The personal property is usually referred to as Section 1245 Property.

Accelerated Depreciation, instead of Straight Line Depreciation, is available for the part of your investment property that is made up of what the IRS classifies as personal property, the Section 1245 Property.

(Although the IRS does allow some types of real property to be classified as Section 1245 Property and claim Accelerated Depreciation, such a Low Income Housing, we won't go into that here becvause it is incredibly complicated).

For more information, see SECTION 20. DEPRECIATION: SECTION 1250 PROPERTY (P. 87) and SECTION 19. DEPRECIATION: SECTION 1245 PROPERTY (P. 84).

Accelerated Depreciation means that you will be able to, for example, deduct each year more than 10% of the book value of an asset with a 10-year life span.

Once more: with Straight Line Depreciation if you had an asset with a 10-year life, you would be allowed to deduct 1/10 (10%) of your purchase price each year as a depreciation allowance.

But with Accelerated Depreciation, you will be allowed to deduct more than 10% each year (at least, for the first few years).

The most popular type of Accelerated Depreciation is called Double Declining Balance, referred to as DDB.

See SECTION 17. DEPRECIATION: DOUBLE DECLINING BALANCE (P. 75).

There are two more types of Accelerated Depreciation.

One is called 150% Declining Balance, referred to a 150DB.

See SECTION 22. DEPRECIATION: 150% DECLINING BALANCE (P. 93).

The other type of Accelerated Depreciation is Sum-of-The-Years-Digits, which is almost never used.

An important distinction for you to note about Accelerated Depreciation is that while you are now using it to shield your income from your current tax bracket liability, you will pay a different tax rate when you eventually sell the property and have to pay a Depreciation Recapture tax.

For Straight-line Depreciation Recapture, the tax rate is 25%.

But for Depreciation Recapture of Accelerated Depreciation, the tax rate is whatever your individual tax rate is for that tax year. And for a tax year in which you sell a large investment property, you could be in a much higher tax bracket.

SECTION 16.

DEPRECIATION: COMMERCIAL PROPERTY

Depreciation is the annual "expense allocation" that the IRS allows you to deduct from the operating income of your investment real estate, even though it is not an actual cash, out-of-pocket expense.

The life of the property determines how much you will be able to deduct each year.

There are two categories of depreciable investment properties.

(Actually, there are three, but I won't deal with Low Income Housing).

The two categories are Residential Rental Property and Commercial Property.

They have different "lives."

Residential Real Estate has a depreciable life of 27.5 years, and Commercial Property has a depreciable life of 39.0 years, both of them being referred to as "investment property."

For more, see SECTION 18. DEPRECIATION: RESIDENTIAL REAL ESTATE (P. 80).

Let's look at an Example.

You bought a Warehouse for $280,000 and did $20,000 in renovations, for a total Basis of $300,000.

But this is not your Depreciable Basis.

First, we must subtract out the value of the land, because the land is not a depreciable asset.

You assign a value to the land of $25,000.

This leaves you a Depreciable Basis of $275,000.

D = (PP + CI − LV) ÷ AL, WHERE D IS THE AMOUNT OF ALLOWABLE ANNUAL DEPRECIATION,
PP IS THE PURCHASE PRICE,
CI IS YOUR CAPITAL IMPROVEMENTS ON THE PROPERTY,
LV IS THE ASSIGNED LAND VALUE, AND AL IS THE ASSET LIFE.

D = (280,000 + 20,000 − 25,000) ÷ 39.0

D = 275,000 ÷ 39.0

D = 7,051.28

Your annual Depreciation Allowance will be $7,051.28.

By way of comparison, if this had been a Duplex, and the numbers were all the same, your annual Depreciation Allowance would be $10,000 because of the 27.5 year life of Residential Rental Property.

CALCULATOR

Let's create a Depreciation Schedule for this Warehouse to see what it looks like. Here is a Free Calculator that you can use:

https://www.calculatorsoup.com/calculators/ financial/depreciation-property-realestate.php

1.) For "Cost Basis" enter 275,000.

2.) For "Recovery Period" select 39.

3.) For "Placed in Service" select "August" for Month and "2018" for Year.

4.) Check "Round to Dollars."

5.) For "Calculate Depreciation" select "Full Schedule."

6.) Click "Calculate."

Your Depreciation Schedule will show you the Depreciation Expense for the year, the Accumulated Depreciation as of the end of the year, and the remaining Book Value of the property at the end of the year.

If this were Residential Real Estate such as a Duplex, instead of Commercial, you would change the "Recovery Period" from 39 years to 27.5 years.

Every single time that you are looking at a potential property purchase, you should run a Depreciation Schedule.

This is information about the property that you absolutely must have in order to make a decision.

SECTION 17.

DEPRECIATION: DOUBLE DECLINING BALANCE

When a taxpayer buys an investment property such as a Duplex, the money he pays for it is not an expense that can be deducted from the income produced by the property before the taxable income amount is determined.

This is true whether he pays cash for the property or finances the entire amount, or any combination of the two.

Most investment real estate is property that the IRS classifies as Section 1250 Property, which usually means that it is a building.

Section 1250 Property must be depreciated using the Straight-line method.

For more information, see SECTION 21. DEPRECIATION: STRAIGHT LINE (P. 89).

But the portion of the real estate investment property called "personal property" by the IRS, even though it is actually business property that is not part of the real estate, is classified as Section 1245 Property.

And Section 1245 Property can be depreciated using Accelerated Depreciation, such as the method described here.

The Depreciation method called Double Declining Balance, referred to as DDB, allows you to deduct more depreciation in the beginning of the life of the asset than you would be able to with Straight Line Depreciation (SD).

If you have a $10,000 asset with a 10-year life, SD would allow you to deduct one-tenth, or 10%, of the value as a depreciation allowance the first year, a total of $1,000.

By using the DDB method, you will be able to deduct twice that amount, 20%, or a total of $2,000.

Here's how that would work.

After the first year, the book value of the asset has declined to $8,000 because you have taken a $2,000 depreciation allowance.

So, for the second year you can deduct 20% again, but not of the $10,000. You can deduct 20% of the $8,000 balance. The balance is declining. This balance is what is being referred to by the title of the depreciation method, "Declining Balance."

Your second year deduction is 20% of $8,000 = $1,600.

This causes the book value balance to decline to $6,400.

Your third year deduction is 20% of $6,400 = $1,280.

Your fourth year deduction is 20% of $5,120 = $1,024.

At this point, you are 40% through the life of the asset, but you have deducted almost 60% of its value ($5,904).

Depreciation is all about recovering your capital expenses as quickly as possible, and the DDB method is the most popular way of doing that.

If you are not in a position to take the maximum depreciation early in your investment holding period, but still can benefit from some form of Accelerated Depreciation, you might consider using the 150% Declining Balance method.

See SECTION 22. DEPRECIATION: 150% DECLINING BALANCE (P. 93).

CALCULATOR

Now that you understand how the Double Declining Balance method of Depreciation works, let's do a Depreciation Schedule.

Here is a Free Calculator:

https://www.calculatorsoup.com/calculators/
financial/depreciation-declining-double.php

1.) For "Asset Cost" enter 10,000.

2.) For "Salvage Value" enter 0.

3.) For "Useful Life" enter 10.

4.) For "Starting Month" select "January."

5.) For "Starting Year" enter 2018.

6.) For "Convention" select "Full-Month."

7.) Check "Round to Dollars."

8.) For "Calculate Depreciation" select "Full Schedule."

9.) Click "Calculate."

Your Depreciation Schedule will show the Depreciation, Accumulated Depreciation, and Year-end Book Value for each year.

You will notice that at the end of the 10-year Asset Life you still have a Book Value of $1,074.

This is because you can never reduce anything to zero by taking 20% of it over and over again. At some point, you would have to take 100% of it.

Therefore, at some point you will have to change your method of Depreciation to Straight Line Depreciation.

Usually, the best time to do this is after the halfway point.

Here, your Book Value after five years is $3,277.

If you switch to Straight Line for the sixth year, you will claim $655 in Depreciation each year and reduce the Book Value to zero at the end of its 10-year life.

On a small-dollar asset like this, the IRS is not likely to be concerned with your changing your Depreciation Method, and if they are, the consequences of having to "recharacterize" your amounts of claimed Depreciation are minimal.

But on high-dollar assets, it is a good idea to consult with your tax professional before doing something like this on your own.

SECTION 18.

DEPRECIATION: RESIDENTIAL REAL ESTATE

Depreciation is the annual "expense allocation" that the IRS allows you to deduct from the operating income of your investment real estate, even though it is not actually a cash, out-of-pocket expense.

The life of the property determines how much you will be able to deduct each year.

There are two categories of depreciable investment properties.

The two categories are Residential Rental Property and Commercial Property.

They have different "lives." Commercial Property has a life of 39.0 years.

For more information, see SECTION 16. DEPRECIATION: COMMERCIAL PROPERTY (P. 71) for details.

Residential Real Estate used for investment property has a life of 27.5 years.

Let's look at an Example, like the one we used for Commercial Property.

You bought a Duplex for $280,000 and did $20,000 in renovations, for a total Basis of $300,000.

But this is not your Depreciable Basis.

First, we must subtract out the value of the land, because the land is not a depreciable asset.

You assign a value to the land of $25,000.

This leaves a Depreciable Basis of $275,000.

D = (PP + CI – LV) ÷ AL, WHERE
D IS THE AMOUNT OF ALLOWABLE ANNUAL DEPRECIATION,
PP IS THE PURCHASE PRICE,
CI IS YOUR CAPITAL IMPROVEMENTS ON THE PROPERTY,
LV IS THE ASSIGNED LAND VALUE, AND
AL IS THE ASSET LIFE.

D = (280,000 + 20,000 – 25,000) ÷ 27.5

D = 275,000 ÷ 27.5

D = 10,000

Your annual Depreciation Allowance will be $10,000.

CALCULATOR

Let's create a Depreciation Schedule for the Duplex to see what it looks like. Here is a Free Calculator that you can use:

https://www.calculatorsoup.com/calculators/financial/depreciation-property-realestate.php

1.) For "Cost Basis" enter 275,000.

2.) For "Recovery Period" select 27.5.

3.) For "Placed in Service" select "August" for Month and "2018" for Year.

4.) Check "Round to Dollars."

5.) For "Calculate Depreciation" select "Full Schedule."

6.) Click "Calculate."

Your Depreciation Schedule will show you the Depreciation Expense for the year, the Accumulated Depreciation as of the end of the year, and the remaining Book Value of the property at the end of the year.

If this were Commercial Real Estate such as a Warehouse, you would change the "Recovery Period" from 27.5 years to 39 years.

You will learn how important Depreciation is in real estate investing after you have been doing it for a while.

Without the deduction for "depreciation allowance" most real estate investments would not be attractive investments.

SECTION 19.

DEPRECIATION: SECTION 1245 PROPERTY

When a taxpayer buys an investment property, such as a Duplex, the money he pays for it is not an expense that can be deducted from the income produced by the property before the taxable income amount is determined.

This is true whether he pays cash for the property or finances the entire amount, or any combination of the two.

Investment property is placed into two different categories.

The building and the main building components are classified as Section 1250 Property.

Section 1250 Property must be depreciated using the Straight-line method, meaning an equal depreciation allowance expense each year for the life of the asset.

The real estate investment property can be depreciated for 27.5 years because it is classified as Residential Real Estate.

If the real estate investment is Commercial Property, it must be depreciated over the life of 39 years.

The other category for your real estate investment property concerns the furniture, fixtures and equipment.

These items are categorized as Section 1245 Property.

It is important to distinguish between the two because Section 1245 Property has a shorter depreciation period, usually either 5, 7, or 15 year periods.

Also, Accelerated Depreciation can be used for Section 1245 Property, such as Double Declining Balance or 150% Declining Balance, which gives you larger depreciation deduction in the early part of the asset life.

In many cases, when Section 1245 Property is purchased, new and used, and put into service, it can provide 100% Bonus Depreciation the first year under Section 179.

It is very important to separate out your Section 1245 Property from your total real estate investment to take advantage of the quicker and larger depreciation deductions.

The only downside to taking the Accelerated Depreciation is that when you sell the investment, and you must pay a Depreciation Recapture tax, the amount of the tax is the same as your individual tax rate instead of the standard 25% tax for Depreciation Recapture of Straight-line Depreciation of Section 1250 property.

SECTION 20.

DEPRECIATION: SECTION 1250 PROPERTY

When a taxpayer buys an investment property, such as a Duplex, the money he pays for it is not an expense that can be deducted from the income produced by the property before the taxable income amount is determined.

This is true whether he pays cash for the property or finances the entire amount, or any combination of the two.

Section 1250 Property is the real estate that you own and use as investment property. It is the building, not the land or the furnishings, fixtures, and equipment, although you can include the value of these items with the building instead of depreciating them separately.

Your property is described in Section 1250 of the Internal Revenue Code.

It can only be depreciated using the Straight Line method, with equal amounts claimed for Depreciation each year.

If the Section 1250 Property is the type classified as Residential Real Estate, the period of depreciation is 27.5 years.

If the Section 1250 Property is Commercial Real Estate, the period over which it can be depreciated is 39 years.

When you sell this property and have to pay the Depreciation Recapture tax, the rate will be 25% because your method of Depreciation was Straight Line.

The furniture, fixtures and equipment in your investment real estate are classified as Section 1245 Property.

For that, see SECTION 19. DEPRECIATION: SECTION 1245 PROPERTY (P. 84).

SECTION 21.

DEPRECIATION: STRAIGHT LINE

Depreciation is the annual "expense allocation" that the IRS allows you to deduct from the operating income of your investment real estate, even though it is not a cash, out-of-pocket expense.

There are different categories of property that can be depreciated, such as real property and personal property.

And there are also different methods by which these properties can be depreciated.

The methods are divided into two types.

The two types are Straight Line Depreciation and Accelerated Depreciation.

For more information, see SECTION 15. DEPRECIATION: ACCELERATED (P. 68).

As for Straight Line Depreciation, it is just what the name implies, equal amounts each year for the life of the asset.

The asset that you are depreciating will have a "life" assigned by the IRS, which may or may not actually reflect the useful life of the item.

For instance, your Duplex, being classified as Residential Real Estate by the IRS, is assigned a life of 27.5 years.

The Depreciation Allowance will be equal and uniform over the life of the asset, and this is called Straight Line Depreciation.

For Example, you bought a Duplex for $280,000 and did $20,000 of improvements. Your total Basis is $300,000.

But this is not your Depreciable Basis, because it includes the land that the building is located on, and land is not a depreciable asset. So we must subtract that value out.

You assign a value of $25,000 to the land.

Let's Calculate your Straight Line Depreciation on the Duplex.

D = (PP + CI − LV) ÷ AL, WHERE D IS THE AMOUNT OF ALLOWABLE DEPRECIATION,
PP IS THE PURCHASE PRICE,
CI IS THE CAPITAL IMPROVEMENTS ON THE PROPERTY,
LV IS THE ASSIGNED LAND VALUE, AND AL IS THE ASSET LIFE.

D = (280,000 + 20,000 – 25,000) ÷ 27.5

D = 275,000 ÷ 27.5

D = 10,000

Your Straight Line Depreciation on the Duplex is $10,000 per year.

DEPRECIATION RECAPTURE

If you hold your property for ten years and claim a total of $100,000 in Depreciation over that time period, when you sell you will have to pay a tax on the Depreciation you have taken.

The tax on Straight Line Depreciation Recapture is 25%.

So, after ten years, you will pay $25,000 in taxes on the $100,000 that you have been deducting from your income.

CALCULATOR

Now that you understand Straight Line Depreciation, let's create a Depreciation Schedule to see what it looks like. Here is a Free Calculator that you can use:

https://www.calculatorsoup.com/calculators/ financial/depreciation-property-realestate.php

1.) For "Cost Basis" enter 275,000.

2.) For "Recovery Period" select 27.5.

3.) For "Placed in Service" select "August" for Month and "2018" for Year.

4.) Check "Round to Dollars."

5.) For "Calculate Depreciation" select "Full Schedule."

6.) Click "Calculate."

Your Depreciation Schedule will show you the Depreciation Expense for the year, the Accumulated Depreciation as of the end of the year, and the remaining Book Value of the property at the end of the year.

If this were Commercial Real Estate such as a Warehouse, instead of Residential Real Estate, you would change the "Recovery Period" from 27.5 years to 39 years.

SECTION 22.

DEPRECIATION: 150% DECLINING BALANCE

When a taxpayer buys an investment property such as a Duplex, the money he pays for it is not an expense that can be deducted from the income produced by the property before the taxable income amount is determined.

This is true whether he pays cash for the property or finances the entire amount, or any combination of the two.

Most investment real estate is property that the IRS classifies as Section 1250 Property, which usually means that it is a building.

Section 1250 Property must be depreciated using the Straight-line method.

For more information, see SECTION 21. DEPRECIATION: STRAIGHT LINE.

But the portion of the real estate investment property called "personal property" by the IRS, even though it is business property, is classified as Section 1245 Property.

And Section 1245 Property can be depreciated using Accelerated Depreciation, such as the method described as Double Declining Balance in another Section.

See SECTION 17. DEPRECIATION: DOUBLE DECLINING BALANCE (P. 75).

A similar method is the 150% Declining Balance method.

It also allows you to deduct larger amounts of depreciation in the early part of the asset life than you would be able to with Straight Line Depreciation (SD), but not the maximum amount.

If you have a $10,000 asset with a 10-year life, Straight Line Depreciation would allow you to deduct one-tenth, or 10%, of the value as a depreciation allowance the first year, a total of $1,000.

By using the 150% Declining Balance method, you will be able to deduct a total of $1,500 the first year.

Here's how that would work.

For the first year, you take the Basis of $10,000 and divide by the 10-year life, and get $1,000. Then you multiply that by 150%, or 1.5, and get $1,500 depreciation allowance.

For the second year, you take the reduced Basis of the property, hence the "Declining Balance," of $8,500 and divide by 10, and get $850.

You multiply the $850 by 150%, or 1.5, and you get $1,275 depreciation allowance.

You continue to do this until your deduction would be more by switching to the Straight Line method, and then you change to that.

Depreciation is all about recovering your capital expenses as quickly as possible, and DDB and 150% Declining Balance are the best ways.

CALCULATOR

Now that you understand how 150% Declining Balance Depreciation works, let's do a Depreciation Schedule, using a Free Calculator.

https://www.calculatorsoup.com/calculators/financial/depreciation-declining-balance.php

1.) For "Asset Cost" enter 10,000.

2.) For "Salvage Value" enter 0.

3.) For "Useful Life" enter 10.

4.) For "Depreciation Factor" enter 1.5.

5.) For "Starting Month" select "January."

6.) For "Starting Year" enter 2018.

7.) For "Convention" select "Full-Month."

8.) Check "Round to Dollars."

9.) For "Calculate Depreciation" select "Full Schedule."

10.) Click "Calculate."

Your Depreciation Schedule will show you the Depreciation, Accumulated Depreciation, and Year-end Book Value for each year.

You will notice that at the end of the Asset Life you still have a Book Value balance.

This is because you can never reduce a number to zero by taking 15% of it over and over again. At some point, you must take 100% of it.

Therefore, at some point you will switch to the Straight Line Depreciation method of Depreciation.

You will need to consult with your tax professional to determine when and how to do this.

SECTION 23.

DEPRECIATION RECAPTURE

When you purchase an asset to be used in your income-producing business, you are entitled to deduct a "depreciation allowance" each year from that income.

But when you sell the asset, and you have a gain, the IRS wants you to pay a tax on the amount of depreciation you have taken. This is called "Depreciation Recapture."

The amount of the Depreciation Recapture tax is 25%.

Let's start by calculating the Depreciation.

**D = (PP + CI – LV) ÷ AL, WHERE
D IS DEPRECIATION,
PP IS THE PURCHASE PRICE OF THE ASSET,
CI IS CAPITAL IMPROVEMENTS MADE TO THE
PROPERTY,
LV IS THE LAND VALUE, AND
AL IS THE ASSET LIFE.**

For example, if you bought a Duplex for $280,000 and made $20,000 of Capital Improvements, and assigned $25,000 value to the land, you would have a Depreciable Basis of $275,000 and you would be able to depreciate the structure over a period of 27.5 years and claim $10,000 in Depreciation each year.

$$D = (280,000 + 20,000 - 25,000) \div 27.5$$

$$D = 275,000 \div 27.5$$

$$D = 10,000$$

Your annual Depreciation Allowance will be $10,000.

If you sell the asset after five years for $375,000 you will have a Capital Gains of $125,000 instead of the $75,000 difference between what you paid for it and what you sold it for.

This is because the $50,000 in Depreciation that you took over the five years reduced your Basis in the property from $300,000 to $250,000.

And now, the IRS considers the first $50,000 of that $125,000 of Capital Gains to be Depreciation Recapture, and they will tax it at a rate of 25%.

The remaining $75,000 of the Capital Gains amount of $125,000 will be considered "pure" Capital Gains and will be taxed at whatever tax rate you are subject to as an individual, probably 15%, but maybe 20%.

Your Depreciation Recapture tax would be .25 x 50,000 = $12,500.

Your Capital Gains tax, if you are in the 20% CG tax bracket, would be .20 x 75,000 = $15,000.

Many taxpayers wonder why they would choose to take Depreciation and reduce their taxable income when they are in a tax bracket lower than 25%, and then have to pay 25% on the Depreciation amount when they sell.

There are two answers, but the more important one is that you do not have a choice.

Even if you do not claim the Depreciation on your tax return, you will still be taxed 25% on what you didn't claim because the rule is that the Depreciation Recapture applies to "depreciation allowed" and not to "depreciation taken."

The only way that you can avoid Depreciation Recapture is to engage in a Section 1031 Like Kind Exchange when you sell your investment property.

Under Section 1031 you can sell your investment property and replace it with another investment property of equal or greater value, within 180 days, and instead of paying taxes on the Capital Gains and the Depreciation Recapture, you just roll those taxes into the new investment property.

I can recommend an excellent book on the subject (yes, I wrote it).

"How To Do A Section 1031 Like Kind Exchange" in both digital and print on Amazon. You can "Look Inside" here:

www.amazon.com/Michael-Lantrip/e/B01N2ZRGUY

SECTION 24.

EQUITY

Equity (E) is the value you have in your real property investment.

Equity is actually "net value," because it must be calculated.

**E = FMV − MPO − L − OD, WHERE
E IS YOUR EQUITY IN THE PROPERTY,
FMV IS THE FAIR MARKET VALUE OF THE PROPERTY,
MPO IS THE MORTGAGE PAYOFF AMOUNT,
L IS LIENS ON THE PROPERTY, AND
OD IS OTHER DEBTS ON THE PROPERTY.**

If you bought a $210,000 Duplex, paying $50,000 down, $5,000 closing costs, and getting a $160,000 mortgage, then your Equity in the property is $55,000 (50,000 plus 5,000).

At the time of purchase, the FMV is presumed to be what you paid for the property, and you paid $210,000 to the Seller and $5,000 to the closing agent and others, for a total of $215,000.

E = FMV – MPO – L – OD

E = 215,000 – 160,000 – 0 – 0

E = $55,000.

But even after you buy the property, you can Calculate your Equity at any time by using the above Calculation.

If you've held the property for at least a year, two of the four elements making up Equity have probably changed, and possibly all four.

Let's say you have held the property for three years.

By looking at comps, you determine that the FMV is now $255,000. This is because the property has appreciated in value about 6% each year, and because you have added a new furnace.

You have made 36 mortgage payments and the principal portion of these payments have reduced your payoff by $6,500.

You replaced the furnace at a cost of $6,000 and the company is allowing you to make payments on the bill in return for you granting them a lien on the property until it is paid, and the balance is $4,500.

Your property taxes will be due shortly, and that amount will be about $1,200.

So, the calculation now looks like this:

**E = FMV – MPO – L – OD, WHERE:
E IS EQUITY,
FMV IS FAIR MARKET VALUE,
MPO IS MORTGAGE PAYOFF AMOUNT,
L IS LIENS, AND
OD IS OTHER DEBT.**

E = 255,000 – (160,000 – 6,500) – 4,500 – 1,200

E = 255,000 – 153,500 – 4,500 – 1,200

E = $95,800

Your Equity has gone up from $55,000 to $95,800 in three years, an increase of $40,800.

The increase is due to asset appreciation and mortgage paydown.

The $40,800 increase in Equity represents a 74.18% increase in three years, which is almost 25% per year. Of course, that does not take into account the time value of money.

See SECTION 47. TIME VALUE OF MONEY (P. 198).

And, of course, this Calculation is for your Equity in the property and assumes that you plan to hold the property for more years into the future.

The amount of Equity that you would realize if you sold the property now is a different number.

The $95,800 amount is not what you would receive in a check at the closing table.

You would have transaction costs to be deducted, such as Sales Commission, a Survey, a Title Insurance Policy for the Buyer, legal costs for document preparation, escrow fees, and others.

The total transaction costs could be as high as $18,000.

That would still leave you with Equity of $77,800, an increase of $22,800.

Your three-year increase percentage would be 41.45% instead of 74.18%, and your annual increase would be 13.8% instead of 25%.

Remember, in the truest sense, Equity is the actual value that you have in your real property, which is expressed in the number of dollars you could put in your pocket if you sold it.

SECTION 25.
FAIR MARKET VALUE

The Fair Market Value (FMV) of a property is usually determined by the free market dynamic of supply and demand.

FMV is the price at which a willing Seller and a willing Buyer agree to transfer ownership.

But that is difficult to predict, and it isn't what the FMV of the property is for you; it's what it is for two other people.

But it is the definition of Fair Market Value, and you can determine it by looking at sales comparisons in your area for similar property.

But you want to Calculate the FMV for you.

The Calculation for determining what the FMV of the property is for you, using your Cap Rate, is:

FMV = NOI ÷ CR, WHERE
FMV IS THE FAIR MARKET VALUE OF THE PROPERTY,
NOI IS YOUR NET OPERATING INCOME, AND
CR IS YOUR CAPITALIZATION RATE.

If you have determined that the CR available to you with other comparable investments is 10%, and you are looking at a Duplex with an NOI of $30,000, and want to calculate the FMV:

FMV = NOI ÷ CR

FMV = 30,000 ÷ 0.10

FMV = 300,000

The FMV of this Duplex, based on your 10% Cap Rate, is $300,000.

But you might not have a Cap Rate that you are comfortable using, but you know other numbers related to the property, such as the Gross Rent Multiplier (GRM).

The GRM is a product of supply and demand.

If Fourplexes in your area with units that rent for $1,250 each are selling for $600,000 then you can calculate the GRM.

**GRM = FMV ÷ GPI, WHERE
GRM IS THE GROSS RENT MULTIPLIER,
FMV IS THE FAIR MARKET VALUE, AND
GPI IS THE GROSS POTENTIAL INCOME.**

GRM = 600,000 ÷ 60,000

GRM = 10

The investors in this area are paying ten times the GPI for multi-family properties.

With this knowledge, and the knowledge of how much the units are renting for, you can Calculate the FMV of a property.

FMV = GRM x GPI, WHERE

FMV IS THE FAIR MARKET VALUE OF THE PROPERTY,
GRM IS THE GROSS RENT MULTIPLIER, AND
GPI IS THE GROSS POTENTIAL INCOME.

If you found a Fourplex with two units renting for $750 and two renting for $950, your GPI is (2 x 750) plus (2 x 950) times twelve.

1,500 + 1,900 = 3,400

3,400 x 12 = 40,800.

We plug that into the Calculation, using a GRM of 10.

FMV = GRM x GPI

FMV = 10 x 40,800

FMV = 408,000

Your Fourplex will have a Fair Market Value of $408,000 based on the Gross Rent Multiplier of ten that is the standard in that market for that type of property.

The Calculations for Fair Market Value are just guidelines for you to use to make your own decision about your next investment.

If there are only five seasonal-rental properties between the Interstate and a popular stretch of beach, and you own three of them, you will likely pay whatever you have to pay to get the other two, because paying over the Fair Market Value and raising rents 25% across the board because you control the market could be a good business decision.

The Real Estate Investing Calculations are just to help you make the decision that is right for your particular situation.

SECTION 26.
FUTURE VALUE

One of the main reasons for investing in real estate is to increase your wealth through the yearly appreciation in property value.

The property will go up in value over the long term.

It will increase in different amounts in different years, maybe losing value in some.

But over time, it will go up in value.

There are many estimates of the historic annual increase in value, but the one that I find has the most credibility is 6.7%.

You wouldn't be using this number in 2008, but it is probably good today.

**FV = PV x (1 + I), WHERE
FV IS THE FUTURE VALUE,
PV IS THE PRESENT VALUE, AND
I IS THE PERCENTAGE INCREASE.**

Let's assume that you have a $400,000 property and you want to know what it will be worth for each of the next five years and at the end of that time if it increases 6.7% each year.

$$FV = PV \times (1 + I)$$

$$FV = 400,000 \times (1 + .067)$$

$$FV = 400,000 \times 1.067$$

$$FV = 426,800$$

The property will be worth $426,800 at the end of Year 1.

Then you take the new value, treat it as the new PV, and Calculate the value for Year 2.

$426,800 \times 1.067 = 455,396$ for Year 2.

And you continue to do that for each year.

$455,396 \times 1.067 = 485,908$ for Year 3.

$485,908 \times 1.067 = 518,464$ for Year 4.

$518,464 \times 1.067 = 553,201$ for year 5.

You can continue to create these Calculations for ten years, or even more, but at some point it becomes random, because the Calculations are initially based on an assumption, then the results are compounded with another assumption, and so forth.

If you just want to know the potential value after five years, based on an annual increase of 6.7%, you can just multiply 6.7% to the fifth power and then multiply the answer by the original property value.

1.067 x 1.067 x 1.067 x 1.067 x 1.067 = 1.383

400,000 x 1.383 = 553,200

The property would be worth $553,200.

CALCULATOR

Now that you understand what the Future Value Calculation is, what it's used for, and how it works, here is a Free Calculator that you can use for quicker results.

https://www.calculatorsoup.com/calculators/financial/future-value-calculator-basic.php

1.) For "Number of Years" enter 5.0.

2.) For "Interest Rate" enter 6.70.

3.) For "Present Value" enter 400,000.

4.) Click "Calculate."

Your Future Value Calculation will be $558,655.39.

You will notice that in the above Calculation with the same information, our Future Value was $553,200 which is a different amount.

This is not a mistake.

The difference is because the Calculator is compounding the 6.7% rate monthly, and we used annual compounding in our Calculation.

This Calculator also allows you to do partial years; in other words, a number of months.

If you want to do the Calculation for three years and nine months, put in 3.75 for the "Number of Years" and get $523,893.34.

Play with the Calculator and see what else it can do for you.

SECTION 27.

INCOME STATEMENT

The Income Statement is the control document for any business.

It's what you use to analyze your company or your investment, and to make management decisions.

It's what a Lender uses to determine whether to lend you money.

It's what a potential Buyer uses to determine if he is interested in purchasing your business, or investment property.

It's what the IRS uses to determine if you have been naughty.

It involves the three elements of Income, Expenses, and Profit.

P = I − E, WHERE
P IS PROFIT,
I IS INCOME, AND
E IS EXPENSES

This is what an Income Statement looks like.

ABC COMPANY

Anytown, USA

1/1/2018 – 3/31/2018

INCOME STATEMENT

INCOME

Total Rental Income	40,500	
Other Income	4,500	
GROSS INCOME		45,000

EXPENSES

Repairs & Maint	6,000
Management	4,000
Taxes	3,500
Insurance	1,500
Utilities	4,200
Landscaping	700
Legal	1,000
Accounting	800
Contract Labor	800

TOTAL EXPENSES	22,500
NET INCOME	22,500

Also see SECTION 29. INCOME: GROSS OPERATING (P. 118) and SECTION 33. INCOME: NET OPERATING (P. 133) for more details on what Income might look like.

Often, a Balance Sheet is prepared at the same time as an Income Statement.

See SECTION 2. BALANCE SHEET (P. 7).

Your Income Statement will end up reflecting the activities of your company or investment and there is no way to know at this point what it should look like.

Once you have worked with it for a while, you will know how to do it.

You will design your Income Statement to tell you what you need to know.

And your Income Statement will probably look different from others.

Just remember that your Net Income (Profit) is your Gross Income minus your Total Expenses.

SECTION 28.

INCOME: BREAK-EVEN RATIO

The Break-even Ratio (BER) will tell you the portion of your Gross Operating Income (GOI) that will be needed for paying your Operating Expenses (OE) and your Debt Service (DS).

**BER = (OE + DS) ÷ GOI, WHERE
BER IS THE BREAK-EVEN RATIO,
OE IS OPERATING EXPENSES,
DS IS DEBT SERVICE, AND
GOI IS GROSS OPERATING INCOME.**

(Note: Gross Operating Income is the Gross Potential Income minus Vacancy and Credit Loss).

If we have ten units renting for $600 and a VACL of 10%, we have a GOI of $72,000 minus $7,200 = $64,800.

Our DS is $14,700 and our OE are $32,600.

BER = (OE + DS) ÷ GOI

BER = (32,600 + 14,700) ÷ 64,800

BER = 47,300 ÷ 64,800 = 0.7299

So, about 73% of your Gross Operating Income is being used to pay the Operating Expenses and Debt Service.

Lenders often use this ratio to determine the amount of risk in the loan.

It tells them that in this case, Gross Operating Income can fall by 27% and the Investor will still be able to cover Operating Expenses and Debt Service.

CALCULATOR

Now that you understand Break-even Ratio, let's use a Free Calculator to run one.

https://www.ajdesigner.com/php_ber/break_even_ratio.php

1.) For "debt service (DS)" enter 14700 (no comma).

2.) For "operating expense (OE)" enter 32600.

3.) For "gross operating income" enter 64800.

4.) Click "Calculate."

Your Break-even Ratio is calculated as 72.9938271.

SECTION 29.

INCOME: GROSS OPERATING INCOME

The Gross Operating Income (GOI) is the Gross Potential Income (GPI) minus the Vacancy And Credit Loss (VACL).

GOI = GPI – (GPI x VACL), WHERE GOI IS THE GROSS OPERATING INCOME, GPI IS THE GROSS POTENTIAL INCOME, AND VACL IS THE PERCENTAGE OF VACANCY AND CREDIT LOSS.

GPI is the monthly rent multiplied by the number of units, then multiplied times twelve months.

It is not actually a realistic number, but we have to start somewhere for any Calculation.

VACL is unpredictable, and depends on all of the factors surrounding the property type and location, as well as the current state of the economy, so the best solution is to just use a figure that is 5% or 10% of gross rents.

The safest number is to use 10% and have 5% of that amount represent the times that the property will be unrented, and have 5% represent the amount of losses you will incur due to such things as hot checks, reversed wire transfers, negotiated move-outs, and similar situations.

For a rent house that rents for $1,000 per month and has a 5% VACL:

GOI = GPI − (GPI x VACL)

GOI = (12 x 1,000) − (12,000 x .05)

GOI = 12,000 − 600

GOI = $11,400

For a 10-unit apartment building with units renting for $500 month and a 10% VACL:

GOI = GPI − (GPI x VACL)

GOI = (10 x 500 x 12) − [(10 x 500 x 12) x .10)]

GOI = 60,000 − (60,000 x .10)

GOI = 60,000 − 6,000

GOI = 54,000

Real estate investing is all about income and expenses.

The better you become at recognizing, measuring, and managing them, the more successful you will be.

CALCULATOR

Let's use a Free Calculator to see how this works.

https://www.ajdesigner.com/php_goi/gross_operating_income.php

1.) For "gross scheduled income (GCI)" enter 60000 (no comma).

2.) For "vacancy and credit loss (VCL)" enter 6000.

3.) Click "Calculate."

Your Gross Operating Income is $54,000.

SECTION 30.

INCOME: GROSS POTENTIAL INCOME

Gross Potential Income (GPI) is the expected income that a property will produce without deduction for Vacancy And Credit Loss (VACL).

Multiply the rent amount times the number of units, then times twelve months.

GPI = RPU x U, WHERE
GPI IS THE GROSS POTENTIAL INCOME OF THE PROPERTY,
RPU IS THE RENT PER UNIT, AND
U IS THE NUMBER OF UNITS.

A rent house that rents for $1,000 per month will have a GPI of $12,000.

A Duplex with each unit renting for $850 per month will have a GPI of $20,400.

A ten-unit apartment building with each unit renting for $500 per month will have a GPI of $60,000.

Of course, you almost never have 100% occupancy and perfect tenants, so this number is only the income "potential" of the property, but it is always the starting point for any calculation about income.

The next step is to Calculate your Gross Operating Income (GOI) by applying your percentage for Vacancy And Credit Loss (VACL).

See SECTION 29. INCOME: GROSS OPERATING (P. 118) and SECTION 49. VACANCY AND CREDIT LOSS (P. 202).

SECTION 31.

INCOME: GROSS RENTAL MULTIPLIER

The Gross Rental Multiplier (GRM) is only a rough estimate to compare properties, but it is a very interesting way to look at investments.

You can use the GRM to tell you how much you must pay for each $1.00 of rental income.

Of course, you want to pay as little as possible.

The Gross Rental Multiplier (GRM) is the Fair Market Value (FMV) of the property divided by the Gross Potential Income (GPI).

GRM = FMV ÷ GPI, WHERE GRM IS THE GROSS RENTAL MULTIPLIER, FMV IS THE FAIR MARKET VALUE OF THE PROPERTY, AND GPI IS THE GROSS POTENTIAL INCOME OF THE PROPERTY.

How much are you paying for $1.00 of rental income if a $400,000 Fourplex has a Gross Potential Income of $48,000?

GRM = FMV ÷ GPI

GRM = 400,000 ÷ 48,000

GRM = 8.33

So, you would be paying $8.33 for each $1.00 of potential rental income.

Of course, it is not a Calculation that you can put on your projected Income Statement, but it is a way for you to initially look at four or five potential property purchases.

And it is a Calculation that helps you get a feel for what it will cost you to acquire a future stream of income.

ALTERNATIVE CALCULATIONS

Also, you can add it to other Calculations to get a broader picture.

For instance, if you are only putting 20% of your own money into the investment, then .20 x 8.33 = 1.67. That means that you are only using $1.67 of your cash to receive $1.00 of potential income.

Then you consider that in addition to acquiring an asset that will produce income, you are also acquiring an asset that will appreciate in value.

Assuming a 6.7% annual appreciation rate, which is historic, the $400,000 Duplex will increase in value $26,800 the first year, and increase in a compound fashion each year after that first year, because the $400,000 will continue to appreciate 6.7%, but so will the appreciation amount each year.

Now you can create another calculation that will tell you how much it will cost you to purchase $1 of a combination of potential income and asset appreciation, and call it Gross Benefit Multiplier (GBM).

$$GBM = FMV \div [GPI + (0.067 \times FMV)]$$

$$GBM = 400,000 \div [48,000 + (0.067 \times 400,000)]$$

$$GBM = 400,000 \div (48,000 + 26,800)$$

$$GBM = 400,000 \div 74,800$$

$$GBM = 5.3476$$

So, you would be paying $5.35 for $1.00 of a combination of potential income and asset appreciation.

And if you only contributed 20% of this $5.35 in the form of a Down Payment, then you are purchasing this $1.00 of a combination of potential income and asset appreciation for $1.07.

Then you can factor in the rental increases each year, and you begin to see that at some point you will be paying less than $1.00 for a return of $1.00 potential every year for as long as you own the property.

Just remember, Gross Potential Income is not actual income. You need to look at SECTION 11. CASH FLOW (P. 43) and SECTION 12. CASH FLOW: DISCOUNTED (P. 52) to get a clearer picture of that.

The good thing about using Real Estate Investing Calculations is that once you understand them, you can create your own Calculations that allow you to know things about a property that other investors do not know. And that's when you begin making the best decisions.

CALCULATOR

Now that you understand what a Gross Rent Multiplier is, let's do a Calculation on a Free Calculator.

https://www.ajdesigner.com/php_grm/gross_rent_multiplier.php

1.) For "market value (MV)" enter 400000 (no comma).

2.) For "gross scheduled income (GSI)" enter 48000.

3.) Click "Calculate."

Your Gross Rent Multiplier is 8.33, the same number that we got when we did the Calculation by hand above.

SECTION 32.

INCOME: NET INCOME MULTIPLIER

The Net Income Multiplier (NIM) is used to compare the prices of different investment properties, or to determine the time required to recoup your investment.

But the Net Income Multiplier will also tell you how much you will have to pay for each $1.00 of annual Net Operating Income (NOI) that will be produced by the investment.

This might be the most valuable of all of the Calculations.

After all, that's what you want to know, isn't it? How much money will this put in my pocket, and how much will it cost me to get it?

NIM = FMV ÷ NOI, WHERE
NIM IS THE NET INCOME MULTIPLIER,
FMV IS THE FAIR MARKET VALUE OF THE INVESTMENT, AND
NOI IS THE NET OPERATING INCOME.

For Example, if we have a $400,000 Fourplex that produces $30,700 of Net Operating Income, then the Calculation is:

NIM = 400,000 ÷ 30,700

NIM = 13.029

So, you would pay $13.03 for each $1.00 of annual Net Operating Income.

ALTERNATIVE CALCULATIONS

The four reasons that investors prefer to invest in real estate are cash flow, appreciation, leverage, and tax advantages.

The tax advantages can only be calculated on an individual basis, and we have already calculated the cost of $1.00 of income, but you can also Calculate the cost of $1.00 of Asset Appreciation (AP).

Asset Appreciation happens over time, so we will assume that the asset will be held for five years.

We could also Calculate an increase in the NOI by raising the rents each year, but that increase would probably be offset by a comparable increase in operating expenses, which lowers the NOI, so it would probably be a wash.

But we can assume an annual Asset Appreciation, and apply the historic rate of 6.7%.

Now we can create a new Calculation to determine how much it would cost to acquire $1.00 of a combination of income and appreciation, which we will call AP. We can call the new unknown the Net Benefit Multiplier (NBM), and our Calculation is:

NBM = FMV ÷ (NOI + AP)

NBM = FMV ÷ [NOI + (0.067 x FMV)]

NBM = 400,000 ÷ [30,700 + (0.067 x 400,000)]

NBM = 400,000 ÷ (30,700 + 26,800)

NBM = 400,000 ÷ 57,500

NBM = 6.957

So, it would cost you $6.96 to purchase $1.00 of combined income and asset appreciation.

But this is only for one year of ownership, and we are assuming a holding period of five years. The AP will increase each year, because it is behaving in a compound fashion.

So we have to know the yearly average of the asset appreciation over the five years.

Here's how that Calculation is done for each year of appreciation.

0.067 x 400,000 = 26,800

0.067 x (400,000 + 26,800) = 28,596

0.067 x (400,000 + 26,800 + 28,596) = 30,512

0.067 x (400,000 + 26,800 + 28,596 + 30,512) = 32,556

0.067 x (400,000 + 26,800 + 28,596 + 30,512 + 32,556) = 34,737

And to determine the yearly average for the five years:

(26,800 + 28,596 + 30,512 + 32,556 + 34,737) ÷ 5 = 30,640

Now we plug the 5-year average AP into our NBM Calculation:

NBM = FMV ÷ (NOI + AP)

NBM = 400,000 ÷ (30,700 + 30,640)

NBM = 6.521

So, it would cost $6.52 to purchase $1.00 of a combination of income and asset appreciation with this investment.

CALCULATOR

Now that you understand what the Net Income Multiplier is, let's use a Free Calculator to do a Calculation.

http://www.danielsoper.com/fincalc/calc. aspx?id=59

1.) For "Net operating income" enter 30700 (no comma).

2.) For "Purchase price" enter 400000.

3.) Click "Calculate."

Your Net Income Multiplier is 13.03.

This is the same number that we got doing it by hand.

Now you can experiment by putting in different numbers.

If your target NIM is 10.00, what NOI and Purchase Price will you need to find?

SECTION 33.

INCOME: NET OPERATING INCOME

Net Operating Income (NOI) is the Gross Operating Income (GOI) minus the Operating Expenses (OE).

NOI = GOI – OE, WHERE NOI IS NET OPERATING INCOME, GOI IS GROSS OPERATING INCOME, AND OE IS THE PROPERTY'S OPERATING EXPENSES.

For Example, you have a Fourplex with units that rent for $1,250 each. You have a Vacancy and Credit Loss (VACL) of 10%. So your Gross Potential Income (GPI) is 4 x 1,250 x 12 months = $60,000.

Your VACL is .10 x 60,000 = $6,000. So your Gross Operating Income (GOI) is $54,000.

Your Operating Expenses (OE) are $32,420.

For complete explanation, see the other Sections on Gross Potential Income (GPI), Gross Operating Income (GOI), Vacancy And Credit Loss (VACL), and Operating Expenses (OE).

NOI = GOI − OE

NOI = 54,000 − 32,420

NOI = 21,580

Your Net Operating Income for this property is $21,580.

The two keys to this Calculation are the percentage that you have assigned for VACL, and the specific items that you have decided to include in Operating Expenses.

However, if you know what your Capitalization Rate is, and you are looking at potential investment properties to meet that target rate, you can Calculate what the Net Operating Income must be for each property.

NOI = CR x FMV, WHERE NOI IS NET OPERATING INCOME, CR IS YOUR CAPITALIZATION RATE, AND FMV IS THE FAIR MARKET VALUE OF THE PROPERTY.

If your Cap Rate is 13% and you are looking at a property with an asking price of $166,000, you can plug in the numbers.

NOI = CR x FMV

NOI = .13 x 166,000

NOI = 21,580

This property must produce a NOI of $21,580 to satisfy your requirement.

CALCULATOR

Let's see how this looks in a Free Calculator.

https://www.ajdesigner.com/php_ capitalization_rate/capitalization_rate_noi.php

1.) For "capitalization rate (CR)" enter 13.

2.) For "value or cost (V)" enter 166000 (no comma).

3.) Click "Calculate."

Your required Net Operating Income is $21,580.

We got the same number with our above Calculation.

Now you can quickly substitute numbers in the mix to see what the various outcomes would be.

SECTION 34.

INTEREST: COMPOUND

First, make sure that you understand Simple Interest (I) by reading SECTION 35. INTEREST: SIMPLE.

Compound Interest (CI) is when you are paying interest on interest.

Normally, when an interest rate is stated, it is the annual interest rate.

With no other conditions stipulated, that means that you will have the use of the money for 12 months and at the end of that time, you will owe an amount of interest that is calculated by multiplying the interest rate times the loan amount.

I = P x R, WHERE
I IS THE INTEREST AMOUNT DUE,
P IS THE PRINCIPAL AMOUNT OF THE LOAN,
AND
R IS THE INTEREST RATE STATED.

For Example:

I = P x R

I = 100,000 x 0.06

I = 6,000

If you borrow $100,000 for one year at 6.0%, at the end of that time you will owe $6,000 in interest, as well as the $100,000 borrowed principal.

If you only borrowed it for one month instead of twelve, you would owe:

6,000 ÷ 12 = $500.00.

However, if you borrowed it for a year, and the interest is compounded monthly, the numbers will all change.

Compound Interest means that at the end of each month the interest due is calculated, and added to the principal, and for the next month the interest rate is calculated for that month based on the unpaid principal and the accrued and unpaid interest.

In other words, the interest is compounded.

At the end of the first month, you would owe $100,500.

As you might notice, this is a monthly interest rate of 0.5%.

To work with calculations involving a monthly time period, it is better to convert the annual interest rate to a monthly interest rate.

Monthly Interest Rate = Annual Interest Rate ÷ 12.

Monthly Interest Rate = 6.0 ÷ 12 = 0.50

To Calculate the interest due the second month:

CI = [(100,000 x 1.005) x 0.005]

CI = 100,500 x 0.005 = 502.50.

For the second month, you would still be paying 0.50% on the $100,000 loan, but you would also be paying 0.50% interest on the interest that was accrued and unpaid the first month. You owe $500 interest on the $100,000 and $2.50 interest on the first month's $500 interest. Total = $502.50.

As you can see, Compound Interest will raise the interest liability each month.

If you want to see what the *annual interest* cost would be on $100,000 at 6.0% that is *compounded monthly:*

CI = 100,000 x 1.005 x 1.005 x 1.005 x 1.005 x 1.005 x 1.005 x 1.005 x 1.005 x 1.005 x 1.005 x 1.005 x 1.005 = 106,167.78

Subtract the loan amount of $100,000 from the total, and you have interest due of $6,167.78.

This compares to $6,000 due when the interest is not compounded monthly.

So, the monthly compounding of the 6.0% interest on $100,000 was an additional $167.78.

Interest rates can be compounded daily as well as monthly or quarterly, or any other period.

Daily compounding is often referred to as "Continuous."

When using the Compound Interest rules, lenders will often stipulate that every month has 30 days, and the year has 360 days.

This makes it easier to have general guidelines that apply everywhere and every time.

CALCULATOR

You have done the Calculation yourself, now let's look at a Free Online Calculator that will do it for you, and allow you maximum flexibility to look at it in other ways.

https://www.calculatorsoup.com/calculators/ financial/compound-interest-calculator.php

1.) For "Calculate" select "Total P+I (A)."

2.) For "Principal" enter 100,000.

3.) For "Rate" enter 6.0.

4.) For "Compound" select "Monthly."

5.) For "Time" enter 1.0.

6.) Click "Calculate."

Your Calculation for Compound Interest will be $106,167.78.

This is exactly what we got with the above Calculation, but quicker.

The point for you to remember here is that Compound Interest will increase your loan cost if you are a borrower, and can increase your profit if you are a lender.

Let's look at what would happen if we compounded the interest on this loan daily based on the 365-day calendar year.

Enter everything the same, but change the "Compound" selection from "Monthly" to "Daily (365/ Yr)" and click "Calculate."

Your new Calculation for daily compounded interest using 365 days is $106,183.13.

If you change the compounding interval to 360 days, the difference is one penny less interest.

And if you change the compounding interval to continuously, the difference is 65 cents more interest.

You will probably not need to do so, but you can also use this Calculator to determine the interest on almost any interval of compounding.

This is also a good Calculator to verify that your lender is treating you fairly if you have a loan with compound interest.

The lender might be "rounding up" at every interval in the calculation, and/or might be calculating to two decimal points instead of eight.

On a $400,000 loan that could make a big difference.

SECTION 35.

INTEREST: SIMPLE

Simple Interest (I) is just the stated interest rate multiplied times the loan amount, with an assumed period of one year.

**I = P x R, WHERE
I IS THE INTEREST AMOUNT,
P IS THE PRINCIPAL OF THE LOAN, AND
R IS THE RATE OF INTEREST.**

If you borrow $100,000 for one year at 6.7%, at the end of the year you will have accrued interest of $6,700:

I = P x R

I = 100,000 x 0.067 = 6,700

So, at the end of the year you will still owe the $100,000 principal, and now you will also owe $6,700 in interest.

If you want to know the monthly amount, you just divide by twelve.

6,700 ÷ 12 = 558.33

So, the monthly amount is $558.33.

(Note: this is not completely true if your loan is a mortgage, see below).

Likewise if you want to know the daily amount, divide by 365.

6,700 ÷ 365 = 18.356

This means that your loan is accruing a daily interest liability of $18.36.

Sometimes, when you request and receive a Loan Payoff Statement from your lender, it will state the Principal Balance as of after the last monthly payment, and then will provide something called "Daily Accrual Amount" and that will be the amount of interest liability accruing daily.

You lender does that so that you, and the closing agent if there is a sale pending, can calculate exactly what the loan payoff amount is on any day after the date of the last payment.

The calculation of Simple Interest is reset each month for mortgages.

This is because you are not only paying interest on the loan, but you are also making monthly payments to reduce the principal.

When you make a payment, the payment is first applied to the Accrued Interest, and the remainder of the payment is applied to the Principal Balance.

The following month, the interest rate of 6.7% is applied to the new loan balance, and a different amount of interest is due. The following monthly payment is applied first to the Accrued Interest and the remainder to the Principal Balance.

You can see an Example of how this works by looking at your Amortization Schedule if you currently have a home loan or an investment property loan.

The lender will have provided you with an Amortization Schedule so that you will know the portion of each monthly payment that is being applied to interest and the portion being applied to reduce the principal.

If you do not have an Amortization Schedule handy, go to one of the websites that provides a free Amortization Schedule. The one I use is:

www.financial-calculators.com/amortization-schedule.

1.) For "Loan Amount" enter 100,000.

2.) For "Payment #" enter 360, for a 30-year loan.

3.) For "Annual Interest Rate" enter 6.7.

4.) Leave everything else as is, and click "Calc."

Scroll down and you will see your Amortization Schedule.

The amount of each of your 360 payments will be $645.28.

This is the amount necessary to pay the monthly Accrued Interest of 6.7%, and pay off the $100,000 loan in 30 years.

Notice the first payment.

You will see that the interest portion of your first payment is $558.33.

This is exactly what you get by multiplying 0.067 times 100,000 and dividing by twelve.

In other words, one month's interest.

This is an annual interest rate of 6.7% on $100,000, computed monthly.

The remainder of the first $645.28 payment, $86.95, is applied to the Principal Balance of the loan, reducing it to $99,913.05.

For the second payment, less interest is due because 0.067 times 99,913.05 and divided by twelve is 557.85.

The required payment is the same, $645.28, but the breakdown of interest and principal reduction has changed.

So, Simple Interest is still used, but at monthly intervals, on a loan where the interest payments are coupled with payback payments of the principal.

CALCULATOR

Simple Interest is the easiest to Calculate.

There is even a Calculator for it.

https://www.calculatorsoup.com/calculators/financial/simple-interest-calculator.php

In our Example above, we assume that the time period involved is one year.

**$I = P \times R \times T$, WHERE
I IS THE INTEREST AMOUNT,
P IS THE PRINCIPAL,
R IS THE RATE OF INTEREST, AND
T IS THE NUMBER OF RELEVANT TIME PERIODS**

1.) For Principal enter $100,000.

2.) For Rate of Interest enter 6.70.

3.) For Time period enter 1.

4.) Click "Calculate."

Your Simple Interest Calculation will be $6,700.

This is the same as what we got with our own Calculation.

SECTION 36.

LATE FEES

Late Fees are not something that you can just impose because you own the property and you call the shots.

Late Fees are like the amount of the rent, a matter to be agreed upon between the landlord and the tenant. And if you ever expect to have to enforce the collection with a legal proceeding in Court, or avoid a charge of Usury lodged against you, the agreement must be in writing.

The Rental Agreement should spell out precisely how much the Late Fee will be. The Late Fee can be a specific amount or a percentage, but it must be one or the other.

If it is a specific amount, it should also state a time period, or time periods, associated with it, such as "$50 due and payable when the initial delinquency occurs, and an additional $50 for each month that the delinquency continues."

If the Late Fee is a percentage of the rent, it should be stated as such, and also state if it will continue for subsequent months that the delinquency continues.

The most important part of the Late Fee stipulation is exactly when the delinquency will occur, such as "midnight on the eighth day following the day that the rent is due."

Your Rental Agreement should state that the stated amount of rent is due and payable on a certain date "in full," and that payment of less than the full amount due will trigger the Late Fee.

The Agreement should also state that any monies received for rent will be applied first to delinquencies and Late Fees in that order, and then to the current amount due. This will avoid an argument in Court about what was being paid, when a payment was made.

Once the Late Fee is adequately spelled out in your Agreement, have the tenant sign it in front of a Notary Public. This avoids the situation where the tenant takes the Agreement away and brings it back with a forged signature, and this also avoids you having to prove the signature in Court.

You might also draw a line in the margin next to the paragraph about Late Fees, and have the tenant initial on the line. This will counter the argument later in Court that "Yes, I read the Agreement, but I didn't see that."

SECTION 37.

OPERATING EXPENSES

Operating Expenses are looked at in a number of significantly different ways.

The first, and most important, is how the IRS looks at them, because this is how your taxes will be determined.

The IRS says that Operating Expenses are expenses that were incurred because they were necessary in order to produce the income that is being reported, and the expenses contributed to the creation of that income.

Actually, the IRS says "reasonable and necessary," so be careful with the "reasonable" part.

See SECTION 27. INCOME STATEMENT (P. 113) to see what these are.

But for purposes of using your Real Estate Investing Calculations, you will also be compiling other, different, lists of Operating Expenses, which will be used for your investment analysis.

Your decision about what to include in your list of Operating Expenses will determine how accurate your Calculations are.

CASH FLOW

Cash Flow is the cash left over after you take the monthly income from the property and pay all of the monthly expenses of the property.

In other words, cash in, minus cash out.

**CF = I – E, WHERE
CF IS CASH FLOW,
I IS ALL OF THE CASH INCOME, AND
E IS ALL OF THE CASH EXPENSES**

The two critical "Expenses" that you will either include in, or exclude from, the Cash Flow Calculation that will affect its accuracy, and its usefulness, are Debt Service (DS) and Capital Expenditures (CE), also called Cap Ex.

If you are projecting Cash Flow of a potential investment, and you are comparing the results of more than one investment, you cannot include Debt Service in the Cash Flow Calculation, because you have not bought the property yet, and there is no Debt Service.

The Cash Flow that you are projecting is what *you will use to pay* the Debt Service.

Besides, Debt Service is not really a characteristic of the property you are evaluating, it is a characteristic of you, and your ability to borrow money.

The other "Expense" that will affect the accuracy, and usefulness, of your Cash Flow Calculation is Cap Ex.

Although it is not an actual monthly cash expense (you hope!), it is an expected expense that will occur at random intervals, and in large amounts, and should be estimated and treated as a monthly expense, and should be paid into a suspense account to be used when the unfortunate happens, such as a roof just wearing out.

See SECTION 8. CAPITAL EXPENDITURES (P. 31) for a more complete explanation on how to do this.

Of course, you can include Debt Service if that suits your purposes, and you can exclude Cap Ex if you want. Just be sure that you understand the meaning of the number that you are getting.

NET OPERATING INCOME

One of the basic Calculations used in investment analysis is the determination of Net

Operating Income (NOI) of a property, so that multiple properties can be compared for investment decisions, or so that a potential lender can make an informed decision about your loan application.

NOI = GOI – OE, WHERE
NOI IS NET OPERATING INCOME,
GOI IS GROSS OPERATING INCOME, AND
OE IS TOTAL OPERATING EXPENSES

As you can see, the first number that you need, GOI, will be easy to Calculate. You just take the number of units times the rent per unit, times the number of months, and you have your Gross Potential Income. Then you subtract your allowance for Vacancy And Credit Loss (VACLE) and you have your annual Gross Operating Income.

But then you must determine what to include in Operating Expenses, and what to leave out.

You can include or exclude Cap Ex, described above, Debt Service (DS), also described above, and Depreciation, which is an entirely different discussion (See all of the Sections on Depreciation).

Decide what you intend to use your Calculation for, and then decide which Expenses in include.

OPERATING EXPENSE RATIO

The Operating Expense Ratio (OER) tells you what percentage of the Gross Operating Income (GOI) is used to pay the Total Operating Expenses (TOE).

OER = TOE ÷ GOI, WHERE
OER IS OPERATING EXPENSE RATIO,
TOE IS TOTAL OPERATING EXPENSES, AND
GOI IS GROSS OPERATING INCOME

Again, your Gross Operating Income will be easy to determine. See the above paragraph.

You will need to decide which Expenses to include in the number that you use for Total Operating Expenses. This will determine the percentage figure that you get as an answer.

So, know what you will be using the percentage for, and then include the Expenses that you want to be reflected in that number.

SECTION 38.

OPERATING EXPENSE RATIO

The Operating Expense Ratio (OER) tells you what percentage of the annual Gross Operating Income (GOI) is being used to pay the annual Total Operating Expenses (TOE).

The Operating Expense Ratio (OER) is one of the first questions that a lender will ask you.

OER = TOE ÷ GOI, WHERE OER IS OPERATING EXPENSE RATIO, TOE IS TOTAL OPERATING EXPENSES, AND GOI IS GROSS OPERATING INCOME.

For Example, if your Fourplex generates a GOI of $60,000 and your TOE is $32,700, then:

OER = TOE ÷ GOI

OER = 32,700 ÷ 60,000

OER = 54.5

You are spending 54.5% of your annual Gross Operating Income to pay your annual Total Operating Expenses.

You can also use this Calculation to determine the ratio for individual Expenses or groups of Expenses.

If you have a multi-family property that is not being individually-metered and you are considering metering it, you can calculate what percentage of your Gross Operating Income is being spent on Utilities.

OER = TU ÷ GOI, WHERE OER IS THE OPERATING EXPENSE RATIO, TU IS THE TOTAL AMOUNT OF UTILITIES, AND GOI IS GROSS OPERATING INCOME.

The profitability of any real estate investment has to do with the relationship between income and expenses, and this is one of the key Calculations.

CALCULATOR

Now let's see what it looks like on one of the Free Calculators.

https://www.ajdesigner.com/php_oer/ operating_expense_ratio.php

1.) For "operating expense (OE)" enter 32700 (no comma).

2.) For "gross operating income (GOI)" enter 60000.

3.) Click "Calculate."

Your Operating Expense Ratio is 54.5%.

This is the same number we got doing it by hand.

If you have a target OER and you want to determine what your Gross Operating Income must be, or what your Operating Expense must be, click on one of the related Calculations in the box at the bottom, and solve for a different unknown.

SECTION 39.
PAYBACK PERIOD

Payback Period (PP) is the length of time it will take to receive back the amount of cash that you put into the investment.

**PP = ICI ÷ CF, WHERE
PP IS THE PAYBACK PERIOD,
ICI IS THE AMOUNT OF YOUR INITIAL CASH INVESTMENT, AND
CF IS THE MONTHLY CASH FLOW.**

If you bought a property for $100,000 and financed $70,000, then you put in $30,000 in cash to make up the difference.

If you paid $6,000 in closing costs, then you will have also put up the cash for that.

So your total "cash in" is $36,000.

The property cash flows $1,000 per month.

PP = ICI ÷ CF

PP = 36,000 ÷ 1,000

PP = 36

If the property cash flows $1,000 per month, it will take 36 months, or 3 years, to return your cash investment.

This is your Payback Period.

If the Cash Flow is only $500 per month, your Payback Period will be 72 months, or 6 years.

Look at SECTION 11. CASH FLOW (P. 43) for a fuller explanation.

There should be a direct relationship between the amount of your cash investment and the Payback Period because a lower amount will be paid back sooner.

But there is an inverse relationship between the amount of your cash investment and the amount of your Cash Flow that you will be able to keep instead of using it for debt service.

A low cash investment will mean a higher debt service which will result in a lower portion of the Cash Flow available to you because you are spending more of it on debt service.

You can decide exactly when you want to have your cash investment back so that you can put it into another investment, and you can create your financing at the beginning to meet that goal.

A caution here about waiting too long to get your cash back. Money in the future is worth less than money right now.

You can actually do a Payback Period Calculation using Discounted Cash Flow instead of just Cash Flow, but it is very complicated. The Calculation is

$$DPP = - \ln[1 - (IR \div C)] \div \ln(1 + R).$$

It gives me a headache just looking at it.

But, good news, you can do a Discounted Cash Flow, and therefore a Discounted Payback Period, with the Calculator below.

Also see SECTION 12. CASH FLOW: DISCOUNTED (P. 52).

CALCULATOR

Now that you understand what a Payback Period is, let's do a Calculation.

The following Calculator will allow you to do a Payback Period based on Discounted Cash Flow, resulting in the very difficult, but very useful, Discounted Payback Period.

http://www.calculator.net/payback-period-calculator.html

1.) For "Initial Investment" enter 36,000.

2.) For "Cash Flow" enter 12,000.

3.) For "Increase/Decrease" select "Increase."

4.) For percentage enter 5%.

5.) For "Number of Years" enter 5.

6.) For "Discount Rate" enter 7%.

7.) Click "Calculate."

As you can see, your Payback Period is 2.851 years.

But your Discounted Payback Period is 3.286 years.

Your annual Cash on Cash return is 23.56%.

You will also have a chart which shows:

Cash Flow

Net Cash Flow

Discounted Cash Flow, and

Net Discounted Cash Flow

This Calculator will also allow you to do Discounted Payback Period even when you will have different amounts of Cash Flow each year.

SECTION 40.

PRESENT VALUE

Present Value is just what the term sounds like.

Present Value (PV) is the value of something today, usually an asset, and usually with the value expressed in dollars.

The assets that we are interested in are real estate and money.

Your Duplex is worth $400,000.

Your CD is worth $100,000 (I mean Certificate of Deposit, not the disc), although that might be debatable, but we'll take it as a given.

PV involves three elements: value, time, and a stated interest rate.

Value and time are usually determined by factors in place.

The interest rate is the key, and probably the most important of the three.

Think of this as the answer to the question: "How much would you pay me to use $100,000 of my money for a year?"

If you would pay me $12,000 for that money, believing that you could use it to make much more than that, then for you the annual time value of money is 12%.

You can use externally-determined interest factors if you want, such as the Federal Discount Rate, or the current maximum amount of interest available from the big banks for a $100,000 Certificate of Deposit.

But you will get results that are more useful for you if you use a stated interest rate that is relevant to you and your business activities, or anticipated activities.

For Example, let's say that you are one of two owners of a Limited Liability Company (LLC) that owns an Apartment Building that is doing very well as an investment.

And someone offers to purchase your ownership interest in the LLC for $600,000 but cannot pay you the full amount up front. Instead, he offers you $100,000 now, $200,000 a year from now, and $300,000 two years from now, in three cash payments, with no interest accruing.

What is the PV of the $600,000?

PV = A ÷ [(1 + R) MULTIPLIED BY ITSELF "N" TIMES], WHERE
PV IS THE PRESENT VALUE,
A IS THE AMOUNT OF MONEY WE ARE DEALING WITH,
R IS THE STATED INTEREST RATE, AND
N IS THE NUMBER OF PERIODS WE ARE APPLYING THE CALCULATION.

It might be too difficult for most people to do, so let's just think about it, and then do it the way it seems like it should be done, and look at the results.

First, the initial payment of $100,000 has a PV of $100,000 because you are receiving it now.

But the $200,000 that you will receive a year from now is a different matter.

You personally believe that the annual time value of money is 12%, so there is an amount of money that, if you had it now, and increased it by 12%, it would become $200,000 a year from now.

$$PV = A \div (1 + R)$$

$$PV = 200{,}000 \div (1 + 0.12)$$

$$PV = 200{,}000 \div 1.12$$

$$PV = 178{,}571.43$$

The Present Value of the $200,000 you will receive a year from now is $178,571.43.

What about the $300,000 you will receive in two years?

$$PV = A \div [(1 + R) \times (1 + R)]$$

$$PV = 300,000 \div [(1 + 0.12) \times (1 + 0.12)]$$

$$PV = 300,000 \div (1.12 \times 1.12)$$

$$PV = 300,000 \div 1.2544$$

$$PV = 239,158.16$$

The Present Value of the $300,000 you will receive two years from now is $239,158.16.

The total Present Value of the $600,000 in three payment is 100,000 + 178,571.43 + 239,158.16 = $517,729.59.

As you can see, time and interest rate are the two most powerful factors at play in real estate investing.

All of your investment analysis should involve calculating the Present Value and its counterpart, the Future Value.

See SECTION 26. FUTURE VALUE (P. 109).

CALCULATOR

Now that you know what Present Value is, what it is used for, and how to use it, here is a Free Calculator you can use for quicker results.

https://www.calculatorsoup.com/calculators/financial/present-value-calculator-basic.php

1.) For "Number of Years" enter 1.0.

2.) For "Interest Rate" enter 12.0.

3.) For "Future Value" enter 200,000.

4.) Click "Calculate."

Your Present Value is $177,489.85.

As you can see, when we did the Calculation above with the same data, we got $178,571.43.

This is not a mistake.

We were compounding the interest rate annually, and the Calculator is compounding the interest rate monthly.

You must remember that the concept of Compound Interest works both ways.

Now, let's use the Calculator to determine the Present Value of the $300,000 that you will receive in two years.

!.) For "Number of Years" enter 2.0.

2.) For "Interest Rate" enter 12.0.

3.) For "Future Value" enter 300,000.

4.) Click "Calculate."

Your Present Value Calculation will be $236,269.84.

And again, you will notice that in our above Calculation we got $239,158.16 for Present Value of the $300,000.

And again, it is because the Calculator is using monthly compounding instead of yearly compounding.

If you ever want to double-check your answer when you do a Present Value Calculation, you can just reverse the process, and take the answer and treat it as the Present Value in a Future Value Calculation.

Here is the link for the Future Value Calculator.

https://www.calculatorsoup.com/calculators/financial/future-value-calculator-basic.php

SECTION 41.

PROFIT

There is no single definition of Profit, but you probably have a feel for what it is, and you probably know it when you see it.

It might be the number on your Income Statement, which you get by subtracting all of your expenses from your income.

In that case, it might be referred to as "Operating Profit."

SECTION 27. INCOME STATEMENT (P. 113).

Or, it might be what you make when you buy a property, clean it up or rehab it, and then sell it.

In that case, it would be your Capital Gains.

See SECTION 9. CAPITAL GAINS (P. 36).

Or, it might be the number that you Calculate as your Net Operating Income, using estimates and excluding some expenses.

See SECTION 33. INCOME: NET OPERATING (P. 133).

You might even want to look at Profit in terms of the Future Value of the investment.

In that case, see SECTION 26. FUTURE VALUE (P. 109).

And, in many cases, Profit is viewed as the return that you receive on your investment.

For those Calculations, see SECTION 43. RETURN ON CASH (P. 173), SECTION 44. RETURN ON EQUITY (P. 180), SECTION 45. RETURN ON INVESTMENT (P. 187), and SECTION 42. RETURN: INTERNAL RATE OF RETURN (P. 170).

Your Calculation of Profit will be whatever you need it to be for you, and that's what all of these Calculations are, tools for your personal use in your investments.

Don't be told what Profit is. Decide for yourself what it is for you, and manage that.

SECTION 42.

RETURN: INTERNAL RATE OF RETURN

Internal Rate of Return (IRR) is not "internal" and it is not a "rate of return."

IRR is the Discount Rate (DR) for an investment applied to the Present Value (PV) of all future After Tax Cash Flows (ATCF), and then compared to the cost of the Initial Capital Investment.

The ATCFs are yearly, but also include the sale of the investment property at some point in the future, say the end of ten years. The net sales proceeds are added to the tenth year cash flow.

This process is almost complete guesswork, as you can see.

Your Discount Rate is a combination of the Weighted Cost of Capital (WACC) and an assumed risk-free rate of return, which are normally set at 10% and 2%, but could really be anything, depending on who is doing the investing.

You must also assume what the annual Cash Flow will be, and then discount that for each year back to the present to get the Present Value.

You must also predict what the investment will sell for ten years from now, and estimate what your transaction costs will be.

And, you must also predict what will happen to the tax laws for the next ten years, and factor that into the calculations.

It looks impressive when you put it on a chart or graph and present it with confidence.

But in truth, the Internal Rate of Return Calculation is not worth very much.

The input data are all assumptions at best, and at worst, what financial analysts call WAGs. I won't offend you by spelling out the term, but the first word is "wild" and the last word is "guess."

And the IRR Calculation is so complicated that there is not even a Calculation that you can use to try it out.

And there are no Free Calculators that can handle this many unknowns.

But there is a perfectly good way to get the results that the IRR promises.

The best thing for you to do is first perform a Discounted Cash Flow on the monthly income from the investment.

Then you calculate the Net Sales Proceeds from a sale in the future and discount that amount to the Present Value.

Then add the two numbers together and divide by the amount of your initial investment.

The main problem with the Internal Rate of Return Calculation is that it is a ratio, and that means that the investment must be cashed in so that you will have a number to compare with your initial investment.

So, it is not very useful for management purposes.

SECTION 43.

RETURN ON CASH

The Cash On Cash Return (COCR) is the relationship between a property's Cash Flow (CF) and the Initial Capital Investment (ICI).

COCR = CF ÷ ICI, WHERE COCR IS THE CASH ON CASH RETURN, CF IS THE PROPERTY'S CASH FLOW, AND ICI IS THE INITIAL CAPITAL INVESTMENT REQUIRED TO ACQUIRE THE PROPERTY.

First, let's establish that ICI is the initial cash down payment and all of the costs of acquiring the property, usually the closing costs that are detailed on your HUD-1 Settlement Statement.

Now, we need to determine how we will define Cash Flow (CF) because CF seems to have a different definition, depending on the purpose for which it is being used.

Cash Flow is actually the cash left over after you take the monthly cash income from the property, and pay all of the monthly expenses of the property.

In other words, it is cash in, less cash out.

It even has its own Calculation.

CF = I – E, WHERE
CF IS CASH FLOW,
I IS ALL OF THE CASH INCOME, AND
E IS ALL OF THE CASH EXPENSES.

The Cash Flow Calculation is used to create a profile of a property so that you can compare it to another property.

Therefore, Cash Flow should only include those characteristics of a property that all other properties also have. Otherwise, you cannot compare them.

So, the Income of the property should be the cash produced by the operation of the property.

Some Cash Flow Calculations include as "Income," proceeds from a loan obtained and secured by the property.

And some Cash Flow Calculations include as "Income," interest on funds held by the owner of the property that came from the past operation of the property.

These two items should not be included in Income. They do not measure the character or the operation of the property.

Also, some Cash Flow Calculations include Debt Service (DS) as one of the Expenses that are deducted from the Cash Income.

How does this make sense? DS is a measure of the credit worthiness of the person who obtained the loan, if it is a measure of anything. You can't use it to compare two properties with different owners.

And finally, some Cash Flow Calculations fail to include a number for Cap Ex.

No, it is not a monthly cash expense (at least you hope it is not), but it is a real expense that will occur at random intervals and will reflect the true long-term Cash Flow of the property.

And including a Cap Ex figure in your Cash Flow Calculation will allow you to compare rundown properties with properties in good condition, because the rundown properties will require more capital expenditures than the properties in good condition.

Your most accurate Cash Flow Calculation, and your most accurate Cash On Cash Return Calculation, will include an allocation for Cap Ex.

Of course, you can leave out the Cap Ex Expense if you want, but if you are negotiating with a Lender, they will want to see it in there, and if you don't have it, they will make one up.

They've had the experience of having a customer come in and tell them that they can't make the note payment because they have to put on a new $15,000 roof.

It means the Lender will have to either take the property, or make a second loan to cover the roof.

So, let's go back to Cash On Cash Return (COCR).

Let's say you can buy a Fourplex for $400,000 and you can get a 75% loan, meaning that your cash down payment will be $100,000. Your closing costs will be $10,000 and you anticipate spending $15,000 to increase the income capability of the property to its highest possible level.

Your total cash investment will be $125,000.

You Calculate your Cash Flow using the method described in the Section on Cash Flow, and it is $23,040.

You haven't yet accounted for Debt Service, but you can Calculate your COCR at this point.

COCR = CF ÷ ICI

COCR = 23,040 ÷ 125,000

COCR = 18.43%

But your most accurate COCR is what you have left to put in your pocket to return what you took out of your pocket.

Your Debt Service is $1,500 per month, $18,000 per year.

This leaves you a true Cash Flow of $5,040.

COCR = CF ÷ ICI

COCR = 5,043 ÷ 125,000

COCR = 4.03%

Your Cash On Cash Return is a good tool for comparing two properties, but probably not as good when you are making a decision to buy and hold a property for ten years.

The COCR Calculation does not take into account the annual increase in Cash Flow as you raise the rents, or the time value of money, both of which will change your Calculation.

The Calculator that I have chosen to use in this Section is the Payback Period Calculator, because it will allow you to track these two items.

CALCULATOR

Now that you understand the concept of Cash on Cash Return, let's do a Calculation.

https://www.ajdesigner.com/php_cash_on_ cash/cash_on_rate.php

1.) For "annual cash flow (ACF)" enter 23040 (no comma).

2.) For "cash invested (CI)" enter 125000.

3.) Click "Calculate."

Your COCR is 18.43%, which is what we got doing it by hand.

You can change the Calculation to solve for different unknowns.

There is another Calculator that will combine your Cash on Cash Return information with your Payback Period, and I think you will find it interesting and useful because the two are closely aligned.

We also use it for the Calculation in the Section on Payback Period.

http://www.calculator.net/payback-period-calculator.html

1.) For "Initial Investment" enter 125,000.

2.) For "Cash Flow" enter 23,040.

3.) For "Increase" enter 5%.

4.) For "Number of years" enter 10.

5.) For "Discount Rate" enter 7.3%.

6.) Click "Calculate."

As you can see, your Payback Period is 4.886 years.

Your Discounted Payback Period is 6.176 years.

And your annual return for the Cash Flow is 17.39%.

Pick one of your own investments and put the numbers in to see what you get.

SECTION 44.

RETURN ON EQUITY

Return on Equity (ROE) can be viewed in two different ways.

One is to Calculate the operating income return on equity. This tells you how much income you are receiving in return for the cash that you invested, or for the amount of cash plus the accrued appreciation.

It is best to look at this under the Calculation for Return on Investment (ROI) or the Cash On Cash Return (COCR), and adjust that to reflect the return on just your equity instead of the entire investment principal amount or cash amount.

You just substitute one number.

Another way to look at Return on Equity (ROE) is to Calculate how much your Equity would return to you if you now sold the property that you invested in. This is something that you should look at periodically.

It is your Investment Return On Equity.

The Calculation is:

**ROE = (NE − OE) ÷ OE, WHERE
ROE IS RETURN ON EQUITY,
NE IS YOUR NEW EQUITY PRODUCED BY A SALE, AND
OE IS YOUR ORIGINAL EQUITY IN THE PROPERTY AT THE TIME OF PURCHASE.**

But we must first Calculate the Equity in the property when you invested, and then Calculate the Equity in the property when you sold.

First, the Calculation to determine Original Equity.

**E = FMV − MPO − L − OD, WHERE
E IS YOUR EQUITY IN THE PROPERTY,
FMV IS THE FAIR MARKET VALUE OF THE PROPERTY,
MPO IS THE MORTGAGE PAYOFF AMOUNT,
L IS LIENS ON THE PROPERTY, AND
OD IS OTHER DEBTS ON THE PROPERTY.**

If you bought a $210,000 Duplex, paying $50,000 down, $5,000 closing costs, and getting a $160,000 mortgage, then your Equity in the property is $55,000.

At the time of purchase, the FMV is presumed to be what you paid to get the property into your name, and you paid $210,000 to the Seller and $5,000 to the closing agent, for a total of $215,000.

$$E = FMV - MPO - L - OD$$

$$E = 215,000 - 160,000 - 0 - 0$$

$$E = \$55,000$$

But if you have held the property for at least a year, then two of the four elements making up Equity have probably changed, and possibly all four.

Let's say you've held the property for three years.

By looking at comps, you determine that the FMV is now $255,000 because the property has appreciated in value about 6% each year, and because you have added a new furnace.

You have made 36 mortgage payments and the principal portion of these payments have reduced your payoff by $6,500.

You replaced the furnace at a cost of $6,000 and the company is allowing you to make payments on the bill in return for you granting a lien on the property until it is paid, and the balance on the account is $4,500.

Your property taxes will be due shortly, and that amount will come to about $1,200.

So, the Calculation now looks like this:

E = FMV − MPO − L − OD, WHERE E IS YOUR NEW EQUITY IN THE PROPERTY, FMV IS THE FAIR MARKET VALUE OF THE PROPERTY, MPO IS THE MORTGAGE PAYOFF AMOUNT, L IS THE LIENS ON THE PROPERTY, AND OD IS OTHER DEBTS ON THE PROPERTY.

Let's use our new numbers.

$E = 255,000 − (160,000 − 6,500) − 4,500 − 1,200$

$E = 255,000 − 153,500 − 4,500 − 1,200$

$E = \$95,800$

But this is not the amount that you would receive if you sold the property.

You would have transaction costs to be deducted, such as Sales Commission, a Survey, a Title Insurance Policy for the Buyer, legal costs for document preparation, escrow fees, and other items.

In a transaction with numbers like these, the Seller's transaction costs could be as high as $18,000 so let's use that number.

Out new Calculation is:

E = FMV – MPO – CC – L – OD, WHERE E IS YOUR NEW EQUITY IN THE PROPERTY, FMV IS THE FAIR MARKET VALUE OF THE PROPERTY, MPO IS THE MORTGAGE PAYOFF AMOUNT, CC IS YOUR CLOSING COSTS OF A SALE, L IS THE LIENS ON THE PROPERTY, AND OD IS OTHER DEBT ON THE PROPERTY.

E = 255,000 – (160,000 – 6,500) – 18,000 – 4,500 – 1,200

E = 255,000 – 153,500 – 18,000 – 4,500 – 1,200

E = $77,800

Remember, in the truest sense, Equity is the actual value that you have in your real property, which is expressed in the number of dollars you could put in your pocket if you sold it. Any other number is the result of assumptions.

Now let's plug this number into our Calculation to determine the Investment Return on Equity.

ROE = (NE – OE) ÷ OE, WHERE ROE IS YOUR RETURN ON EQUITY, NE IS YOUR NEW EQUITY IN THE PROPERTY RESULTING FROM THE SALE, AND OE IS YOUR ORIGINAL EQUITY IN THE PROPERTY.

ROE = (77,800 – 55,000) ÷ 55,000

ROE = 22,800 ÷ 55,000

ROE = 41.45

Your Return On Equity, for investment purposes, was 41.45% over a three-year period.

That is equal to an annual return of 13.8%.

Your return would have been higher, about 23%, if you could have avoided the Sales Commission by finding your own buyer.

This Calculation does not account for the taxation of Capital Gains or Depreciation Recapture, or for the Time Value of Money.

See SECTION 9. CAPITAL GAINS (P. 36), SECTION 23. DEPRECIATION RECAPTURE (P. 97), and SECTION 47. TIME VALUE OF MONEY (P. 198).

CALCULATOR

Now it's time to use our Calculator.

https://www.ajdesigner.com/php_roe/return_on_equity.php

1.) For "cash flow after taxes (CFAT)" enter 20600 (no comma).

2.) For "initial cash investment (ICI)" enter 100000.

3.) Click "Calculate."

Your Return on Equity is 20.6%.

You can also enter the number for Cash Flow before taxes, which you are more likely to have, and still get a useful answer.

SECTION 45.

RETURN ON INVESTMENT

There are many ways to Calculate your Return On Investment because there are many definitions of "Return" and many definitions of "Investment."

CAPITALIZATION RATE

Even your Capitalization Rate (CR), referred to as Cap Rate, is an overall rate of return on the value of your asset, because it is the ratio of the Net Operating Income (NOI) to the Fair Market Value (FMV) of the property.

CR = NOI ÷ FMV, WHERE CR IS YOUR CAP RATE, NOI IS YOUR NET OPERATING INCOME, AND FMV IS THE FAIR MARKET VALUE OF THE PROPERTY.

But this Calculation depends on the specific numbers that you decide to use, and there is more than one acceptable number for NOI and FMV .

See SECTION 10. CAPITALIZATION RATE (P. 40), SECTION 33. INCOME: NET OPERATING (P. 133), and SECTION 50. VALUE (P. 205).

CASH FLOW

Your Cash Flow (CF) is a type of Calculation for your Return on Investment, which you will insist on knowing before you enter into an investment.

CF = I − E, WHERE
CF IS CASH FLOW,
I IS ALL OF THE CASH INCOME, AND
E IS ALL OF THE CASH EXPENSES.

Your CF is what is left to pay your Debt Service (DS) after you pay all of your expenses.

Included in your "Expenses" will be one expense that is not an actual cash expense, but is a specified amount put into an accrual account called "Cap Ex" to cover future Capital Expenditures.

See SECTION 11. CASH FLOW (P. 43), SECTION 12. CASH FLOW: DISCOUNTED (P. 52), and SECTION 8. CAPITAL EXPENDITURES (P. 31).

CASH ON CASH RETURN

Another type of Return on Investment is the cash return on the cash that you invest.

COCR = CF ÷ ICI, WHERE COCR IS THE CASH ON CASH RETURN, CF IS THE PROPERTY'S CASH FLOW, AND ICI IS THE INITIAL CAPITAL INVESTMENT REQUIRED TO ACQUIRE THE PROPERTY.

The ICI will be the initial cash down payment and all of the costs of acquiring the property, which is usually listed on your HUD-1 Settlement Statement.

The Calculation will tell you what percentage rate of return you are earning on the amount of cash that you have invested.

Remember what you saw when you looked at the Section on Cash Flow and the Section on Discounted Cash Flow.

Remember specifically, that the Cash Flow number used in this Calculation is before you have paid the Debt Service. So, if your Debt Service is more than your Cash Flow, you will have a negative Return on Cash.

RETURN ON EQUITY

Not all investors are primarily interested in creating a stream of income, and so are not concerned about its percentage in relation to the amount invested.

Some investors would rather break even and have a property with a strong appreciation in value, so they can enjoy the benefits, and delay the taxes, far into the future.

There are two Calculation for Return on Equity and there are even two Calculations for determining the number to use for Equity.

See SECTION 44. RETURN ON EQUITY (P. 180).

OTHER RETURNS

You might evaluate your investment based on the value it will have in the future, rather than the value of the current income.

In this case, you should look at SECTION 26. FUTURE VALUE (P. 109) to see how to estimate that number under other assumptions. If you just want to break even, see SECTION 28. INCOME: BREAK-EVEN RATIO (P. 116).

If you are approaching Return on Investment in reverse order, and already know the total dollar amount of Gross Income you want to receive, and now you want to know the amount of the investment required, use SECTION 31. INCOME: GROSS RENTAL MULTIPLIER (P. 123).

It will tell you how much you must pay for each $1.00 of Gross Potential Income.

If you want to know how much you will have to pay for each $1.00 of Net Operating Income instead of Gross Operating Income, go to SECTION 32. INCOME: NET INCOME MULTIPLIER (P. 128).

RETURN ON SALE OF INVESTMENT

If your investment scenario involves selling your investment property for capital gains as part of your Calculation, then you want to use this:

**ROI = (P − O) ÷ O, WHERE
ROI IS RETURN ON INVESTMENT,
P IS PROCEEDS FROM THE SALE, AND
O IS YOUR ORIGINAL INVESTMENT.**

But be aware that the Proceeds of the sale are not what you sell the property for, because there are transaction costs that must be deducted from that.

And your Original Investment will also include all of the capital improvements made on the property since you bought it.

So, the best way to Calculate your Return on Investment is to decide exactly which part, or parts, of the investment is most important to you and Calculate that.

SECTION 46.
RULE OF 72, 69 AND 113

The Rule of 72 calculates the number of years required to double the amount of money invested.

It assumes that the principal is compounded annually. This means that the interest earned by the principal is added to the principal each year, and creates a new principal amount to be used the following year.

Y = 72 ÷ I, WHERE
Y IS THE # OF YEARS REQUIRED TO DOUBLE THE PRINCIPAL,
72 IS JUST 72, AND
I IS THE ANNUAL INTEREST RATE, WITHOUT CONVERTING TO THE DECIMAL EQUIVALENT.

For example, if your investment principal is returning 20%.

Y = 72 ÷ I

Y = 72 ÷ 20

Y = 3.6

You will double your investment principal in 3.6 years.

ALTERNATIVE CALCULATION

If you set out to double your investment principal within a certain number of years and you want to know what rate of return you must have, the Calculation becomes:

I = 72 ÷ Y, WHERE
I IS THE ANNUAL INTEREST RATE, WITHOUT CONVERTING TO THE DECIMAL EQUIVALENT, 72 IS JUST 72, AND
Y IS YOUR TARGET NUMBER OF YEARS FOR DOUBLING YOUR PRINCIPAL.

Assume that you want to double your investment principal in six years.

I = 72 ÷ Y

I = 72 ÷ 6

I = 12

This tells you that if your principal investment earns 12%, it will double every 6 years.

As a point of reference, if you can double your investment every six years, $50,000 becomes $1.6M in 30 years.

RULE OF 69

Instead of using the Rule of 72, there are some investors who use the Rule of 69.

It is meant to Calculate the same thing, but it is said to be more precise.

Y = (69 ÷ I) + 0.35, WHERE Y IS THE NUMBER OF YEARS TO DOUBLE THE PRINCIPAL, 69 IS JUST 69, I IS THE ANNUAL INTEREST RATE WITHOUT ADJUSTING TO THE DECIMAL, AND 0.35 IS AN ADJUSTMENT FACTOR.

Let's compare it to the Rules of 72, where we used an annual interest rate of 20%.

Y = (69 ÷ I) + 0.35

Y = (69 ÷ 20) + 0.35

Y = 3.45 + 0.35 = 3.8

You will double your investment principal in 3.8 years.

This compares to a result of 3.6 years using the Rule of 72.

RULE OF 113

As you would expect, if there is a Calculation for the period of time necessary to double the amount of money invested, there would also be a Calculation for the amount of time necessary to triple the amount of money invested, and this is it.

Y = 113 ÷ I, WHERE
Y IS THE NUMBER OF YEARS REQUIRED TO TRIPLE THE PRINCIPAL,
113 IS JUST 113, AND
I IS THE ANNUAL INTEREST RATE WITHOUT ADJUSTING TO THE DECIMAL.

Again, using the interest rate of 20%:

Y = 113 ÷ I

Y = 113 ÷ 20

Y = 5.65

If you have principal invested that is returning you 20%, you will triple the amount of that principal in 5.65 years, according to the Rule of 113.

These Calculations are not precise, but they are as close as you need to be to make your investment decisions.

If you need to pinpoint it to a specific date, see SECTION 26. FUTURE VALUE (P. 109) for that Calculation.

CALCULATOR

Here is a Rule of 72 Calculator.

https://www.calculatorsoup.com/calculators/financial/rule-of-72-calculator.php

It will allow you to enter any interest rate that you like, and it will Calculate the number of years it will take to double your investment.

Alternatively, if you want to Calculate the interest rate necessary to double your investment in a specific number of years, you can do that.

SECTION 47.

TIME VALUE OF MONEY

The Time Value of Money (TVM) just means that money in your hand right now is worth more than the same amount of money that you will receive in the future.

There are two reasons for this, and two ways to look at it.

The first way is to look at your savings.

If you have $100,000 cash and purchase a 12-month Certificate of Deposit that will pay you 1% interest, then a year from now you will have $101,000.

So, $100,000 in your hand right now is worth more than $100,000 that you will receive a year from now, because you can invest the $100,000 that you will receive now and turn it into $101,000 a year from now, which is $1,000 more than $100,000.

The second way to look at it is to look at your mortgage.

If you get a $100,000 30-year mortgage at 3%, your monthly payment is $421.60 and in 360 months you will pay back $151,776.

This is the Time Value of Money.

It cannot be ignored, and it will play a part in all of your Real Estate Investing Calculations.

You can see more detailed explanations in SECTION 40. PRESENT VALUE (P. 162), SECTION 26. FUTURE VALUE (P. 109), SECTION 35. INTEREST: SIMPLE (P. 142), and SECTION 34. INTEREST: COMPOUND (P. 136).

CALCULATORS

There are two Calculators that you can use to test your understanding of the Time Value of Money.

The first is the Future Value Calculation Calculator.

And the second is the Present Value Calculation Calculator.

Future Value:

https://www.calculatorsoup.com/calculators/financial/future-value-calculator-basic.php

Present Value:

https://www.calculatorsoup.com/calculators/financial/present-value-calculator-basic.php

SECTION 48.

TRUE PURCHASE PRICE

If you pay cash for your property, then the amount that you paid, plus your Closing Costs, make up the Purchase Price (PP) of your investment property.

But you probably made a Down Payment (DP) and then borrowed the balance of the needed funds, and you will be making Monthly Payments (MP) on the debt for a number of months (#).

So, your True Purchase Price (TPP) is probably a different amount.

TPP = DP + CC + (MP x #), WHERE TPP IS YOUR TRUE PURCHASE PRICE, DP IS YOUR CASH DOWN PAYMENT, CC IS YOUR CLOSING COSTS, MP IS YOUR MONTHLY PAYMENT ON YOUR NEW MORTGAGE, AND # IS THE TOTAL NUMBER OF PAYMENTS IN THE LIFE OF THE LOAN.

Let's say you bought a $400,000 Duplex. Your closing costs were $10,000. You paid 20% down, and financed the remaining $320,000 for 30 years at 3.35%, with monthly payments of $1,410.28.

TPP = DP + CC + (MP x #)

TPP = 80,000 + 10,000 + (1,410.28 x 360)

TPP = 90,000 + 507,700

TPP = 597,700

Your True Purchase Price is $597,700.

But, of course, this amount is paid over a 30-year period.

It is larger than the purchase price of $400,000 because of the time value of borrowed money.

Your $507,700 total payments included repayment of the $320,000 loan, plus interest payments of $187,700.

However, the other side of the coin is that while you were paying 3.35% annually for the use of the $320,000, the value of the property was increasing 6.7% annually, based on the initial Fair Market Value (FMV) of $400,000.

$400,000 increasing 6.7% annually results in a FMV of $2,798,933.46 after 30 years.

You would take that deal any day.

SECTION 49.

VACANCY AND CREDIT LOSS

Vacancy And Credit Loss (VACL) is the percentage factor that you must apply to your Gross Potential Income (GPI) amount in order to Calculate your Gross Operating Income (GOI).

Your investment property will probably not be rented 100% of the time, and you will probably never have a tenant who always pays on time and never has a bouncing check. That's why your GPI is called "Potential."

One of the costs of doing business in real estate investing is having an empty property occasionally.

This is the vacancy factor.

Another cost is to have a check bounce, or a wire transfer be reversed on you (yes, it's called an "ACH" wire transfer, it can be taken back at any time up to 90 days, and there is nothing you can do about it, and you should look out for them). This is the credit factor.

Together, empty units and credit problems are called Vacancy And Credit Loss (VACL).

You must account for these just as though they were regularly scheduled expenses, the same way that you account for Cap Ex.

See SECTION 8. CAPITAL EXPENDITURES (P. 31).

The costs when units are vacant also include advertising for a new tenant, doing minor maintenance, repainting and rehab for a new tenant, and management cost for a new lease.

But these expenses are accounted for elsewhere.

For now, we are just interested in setting a figure for the amount of vacancy you expect to experience, and the amount of loss you expect to suffer directly from credit problems.

You are the only person who can do this because you know your property and your market better than anyone else.

The usual vacancy rate is set at 5%. This means that about every eighteen months you will have an empty unit.

This is probably a good thing. You need to get in there and do a thorough cleaning and inspection, and probably some preventive maintenance. The tenant certainly will not do it before leaving.

The usual credit loss rate is set at an additional 5%. It is almost impossible to prevent fraud, and even with your best efforts you will probably suffer some loss.

So, a safe amount to assign to VACL is 10%. That should cover most situations. And if you suffer no VACL, it's just a bonus for you.

For a Calculation on how VACL affects your income projections, see SECTION 29. INCOME: GROSS OPERATING (P. 118).

VACL is very important, because other than raising the amount of your rents, the only way to increase your Gross Operating Income is to reduce your VACL.

SECTION 50.
VALUE

Value is a matter of opinion. And there are two ways of looking at it.

WHAT THE PROPERTY IS WORTH TO YOU

One way is to calculate value based on what the property is worth to you, or what the property is worth to anyone similar to you who seeks a specific return on investment, or seeks a specific Cap Rate.

You do this by calculating the Economic Value of the property.

$V = NOI \div CR$, WHERE
V IS THE ECONOMIC VALUE,
NOI IS THE NET OPERATING INCOME, AND
CR IS THE CAPITALIZATION RATE

If you are looking at a property that produces $3,000 per month of net income from operations, then your NOI will be $36,000.

If you are expecting to earn a 10% rate of return on your investment, then your CR will be 10% (0.10).

Therefore:

$V = NOI \div CR$

$V = 36,000 \div 0.10$

$V = 360,000.$

This property will have an Economic Value to you of $360,000.

WHAT YOUR PROPERTY IS WORTH TO SOMEONE ELSE

You can also use the Value calculation to determine what your property will be worth to someone else. Just find out what their expected Cap Rate is and plug it into the calculation.

Chances are, there is a similar target Cap Rate that is in play for the general community of real estate investors for a particular type of property.

If you know this number, and you have a property for sale, you will be able to determine what someone would be willing to pay.

If multi-family investors in your area are currently willing to accept a 6% Cap Rate, then your calculation is:

V = NOI ÷ CR

V = 45,000 ÷ 0.06

V = 750,000

You would be safe to market your property for $750,000 and expect to be negotiating with serious buyers.

HOW TO DETERMINE THE CAP RATE

In the above Example, you might want to get an advantage in the market by promoting your property as the one that is offering a higher Cap Rate than the other properties available.

Let's say that you are willing to take $710,000 for the property, and wonder if that will raise the Cap Rate enough to get buyers' attention.

This is the Calculation to determine the Cap Rate:

**CR = NOI ÷ V, WHERE
CR IS THE CAP RATE,
NOI IS THE NET OPERATING INCOME, AND
V IS THE ECONOMIC VALUE OF THE
PROPERTY**

$$CR = NOI \div V$$

$$CR = 45,000 \div 710,000$$

$$CR = 0.634$$

Lowering your asking price to $710,000 would allow you to market the property as having a Cap Rate of 6.34%.

LOAN TO VALUE RATIO

Another way to look at "Value" is when a Lender is determining how much to loan you for the purchase of an investment property.

That Calculation for Loan-to-Value Ratio is

**LVR = LA ÷ V, WHERE
LVR IS THE LOAN-TO-VALUE RATIO,
LA IS THE LOAN AMOUNT, AND
V IS THE LESSER OF THE SELLING PRICE OR
THE APPRAISED VALUE.**

Let's say you find a Fourplex with an asking price of $400,000 and both the tax records and the NOI support the price, but it needs work and you sign a contract for $360,000.

Your Lender has promised a 70% loan.

How much will you be able to borrow?

LVR = LA ÷ V

.70 = LA ÷ 360,000

.70 x 360,000 = LA

252,000 = LA

LA = 252,000

Your Loan Amount will be $252,000 based on a Loan-to-Value Ratio of 70%, when the Value is identified as the lesser of the real world Value or the Selling Price.

So, Value is used in a number of different ways, and all are correct within the context of their use.

There are even two different types of Appraised Value, and both are correct.

The Taxing Authority will do what they call a Tax Appraisal, which is placing a Value on your property so that the Property Tax Rate can be applied and the amount of your Property Taxes determined.

These were once wildly inaccurate because the appraisals were being done by unqualified, virtually-untrained employees, hired because they were willing to work for the salary being offered, and not because of their knowledge of real estate.

Today, the process is done by a very good computer program using a database of historic data, and the appraisals are much more accurate.

The other type of Appraised Value is an Appraisal, hopefully done by a licensed Appraiser, and including a multi-page report with comparable sales ("comps") and pictures of all properties, and an explanation of how the Appraised Value was determined.

They were also once wildly inaccurate because the Appraiser would use whatever number you needed, but now that some of those people have gone to jail for being part of a process of defrauding lenders, it is almost impossible to get anything but a totally accurate Appraisal.

CALCULATOR

Now that you understand the various ways to look at Value, let's use a Free Calculator to determine Value based on your Capitalization Rate.

https://www.ajdesigner.com/php_capitalization_rate/capitalization_rate_v.php

1.) For "net operating income (NOI)" enter 36000 (no comma).

2.) For "capitalization rate (CR)" enter 10.

3.) Click "Calculate."

Your Value is Calculated to be $360,000.

This is the same number that we got when doing it by hand.

You can substitute various factors here and see exactly what investment numbers you need to meet your objectives.

CONCLUSION

I hope you have benefitted from the material in the book. If so, you can help others find their way here by going to Amazon.com and leaving a review that will let them know what your experience has been, and help them decide whether to add this book to their library on Real Estate Investing.

Thank you.

Made in the USA
Columbia, SC
08 April 2019

Color Alchemy

Self-Mastery with the Endless Supply of Color

Vitality

Creativity

Power

7 Days
7 Colors

Love

7 Triumphs

Focus

Jami Lin

Bliss

Intuition

ColorAlchemy
Self-Mastery with the Endless Supply of Color

EarthDesign, Inc.
PO Box 530725, Miami Shores, Florida 33153 U.S.A.
JamiLin.com & ColorAlchemy.com

Printed in India by Replika Press Pvt.Ltd.

DISCLAIMER

Recommendations made in this publication do not prescribe the use of any techniques as treatment for physical, emotional, or medical problems. This information is provided with our most positive intentions to help you in your quest for emotional and spiritual well-being. The authors, publishers, programmers, and/or their affiliates do not assume any responsibility for your actions.

Lin, Jami.
   ColorAlchemy : self-mastery with the endless supply
of color / [Jami Lin].
   p. cm.
   Includes bibliographical references.
   "7 days, 7 colors, 7 triumphs, vitality, creativity,
power, love, focus, intuition, bliss."
   ISBN-13: 978-0-9643060-2-8
   ISBN-10: 0-9643060-2-6

   1. Color—Psychological aspects.
2. Self-actualization (Psychology)   I. Title.

BF789.C7L56 2008   152.14'5
                    QBI07-600332

You are the Light
unto Yourself
-Buddha

Table of Contents

How to use ColorAlchemy   vi
Preface: Dr. Burton Jacknow PhD   vi
Foreword: Dr. Darren Starwynn, OMD   vii
Introduction: Jami Lin   viii
Acknowledgments   256
End Notes   256
Graphic Credits   257
About Jami Lin   258

Part 1

ColorAlchemy Quick Start   1
Living ColorAlchemy   13
Mental ColorAlchemy   25
Physical ColorAlchemy   51
Spiritual ColorAlchemy   67

Part 2: Daily ColorAlchemy Triumphs   81

Week #1
Colors of Your Mind

Monday   88
  Enhance Color Breathing   88
  Adding Visualization   90
Tuesday   91

Wednesday   93
  Daily Habits   95
  Journaling   96
Thursday   99
  Blessing Your Materials   101
  Complementary Breathing   104
Friday   105

Saturday   107

Sunday   109

Week #2
Colors of Your Body

Monday   113

Tuesday   119
  Healing Hands   124
Wednesday   125

Thursday   131
  As Above, So Below   136
  Liquid Light Meditation

Friday   137
  Blessing Your Body   142
Saturday   143
  Color Rays & Healing   147
  Color Ray Guide   148
Sunday   149
  Reading Auras   153
  Diagnosing Auras   154

Week #3 **Colorful Activators**	**Week #4** **Colors of Your Spirit**

Monday	**157**	**Monday**	**205**
On the Body	158	Dance your Spirit	207
In the Body	161	Chakra Dance	208
		Moving Mediations	209
Tuesday	**163**	**Tuesday**	**211**
Around the Body	164	ColorAlchemy Music	
Office ColorAlchemy	167	by Maestro Steven Halpern	212
Journaling Success	168	Chanting to Open Chakras	217
Wednesday	**169**	**Wednesday**	**221**
Frozen Light: Gemstones	170	Healing Core Issues	222
Cleanse & Bless Stones	172	BETA Scan	224
Using Stones	173		
Thursday	**175**	**Thursday**	**227**
Liquid Light: Essential Oils	176	Astrology & ColorAlchemy	228
Fragrance and the Mind	178	Numerology	231
Working with		Dreams & ColorAlchemy	232
Essential Oils	181	**Friday**	**233**
Friday	**185**	Fire Rituals	233
Making Collages	186	New Moon Rituals	237
Drawing Mandalas	187	Candle Rituals	238
		Saturday	**241**
Saturday	**191**	Precious Time	242
Color Toning	192	ColorAlchemy Meditations	243
Sunday	**197**	**Sunday**	**247**
ColorAlchemy Elixirs	197	Affirmations	248
Creating Elixirs	198	Initiations & Triumphs	250
Bathe ColorAlchemy	201	Initiation Celebrations	253

A Personal Note from Jami Lin

Spend a few minutes each morning with the appropriate Daily Color to have enlightening ColorAlchemy all day long. Experiment and have fun with all the ColorAlchemy Activators. In just one short month, you'll *Live ColorAlchemy* to create easy, life-transforming habits that will be yours forever. You'll see what I mean as you experience greater joy as you grow your colorful life.

Will you let me know how you do? Share your ColorAlchemy experiences with me on my special blog: JamiLin.com/blog.

Have fun and enjoy your day full of color … With love and in living color,

Jami Lin

How to Use ColorAlchemy

Every day is an opportunity to maximize all aspects of life using color. Every color moment is an occasion for joy. ColorAlchemy coaches you to live in the moment, in the *colorful place*, to accomplish goals and to be happy. ColorAlchemy is divided into two sections:

Part 1: Living ColorAlchemy
Appreciate the universal mental, physical, and spiritual connections among the science, history, and psychology of color to discover why ColorAlchemy is consistently effective.

Part 2: Daily ColorAlchemy Triumphs
Every day of the week is a different color that aligns with all the universal qualities to enhance your life. For a total of twenty-eight days, each Daily Color provides simple and fast ways to enhance your life with *Living ColorAlchemy*.

Experience the Daily Color and absorb its life-enhancing attributes every day. Leisurely discover *Living Color Alchemy* (part 1) as a proven, reliable, and ever-present resource.

Preface

During my fifty years as a scientist and an inventor, I have appreciated the healing value of how colored light has a beneficial influence on the body and human psyche. Even before NASA's clinical trials using colored LED lights to accelerate healing in space that delivered light deep into tissues of the body to promote wound healing and human tissue growth, the science that explains how color wavelengths influenced the body's chemical structure to stimulate its natural healing process was unmistakable.

Dating back to Hippocrates, healers understood that every aspect of our bodies, including all physiological and psychological processes within, are in resonance with various colors of the visible and invisible light spectrum. They also understood how limited absorption of color has been linked to depression and mental illness. Clinical studies made by such world renowned scholars as Dr. Norman E. Rosenthal, MD (Senior Researcher at the National Institute of Mental Health and Clinical Professor of Psychiatry at Georgetown University), explicitly reveal that when a subject is receiving normal doses of full-spectrum, environmental light as compared to those with suppressed light (SAD: seasonal affective disorder), proper levels of melatonin is released in the body, depression is minimized, and mood is positively elevated.

Jami Lin's *ColorAlchemy* simplifies the science and allows readers easy access to the physical, emotional, and psychological benefits of color healing.

Burton Jacknow, PhD in Physical Organic Chemistry, Columbia University

Foreword

All of us are in an intimate relationship with color, all the time and every minute, whether or not we are conscious of it. While most people easily recognize the role of color in clothing, in interior decorating, and in the sights of our marvelous Earth, our relationship with color goes much further.

Every aspect of our bodies, including all physiological and psychological processes, are in resonance with the various colors of visible and invisible light. Resonance means how a vibrating energy field, such as an organ in the body, a cell, or even a thought, influences another while communicating beneficial or depleting information at the same time.

Although our bodies and the physical world appear solid, it is an illusion of our senses. All organic and inorganic structure is empty space between atomic and subatomic particles. These particles are in a constant dance of vibration and interaction—and one vital language of these particles is color wavelengths. Color is pure information for our body/mind. You can heal a toxic or stressed liver with green light, build up depleted adrenals with magenta, help ace a test requiring a lot of mental concentration with lemon light, and soothe inflammation or stressed-out emotions with violet or blue.

Color is the language our organs, glands, cells, and energy centers use to communicate. Color is the biggest way we experience each other and the environment through either seeing with our eyes or sensing through our hearts and other feeling centers.

All the substances we use for medicine possess chemical bonds that release color wavelengths when metabolized by our bodies. Through using color, light, and microcurrent successfully with my patients for many years, I am confident that future research will confirm that the release of color is what heals the body—not the chemicals themselves.

Jami Lin understands the *mental medicine* of color as it works through the mind, heart and emotions. She makes a deep and complex science easily accessible for anyone using color for healing, peace, and comfort in our challenging world. Her bite-size gems of color wisdom provide profound results with only a few minutes of guided awareness.

Travel beyond how you have unconsciously worked with colors all your life and through every cell of your body. Nurture yourself with healing and balancing ColorAlchemy each day with simple and highly practical exercises, meditations, and tools for daily living. Consciously, take greater charge of your own happiness and destiny. Even a little ColorAlchemy goes a long way!

Darren Starwynn
OMD, Doctor of Chinese Medicine
Color-Medicine Healer and CEO of MicroLight Research

Introduction

ColorAlchemy is a simple method of converting darkness into light. ColorAlchemy is the convergence of spirituality and science for immediately reducing stress and making long-term, beneficial life changes. Explained by twenty-first-century science, it has roots in almost all ancient traditions. Twenty years ago, I could tell you that working with color is an inspirational vehicle for personal growth and happiness. Today, I can explain why it is so effective!

Light is energy that human beings see with the naked eye, the spectrum from red to violet. ColorAlchemy guides your adventures through the spectrum while satisfying your intellectual curiosity about the energetic powers of light.

Quantum scientists agree that the energy of matter is an intangible subatomic substance that holds molecular structure together like some grand intelligence. Knowing that made me wonder, Is this the intelligence that governs mind over matter? Is this the energy of creation represented by all spiritual traditions as the light of the Creator?

By trusting the logic of my intuition, and acknowledging that colors are light, and that humankind embodies the energy of the Creator, you too can use color to "let there be light" in your life.

Since recorded history, some level of societal darkness has always existed. Current times are no exception. Humankind continues to struggle amid the gray tones of self-sabotage, fear, confusion, lethargy, and pessimism.

Even during life's most stressful challenges, I refused to fall prey to the dark side of life, and always have. Before I could reach my mother's art easel at age three, I was hypnotized watching her paint and enjoyed how her brushes recreated light onto a canvas. In spite of Mom's misgivings with the mess created with my first finger paints, it initiated my love of color. From that day on, I wanted to express myself with the source of all beauty—just like Mom.

I graduated with a BA in interior design from the University of Florida, School of Architecture, and have practiced professionally ever since. I love how color excites the senses and enhances emotions. As day transforms into night or when different qualities of light are introduced (whether natural, incandescent, halogen, etc.), it is fascinating to experience how their unique characteristics alter the color and feeling of a space. I delight in the way painting a room transforms its energetic personality, influences surrounding areas, and changes the mood of occupants.

As a Feng Shui master, my privilege and goal is to improve the quality of people's lives with the colors of the Chinese five elements and incorporate age-old observations with contemporary scientific breakthroughs.

The more I research and continue my experiments with color, the more my excitement grows. By spending only a few minutes a day in *color consciousness*, I am more relaxed and I accomplish more with greater ease—plus, I am happier than ever before! I am constantly discovering profound understandings within my psyche and have greater confidence. The lives of my clients and students improve.

Motivated by these revelations, I wrote *ColorAlchemy* to show you how to physically and mentally benefit with color and light.

Psychological studies about people affected by Seasonal Affective Disorder (SAD) document that the human body (matter) requires spectral-light energy to alleviate debilitating conditions of the mind, such as depression and despair. As a result of mental dis-ease (not-so-good energy), one's immune system is compromised, making the body a magnet for physical illness. With proper light absorption and ColorAlchemy's color consciousness (positive mind energy), anyone can conquer mind over matter, heal mind and body, and soulfully, appreciate the simple joys of life.

ColorAlchemy's universal responses mimic current sociological global conditions. We can choose to be indifferent and surrender to the dark trappings of life or we can take conscious steps to live in the light.

ColorAlchemy practice also diminishes human failure and enhances success. Applying the *alert colors* of Homeland Security's Advisory System, we can use Red for the most intense warning, or consciously choose to use its positive qualities to stimulate vitality and motivation. The positive or negative influence of Orange's high emotion, just like all the rainbow colors, is determined by how it is integrated and controlled. Yellow's powerful brightness may still be too hot for comfort, but conversely it helps influence the world with intellectual brilliance. The scientific sequence of color wavelengths continues to follow the psychological progression. Green, Blue, Indigo, and Violet progressively soften into the more loving, quiet, and inward parts of ourselves.

The positive and negative traits of every color provide clues for creating personal happiness and tips for transforming the layers of bleak darkness into radiant joy. ColorAlchemy helps you release what doesn't promote positive potential. Absorbing the positive aspects of color sweetens life even further.

In these fast-paced times, living with less stress and loving one's self more are just a few of the golden nuggets at the end of ColorAlchemy's beneficial rainbow.

Instantaneous accessibility to information on the Internet accelerates our lives. Most people *want IT NOW*. By moving so quickly, we often lose the focus of our birthright, our priorities, and our essential spirit. More often than not, we overlook easy and readily available tools that can connect us to the deep, quiet, luminous, divine aspects of *BEing a human being.*

ColorAlchemy's simplicity is as powerful and seductive as the blissful calm of discovering an unexpected rainbow. With ColorAlchemy's quick methods, mind over matter and inner peace are vibrant triumphs. Accessibility is simply one colorful breathing exercise away.

Experience and enrich your life with the Daily Colors: wear them, drink them, breathe them, bathe in them, draw with them, and live the profound influence for yourself.

Deepen your relationship with the colors that are already a part of your energy. BE all that you can be. Your heart and spirit will instantly be transformed. Capture the beauty of your inner rainbow.

Celebrate your colorful triumphs. Enjoy and discover the beautiful colors that are your birthrights. Let there be light within you and through you. I know that we can bring the darkness into the light. Enjoy your colorful adventure for the rest of your life.

Jami Lin
Summer 2008

Color creates Love, Joy and Peace in any language.

A color stands abroad on solitary hills
that science cannot overtake,
but human nature feels.

—Emily Dickinson

Color Alchemy
Quick Start

Day	Body Part Chakra	Life Qualities
Monday	Root Chakra Base of Spine	**Vitality, Courage, Security, Confidence, Strength, Stamina** For the first day of the workweek to get-up-and-go color. Ground your week: think courage, strength, and enthusiasm.
Tuesday	Sacral Chakra Sex Organs	**Happiness, Desire, Creativity, Emotion, Pleasure, Intimacy** Creative juices are flowing. Get out there! Propagate new projects. Feel passion. Feel and experience the momentum!
Wednesday	Will Chakra Solar Plexus	**Personal Power, Dedication, Commitment, Drive, Ambition** You are in the flow. Shine! Communicate. Commit. Take command of your projects.
Thursday	Heart Chakra Heart	**Love, Forgiveness, Compassion, Trust, Balance, Renewal, Growth** Supported by the green of the earth, mid-week provides joy about this week's accomplishments. Share it with love.
Friday	Throat Chakra Throat	**Decisive, Truth, Clarity, Communication, Focus** Supported by the oceans and sky, experience clear communications. Wind down with family, friends, and YOU.
Saturday	Third-Eye Chakra Forehead	**Intuition, Vision, Psychic Powers, Seeing Beyond** Rejoice with the deeper colors of the soul. The weekend has slower energy. Finish your chores. Relax and play.
Sunday	Crown Chakra Top of Head	**Peace, Bliss, Spiritual Love, Divinity, Inspiration** The day of quiet and time for completion. Be introspective and meditate. Rejuvenate for the cycle ahead.

Notice how the seven spectral colors align with the seven days of the week and seven chakras (or body areas). In the following chapters, discover how each color, day, and chakra has a unique quality that is common to all three. It connects them and shows how to absorb their benefits.

What is ColorAlchemy?

The word *alchemy* originated in the Middle Ages and is the wizardry of changing base metals into gold. For me,

The magic of alchemy is improving something through science, commitment, and intention.

ColorAlchemy's *something* is YOU!

ColorAlchemy is a sacred process for improving your life. ColorAlchemy's transformational soul purpose is to:

- Create positive thought and behavioral patterns,
- Develop greater inner peace and outward joy,
- Expand intuition,
- Reduce stress, and
- Awaken to your greatest potential.

ColorAlchemy is color-consciousness training.
ColorAlchemy is an all-encompassing method of self-actualization

ColorAlchemy captures the endless supply of color and absorbs its life-enhancing benefits.

Harness the mental, physical, and spiritual influence of ColorAlchemy to support individuality and enhance personal desire

Why use color?

Color is beautiful. Color exists in every moment of every day, in dreams and if you look and pay attention, on the inside of your eyelids. Instead of taking color for granted, Live ColorAlchemy by paying attention to color's profound influence on every aspect of your life and on your ver

Like all artistry, the colorful canvas of life that surrounds you is perfectly balanced. Throughout Jami Lin's *ColorAlchemy*, you'll discover how color balances your mental, physical, and spiritual worlds. You'll experience how color immediately helps heal the body, tempers emotions, improves the mind, and raises spiritual consciousness.

Color Always Makes an Impression

Our relationship with color runs deep within our consciousness. Even our recollections and feelings are *colored* and expressed through language. With words, color is associated with emotions, such as feeling blue, seeing red, or being green with envy.

Colorful impressions and emotions are easily traced to our earliest memories. I remember the first time I saw *The Wizard of Oz* with the advent of color television. When Dorothy stepped into the colorful world of Oz from her black-and-white life in Kansas, it was comforting, uplifting, and exciting. In that magical, alchemical moment, life was real. ColorAlchemy shows you exactly what Dorothy learned: to experience how colorful life is (or can be) right in your own backyard.

What was your initial reaction when you stepped into Oz for the first time? It took my breath away. *Did it make enough of an impression that you remember exactly where you were and who you were with? What was your experience?*

Notice how color provides the opportunity for each of us to stand in our own colors. We are all unique and integral to the entire spectrum of life.

Living ColorAlchemy Is Easy

Living ColorAlchemy is integrating color into your consciousness as part of your daily routine.

Be aware of the colors around you to stimulate creative energies and inspire your *inner colors*. Color awareness awakens your greatest personal potential. Pay attention to how some colors promote positive attitudes and transform darkness into light while others can be nonsupportive, depressing, and debilitating.

Invest a few minutes with the Daily Colors and their attributes.

By the end of each week,
you'll absorb the:

**Specific benefits of
each daily color**

and the

**Combined energies to align
with nature's perfection and
the Light of the Creator.**

*Pause for a moment, consider how
you feel when witnessing a sunset,
a rainbow, the diversity of bird
and butterfly wings,
the color of the ocean's creatures,
or a field of wildflowers.*

Practice two colorful minutes a day, for ColorAlchemy to become second nature and to:

1. Receive colorful energy at a moment's notice by:

● Looking around, recognizing, and
● Absorbing the needed color through your mind's eye and visualization.

2. Using color to support daily tasks.

Consider your daily schedule. When you wake up feeling sluggish or you have an important event, after being colorfully aware, it is easy to choose the appropriate color(s) to enhance the opportunities of your day.

Create ColorAlchemy moments of inner peace, clarity, and inspiration.

In the same way that you experience a fleeting rainbow, consciously create colorful moments to pause and enhance your daily routine.

How ColorAlchemy Works

In every moment, there is an unlimited source of color. Because the brain is activated and responds to color thousands of times a day, color is the perfect mental trigger.

As above. So below.

*The unlimited supply of
color is a treasure and a gift.*

*From heaven above,
the Aurora Borealis
in the sky,
to the Grand Canyons
of the earth,
to a reefscape below the sea,
color is a feast for the senses.*

Mentally incorporating positive associations of each color, the mind builds a calming and beneficial influence, which deepens every time you consciously experience color. The more you engage with color, the greater its cumulative and positive influence. Then as you practice ColorAlchemy, every time you consciously or unconsciously respond to color, the brain effortlessly incorporates its life-enhancing attributes.

When your mind is colorfully programmed, ColorAlchemy becomes second nature for instantaneous benefits.

Live ColorAlchemy. Pause your daily routine to capture magical colorful moments many times as needed during the day. In these brief moments, experience immediate joy, greater ease, and increased comfort.

ColorAlchemy shows you how the science, artistry, and psychological influence of the color spectrum are *living color*, alive through the perfection of:

- Physical Science: earth, heaven, and our bodies
- Quantum Physics: the energy of creation that binds all molecular structure together on a subatomic level
- Metaphysical Science: the colorful relationship to the Creator

In ColorAlchemy's simplicity, you already know that every day has the qualities of a different color with different energetic attributes.

Notice how when all the life attributes combine, you have all the components you need for mind, body, and spiritual balance.

**Red & Orange
ground & stabilize**

PHYSICAL: Vitality, Courage, Security, Strength, Stamina
PHYSICAL: Physical Desire, Pleasure, Intimacy, Creativity, Emotion

**Yellow, Green & Blue
focus your mind**

EMOTIONAL: Personal Power, Commitment, Drive, Ambition
EMOTIONAL: Love, Forgiveness, Joy, Compassion, Trust, Balance
EMOTIONAL: Decision Making, Inner Truth, Clarity Focus

**Indigo & Violet
expand consciousness**

SPIRITUAL: Intuition, Vision, Psychic Powers, Seeing Beyond
SPIRITUAL: Peace, Bliss, Spiritual Love, Divinity, Inspiration

Live ColorAlchemy

When all life qualities are holistically in balance, you have the formula for happiness.

Body + Mind + Spirit = Happiness

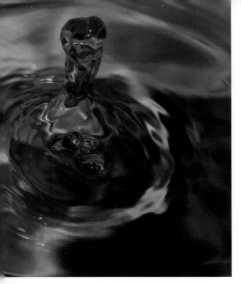

Discover why water is a special *ColorAlchemy Activator,* p. 22.

Notice that of the seven colors, there are more attributes governed by the mind and emotions. The mind is the common denominator that connects the beneficial influence of color to the physical, emotional, and spiritual parts of ourselves.

Evolving the mind is key to personal development and the first step in *Living ColorAlchemy. Mental ColorAlchemy* is the place to start because *Physical ColorAlchemy* and *Spiritual ColorAlchemy* begin with thinking ColorAlchemy.

Quick ColorAlchemy

At a moment's notice, it only takes a few seconds to absorb whatever color you need. The key is remembering to:

Consciously pause your day to live ColorAlchemy.

Start *Living ColorAlchemy* right now!

Pause with a breath of today's color and attributes.

As above. So below.
(And its magical meditations, p. 136)

From heaven to the depths of the sea,
experience all the details from
the unlimited supply of color.

Close your eyes, take a long, deep, relaxing breath. As you
repeat two more breaths, visualize your favorite color.

Experience the calm and relaxing *space* of
your periodic momentary mental break:

It's a refreshing stillness, a pause from the ordinary.

Don't wait to capture a rainbow or sunset;
create one with a visualization in your mind's eye!

In less than a week, you'll remember the seven colors, their connection
to the seven days of the week, and their attributes because of their logical,
scientific, and spiritual sequence.

Do you want to make it even easier? If you don't remember today's color,
you have two choices:

1. Refer to the chart on p. 2 and breathe the Daily Color.
2. Breathe in any color that intuitively feels right.
   Learn how to enhance your breathing on p. 88

Pause. Create a ColorAlchemy moment.

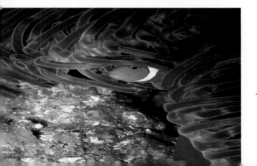

Create Colorful Habits

It takes twenty-one days to create a new habit. ColorAlchemy consistency is essential. Because I love giving more than expected, I happily give you seven extra colorful days (to align with the twenty-eight-day lunar cycle) and lots of *ColorAlchemy Activators* to be sure ColorAlchemy really sinks in!

You'll see what I mean as you live ColorAlchemy with these habits:

1. **Enjoy color.** You don't have to be an artist or pick up a crayon. All the exercises in ColorAlchemy show you how to absorb color's attributes to reawaken the artistry of happiness.

Make ColorAlchemy a daily habit. Each day, practice two minutes in the morning, two minutes in the evening, and pause during your day to absorb color as needed.

2. **Train the mind, the most important foundation of happiness.** The mind is the only thing that we have any control over. It is the catalyst for ColorAlchemy and the basis for success in everything.

Throughout the text, I'll share fun and quick ways to incorporate color into your life. For now, pay attention to the color around you.

Get into the easy habit of thinking, breathing, and practicing ColorAlchemy while doing routine activities such as:

- Brushing your teeth/washing your face
- Taking a shower or bath
- Waiting in line at the grocery, bank, post office, etc.
- Filling your car with gas
- Driving
- During television commercials
- Holding on the phone
- **Pausing for two-colorful minutes in the morning, in the evening, and periodically during the day.**

With a little daily consciousness (and very little effort):

Each day, enlighten your day!
Each week, absorb and balance all the attributes of happiness.

ColorAlchemy is a process that keeps getting better. Experience the Daily ColorAlchemy Triumphs each day!

And in one short month, you'll:

Create life-transforming benefits to live ColorAlchemy forever.

Want a teaser?
Wear an article of clothing or an accessory in today's Daily Color.

ColorAlchemy is so easy.
Have fun *Living ColorAlchemy*!

Whether natural color or that which is created by man, color surrounds you in every moment.

Color, unspoiled by meaning, and unallied with definite form, speaks to the soul in a thousand different ways.

—Oscar Wilde

Living Color Alchemy

Experience Your Daily Colors

Have you done your color breathing today?

"When atomic nuclei smash together, physicists hope to create states of matter abundant only during the first instants of the universe. One particle they seek is the so-called God particle. It is the missing evidence in a theory that explains a basic characteristic of the universe: how fundamental particles acquire mass." [1]

—Joel Achenbach
National Geographic, March 2008

Living ColorAlchemy refers to:

- YOU, *Living ColorAlchemy*
- Integrating ColorAlchemy into your daily consciousness
- ColorAlchemy is living energy
  through physical and quantum science

As a student, perpetually hungry for knowledge, I love how the universal concepts of ColorAlchemy are **alive** and found throughout history, science, physiology, and philosophy. Each field offers multiple justifications of why and how ColorAlchemy works. With such diverse validation, this understanding reinforces the reasons to *Live ColorAlchemy* and absorb its transformational power.

Discover as much as you'd like about the physical science of ColorAlchemy in this fascinating section. If it seems complicated to you, relax, enjoy the simplicity of color breathing and continue with *Mental ColorAlchemy*.

Colorful Science

Experiencing the effects of color is nothing new. Cross-culturally and throughout the millennia, color has been used for healing by the Egyptians, Chinese, Mayans, and Native American tribes.

Many traditions, such as in Chinese Feng Shui, integrate the experience of color through the representation of the cardinal directions and how each direction feels different. Color has always reinforced personal connection to earth's energies.

Doesn't the color and vibration of a sunrise (east) feel different than a sunset (west)?

Color magnifies the experience of living. The colors of earth influence our body, mind, and emotions. Color stimulates our nervous system, affects our perceptions, and generates mental associations.

When the sun's light is shining its colors, we feel energized, full of life, and vibrant. We may feel lethargic and gray on a cloudy day. Did you know that to be healthy, we need a minimum of twenty minutes of sunlight to nourish our cells as well as to help prevent depression and mental illness? There is even a mental affliction called SAD (Seasonal Affective Disorder). Caused by the absence of sunlight and its full-spectrum color, SAD begins during the shortening of days in fall and winter, is especially prevalent in longitudes closer to the poles, and creates severe depression in some people.

Color Is Pure Energy

Light is pure energy and it is our most valuable resource. The sun's energy, our largest source of light, brings life into our world and sustains everything that exists on the planet.

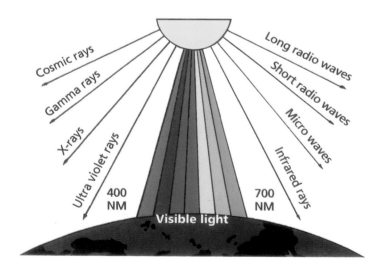

Sunlight is perceived through our eyes as white light and is composed of energetic vibrations or frequencies carried by waves, just like heat or sound. Light is either visible or invisible to the eye.

Invisible light energies are cosmic, gamma, ultraviolet (which gives you a sunburn if you are not careful), long and short radio waves, microwaves, infrared rays, and x-rays.

ColorAlchemy uses the visible aspects of light. Visible light is the light accessible to the human eye. It is composed of the rainbow colors that Sir Isaac Newton observed in 1666 when a ray of sunlight passes through a prism.

Newton discovered what he described as the *seven-color body*. Was Newton intuitively talking about the chakras in *Body ColorAlchemy*? Every time Newton held a prism up to the sun, the light refracted and dispersed into its colorful components.

This duplication is the reason ColorAlchemy is consistently effective.

Each color has a unique vibration, or energetic speed. Between the lowest and highest vibration, we experience the visible spectrum. We see the color Red because it has the lowest frequency of visible light and Violet because it has the highest vibration. If a light wave changes frequency, the color changes.

"Each thing—the human body, flowers, animals, etc.—contains pigment molecules responsible for absorbing particular colors and reflecting others—each with its own unique way of absorbing and reflecting. Absorption occurs when a pigment is resonating with a particular color wavelength. When there is no resonant pigment for a wavelength, the color is turned away, reflected. Absorption and reflection are the process of vibrational selectivity." [2]

Affectionately known as *ROYGBIV* by scientists and colorists, the full-spectrum sequence is Red, Orange, Yellow, Green, Blue, Indigo, and Violet. This is the exact same vibrational and energetic order of the Daily Triumphs (Monday through Sunday) and the colors of the chakras—the energy centers in the human body.

These are the colors and vibrations of the ColorAlchemy rainbow. On the ColorAlchemy chart on p. 2, notice how the energies climb the vibrational ladder. The energies of the week build with each day, starting with the lower, primal energies, and evolve toward higher spiritual daily energies. In *Body ColorAlchemy*, discover how the energy of each chakra and its color follows the ROYGBIV sequence and grows from the ground to the highest spiritual location of the body.

Each color is an energy with its own set of unique life-enhancing attributes. ColorAlchemy incorporates each color's vibration into the body's vibrational field and trains it how to receive the highest benefit.

Integrate color into consciousness to balance the rainbow of *vibrational energy* and each color's life qualities in the mind, body, and spirit.

Rainbow Colors: *Living ColorAlchemy*

When earth conditions are just right, we experience *Living ColorAlchemy* such as rainbows, sunrises, sunsets, and the Aurora Borealis. Because rainbows include all spectral colors, they are considered the favorite of all colorful phenomenon.

Rainbows consist of Newton's duplicatable, low-to-high (ROYGBIV) light frequencies that are visible when they "prism" through water droplets in the atmosphere. Rainbows are a magical, yet scientific event.

Rainbows are a positive moment that pauses the day from its ordinary routine.

When you experience a rainbow, there is a sense of excitement through the calm and peacefulness. Part of why a rainbow is magical is because its energy is so fleeting. The perfect, colorful moment needs to be captured before it fades away.

"That translucent instant (before the dance of daily life returns) is like standing inside a bubble of our primal being, listening to the echoes of almost a forgotten unity." [3]

Witnessing a rainbow is *Living ColorAlchemy*. As you will learn in *Mental ColorAlchemy*, rainbows are symbols of living in the present, not in the past or in future mental wanderings.

A rainbow is a spiritual metaphor for life and a precious reminder to live in the present moment.

Because you receive color and benefit from it through the eyes and skin every moment, you can live ColorAlchemy in an instant. All you need to do is duplicate the moment with your inner rainbow:

- Be conscious of daily challenges
- Observe when you need to pause your day
- Create a ColorAlchemy moment

Capture and absorb your needed color(s) by:
- Noticing the colors that surround you at all times
- Visualizing the colors with the power of the mind

Live ColorAlchemy: Create Colorful Habits

Capture two minutes in the morning, two minutes in the evening, and, just like a fleeting rainbow, periodically during the day.

Enjoy the colors of NOW before the moment slips away and is gone.

Enjoy the precious moments of YOU.

Color is the Source of Creation

Through science, we already know that color is pure energy and energy is the foundation for everything that exists. Thanks to what I learned from the PBS television show *Nova*, I feel confident to say that color is the source of Creation.

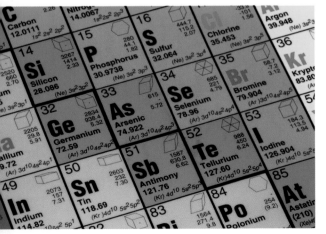

One *Nova* segment discussed whether there was life on other planets. Scientists explained how the universe evolved through the creation of the elements with the genius of the periodic table.

The periodic table is a big grid and contains the smallest recognizable building blocks or elements in the known universe.

The elements are hydrogen, helium, oxygen, and carbon, the stuff our human bodies are made of, along with all the other elements that chemists use when working with molecular structures.

These are the elements of the universe.

Because these elements are the building blocks of the universe, ColorAlchemy is further validated by the way scientists use color to consider whether there is life on other planets.

To scan the universe, astronomers use a spectrograph, or a direct imaging camera. A spectrograph splits, or disperses, the light from an object, such as a planet, into its components, or wavelengths. Sound familiar? This is where Newton comes in. The same way a prism splits light from the sun into the wavelengths that we see as color, a spectrograph splits the light from a planet and takes a picture.

Here's the complicated and real scientific part, and I am not sure I'm supposed to really understand it in this lifetime, but here goes!

According to the physical science known as hyperphysics, by using the colors transmitted through the photons emitted from specific frequencies, or color wavelengths, scientists can calculate the quality and quantity of the elements that are present.

Think about it. Millions of miles away, astronomers know which heavenly bodies contain the elements that could support life.

The fascinating connection to ColorAlchemy is that

Color is the Source of all Creation!

"Colors are emanations from the unseen threads in the fabric of all creation; they are atomic forces that hold the cosmos together." [4]

From the smallest subatomic particle to the grand scale of the universe, you now know why the magnificent photographs of nebulas and other heavenly bodies include all the colors of the rainbow.

They are *Living ColorAlchemy.*

The life cycle of a star goes through the entire spectral sequence of color from its birth to its death ... the colors of the rainbow.

"It may come as a shock to learn that all the atoms in your body and in the earth were once part of a star that exploded and disintegrated, and it is probable that those same atoms were once the debris of an earlier star."[5]

Given the theory that the color of light is the source of creation and the physical composition of all life, then color is the source of everything in our body, too. The body is composed of approximately 65% water (H_2O, the combination of hydrogen and oxygen). The remaining 35% is carbon and trace elements which have their own colorful representations.

Just as water droplets reveal the mystical rainbow in the sky, the water in body holds the energies of spectral color to create an etheric, spiritual rainbow within called the aura and its colorful chakra system.

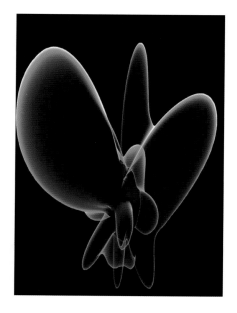

One of the reasons that water ColorAlchemy Activators are so beneficial is because the body needs water to feed its colorful composition.

This fascinating science provides further validity to the following *Spiritual* and *Body ColorAlchemy* chapters.

And the science gets even more exciting...

I was introduced to String Theory while watching another *Nova* episode. I was so intrigued that I did more research.

While not significant to this fascinating discussion, I can't hold back my excitement in telling you that matter and energy are the keys to ColorAlchemy!

The relevance is in the universal nature of how everything sacred in life is interconnected.

Quantum-mechanic scientists explained that strings are elementary particles. These particles are a billionth of a billionth of a billionth of a centimeter, which means that they are too small to be seen with current or even expected technology.

Quantum scientists suggest that strings are not matter but the *consciousness of matter*. **Why are they saying that strings are the consciousness of energy?**

If you listened carefully in between the lines, these scientists sound more like theologians and spiritual theorists as they speculate on What consciousness is. Are they referring to consciousness as the *Creator*? Are strings the scientific proof that unify physical reality and spirit?

"Vibration is the same energy as life itself, originating from God's movement, which has in this plane of existence been condensed into matter. Matter is spirit in motion to such a degree that it gives material expression. The urges of the atom bear the imprint of those fruits born of the Creator from the beginning of time." [6]

Isn't that awe inspiring?

To recap, *Living ColorAlchemy*:

- Integrates color into your daily routine
- Holistically unifies the physical, mental, and spiritual energies of the rainbow colors into the formula of happiness

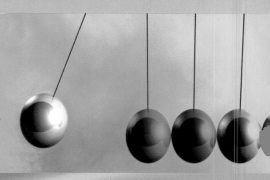

*Newton's Cradle is the perfect symbol for creating ColorAlchemy momentum. **Action** instantaneously creates transformational **reaction** with scientific validation and your ColorAlchemy Activators.*

Be empowered with your Daily Triumphs!

In the previous chapter, I suggested that controlling the mind is the catalyst for happiness because more color-life qualities are governed by the mind and emotion.

Now that you understand the physical and colorful science of the source of creation and the quantum science of String Theory, is the spirit of God the link between our mental and physical worlds?

Perhaps... Either way, the more you learn about the physics of physical reality, the more its science integrates into our spiritual world.

In addition to that transformational concept, it is even more important to use the mind to consciously connect to our spiritual world. Don't just see color. Consciously experience the color around you.

With String Theory and color as the source of creation,

Who or what is God?

"Light is the shadow of God"
—Plato

ColorAlchemy does not conflict with your religious or spiritual beliefs.

*When I speak of God, it refers to the universal intelligence that we are all connected to. God is the energy of all that exists. This God-energy of innate pure light is the source of my interpretation of **what God is**.*

Mental Color Alchemy

The mind is the key to connecting
the beneficial influence of color to the
physical, emotional and spiritual parts of yourself.

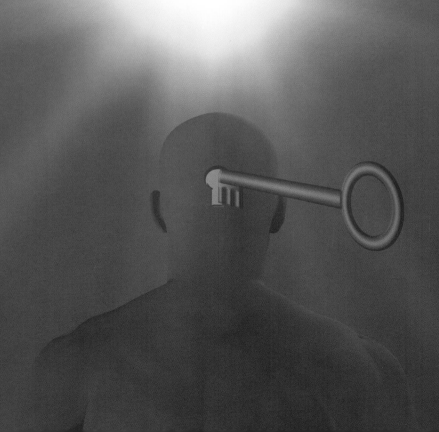

Yellow, Green & Blue are the Mental Colors.

Wear, breathe, and experience them
to focus the power of your Mind.

The Mind

Colorful Mind? Uncontrolled Mind? Which one do you have?

Both?

Colorful Mind

You wouldn't be reading these words if you didn't have a colorful mind. If you are aware of color that surrounds you, your colorful mind is capturing and absorbing life-enhancing, mental breaks from your ordinary routine.

Practicing ColorAlchemy expands your colorful mind and improves the ability to create happiness. Adding conscious intention with controlling the mind deepens your ColorAlchemy and positive life-enhancing choices.

Uncontrolled Mind

How often does your mind replay the same tape reminiscent of the classic movie *Groundhog Day*? Over and over, your mind spins with thoughts about past events or the future.

With thoughts dwelling in the past, present experience often passes unnoticed. That experience is gone, missed, and lost forever! Although it is beneficial to gain wisdom from experience, past thoughts keep the mind from living in the present.

Time spent mentally wandering in the future is equally as wasteful. Let's be honest. With such musings, how often do events occur as you created them? Almost never! When thoughts are spent in future speculation, what subtle and magical moments do you miss in the present?

**Experience happiness.
Live in the moment.**

Capture thousands of life moments
with the joy of a fleeting rainbow.

Look around, be present, and
breathe the color around you.

An undisciplined mind is often filled with detrimental thoughts and negative behavioral patterns. These create stress, flush the body with toxins, and cause premature aging. These stress-producing and habitual toxic cycles of negativity, such as frustration and anger, get reinforced and thus, through perpetuation, become addictions.

Prolonged negative thought addiction:

- Creates imbalance in cardiovascular function
- Disrupts the immune system
- Upsets the endocrine system
- Negatively impacts physical health

In fact, science has proven that habitual negative behavioral patterns and toxic body flush become harmful, habitual physical and mental addictions through the adrenaline rush. Nonsupportive thoughts reconfirm mental insecurities and ultimately produce limitations in life, as well as bitterness and unhappiness.

The easiest way to recognize the uncontrolled mind is through repeated stressful activities, such as when driving a car. For example, how often does a "stupid driver" influence a response? (I usually have this one under control.) Although embarrassing to admit, perhaps you mouth off or drive faster to "show who is in control." But who or what is really in control?

The automated response of the uncontrolled mind is in charge.

No doubt, driving is a stressful activity. The negative reaction may be a reflection of another circumstance that triggered your anger unconsciously compounded by the stress of driving. Whatever the root of the cause, you most likely have no control over the situation.

When driving, create a *pause in the moment* for logic to tell you that:

- You have no control over the other driver, red light, or train.

And most important,

- You have no control over anyone else's thoughts.

- Getting upset is wasted energy.
  The heat of your body is the obvious indicator that mental stress is destructive and shortens life.

Perhaps you believe that there is no choice and that life is spinning out of control. But you do have control. When the mind is trained, the programming of the automatic, nonsupportive response is replaced with positive action.

Throughout your day, or as I like to say, *being out in the world*, how often are you *set off* by assumptions and preconceived notions about others and/or circumstances that do not meet your expectations?

With acceptance that you have no control over most everything, there is a liberating and calming freedom. Please note that I am not suggesting that you be nonchalant, that you procrastinate, or that you avoid situations. Instead, with a calm, controlled, and stress-free mind, you have greater clarity to make decisions and greater ease in completing tasks.

No longer allow yourself to be upset over that which you have no control.

By making conscious choices of how you respond, you change behavioral patterns with the one thing that you do have control over: your mind!

Conscious thought changes behavioral patterns, revealing new options and potential.

ColorAlchemy rewires your brain and transforms you from the inside out.

What does *Your Happiness* look like?

Take a moment to breathe happiness into your vision. Experience it with all your senses. Where are you? What does the space look like? Who are you with? What does it smell like? What are the physical sensations? What colors are surrounding you and what are they saying? How do you feel? How are you inspired? What turns you on? Visualize your happiness as if you are watching yourself in an enjoyable movie.

What positive action is needed to create your world?

Control the Brain with Color

The brain is like a computer. Using the five senses, the brain imprints every favorable and unfavorable experience. Whether conscious of the details or not, the brain processes thousands of subtle bytes of information and stores them. Whatever habit the brain creates, it propagates thought, response, and action. Negative thoughts manifest stress, toxic reactions, and unhappiness. When thoughts are of love, respect, and compassion for yourself and others, you live in peace, happiness, and joy. Unless *software patterns* are altered, reactions and responses continue to be the same.

Change your thoughts. Create your reality.

With conscious intention, your mental ability adds positive meaning and purpose. Imprint life-enhancing qualities of color with your controlled mind.

Positive thoughts create grooves in the mind according to the power of will. Repetition penetrates the mind and transforms thought into reality.

Whether or not you are consciously thinking about color at any moment,

Consistent ColorAlchemy deepens the absorption rate of color's beneficial influence.

The Unconscious Mind Runs Deep

I have read many books and attended many lectures that describe *dis-ease*. Dis-ease, as it is so wonderfully described, is being *ill at ease with something in your world or within yourself*. When there is dis-ease in your consciousness or daily routine for an extended time, it roots in your unconscious mind. Unless there is healing in the unconscious, which comes from changing conscious patterns, the body becomes diseased.

Perhaps you have had similar experiences to confirm this concept. I know when I am stressed, toxins flush my body, immune systems don't work properly, and my body rebels with a cold or zit-fest.

A recent experience further clarified the trickle-down influence of how deep and fast the unconscious stores experience and influence mental and physical health.

While anxious to sell a house and move to a smaller city, I thought the perfect buyers showed up, as the buyers actively pursued us with an acceptable price and terms.

Because everything was flowing smoothly, the deal felt complete and my thoughts were on packing and our new life. As the agreement was to be inked, the buyers bolted.

After sleeping off my letdown, a fresh morning brought conscious logic: "Move on, get over it, the right deal will be better, etc." That night, I thought my reaction to the experience was under control. The following morning, in waking between unconsciousness and consciousness, the buyers were on my mind. The disappointment went deep very quickly.

This was compounded by a complicated and frustrating computer problem, which I thought I was handling reasonably well. However, within minutes of my tech coming over that same morning, I unexpectedly threw up!

Because I rarely get sick, I observed the experience. I was shocked by how fast the combined stress processed through my unconscious and produced toxins in my body. With conscious mental confidence and my body unconsciously trusting my tech, I "let go."

After mentioning this story to my students, one told me she experienced the same thing.

Did the power of suggestion afford her the freedom to release her stress before it had a chance to toxify her body more seriously?

You will not fall of the edge!

Make a commitment to yourself right now: when you encounter extreme situations, give yourself permission to let your body involuntarily cleanse you.

While this short, two-week experience will not be a major influence on my life, it taught me very valuable lessons.

The more controlled the conscious mind, the more the unconscious will be at peace and the less toxic influence it will have on the body.

The less dis-ease you have, the longer and certainly happier life will be.

The choice: internalize stress or calmly handle it.

Happy to have released the toxic stress from my body, I realized I had to work a little harder with my conscious mind.

On a larger scale, what are the emotional, physical, and spiritual effects of long-term, stressful influences: a bad childhood; an abusive parent, lover, or employer: working in an unsatisfying job or ????

What are the unfavorable experiences that you have been holding for a long time? How deep do they go? The rest of *Mental ColorAlchemy* is dedicated to "throwing them up" and getting rid of them!

Creating Your Colorful, Stress-Free World

Color excites the eye and lifts the soul. Color influences mood, feelings, and behavior. Making color-life qualities a part of your consciousness and conditioning the mind, you program good habits and positive thoughts. These new behavioral patterns reduce age-producing stress and stimulate a more youthful outlook.

Put the mind, body, and spiritual aspects of the ColorAlchemy puzzle together. Pay attention to the colors in nature and in human creativity.

1. Be aware of color. *The easy part!*

Bring color and its healing life qualities into your mind, body, and spirit. Spend a few minutes daily with the Daily Color and its life-enhancing techniques.

If you haven't practiced your *two colorful minutes*, go to the *Daily ColorAlchemy Triumphs* and breathe today's color!

Remember, ColorAlchemy is a conscious pause in your day. Enjoy the moment.

2. Cultivate the Observer of your thoughts.

The more challenging part!

Consciously replace unfavorable behavioral patterns and with good ones.

Cultivate Your Observer

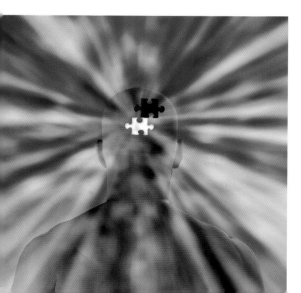

Your Observer is your most inner self, the spirit voice within, and the consciousness behind all that you experience. To create beneficial patterns and profound life-enhancing results with any transformational discipline, your Observer must be put into action. Cultivating your Observer is necessary for personal growth.

The best way I can describe cultivating your Observer is with two examples.

1. May I assume you experience lucid dreaming? While asleep, your conscious mind comes forward and says, *"I am dreaming."* In the moment your conscious mind comes through, you become the Observer of your dream.

Cultivating your Observer while awake is the key.

2. There is a children's cartoon whose character is conflicted about a decision to do the right or wrong thing. On one shoulder is an angel whispering honorable guidance. On the other shoulder is the *inner demon* offering naughty temptation. The cartoon character, caught in the middle, is presented with a conscious choice.

Paying attention to making conscious choices is recognizing your Observer.

Cultivating your Observer in your moment-to-moment thought is being aware of what your mind is thinking.

Train Your Observer

Being present in the moment is being conscious of options. Acknowledge your Observer when presented with a choice: Are you responding to your angel or inner demon? Are you giving thought to the choice, or is your uncontrolled mind running on automatic?

Know your *Observer is observing* when it recognizes:

Angel moments are positive thoughts or reactions.

Perhaps you and your Observer dialogue, *"Stop, take a color breath. I choose not to respond automatically. My conscious choice is in everyone's highest interest.*

My Observer taught me something and I have grown. In the past I may have not handled that as well."

Now the most important part!

Say, *"I AM proud of myself!"*

The words *I AM* are a powerful statement of commitment. They define self-worth, individuality, and commitment. Say them often enough and their truth becomes reality.

I have changed my behavior to that which is positive. I AM growing physically, mentally, and spiritually every day. Using your own words, affirmations like these reinforce *Observer skills* and positive behavior.

Demon moments are negative thoughts or reactions.

The key to transforming your life is to make peace with your inner demon.

1. Through your Observer, realize that you are caught in an automated, preconditioned, self-destructive, negative addiction. Stop it. Take a color breath. While always being kind to yourself, make a conscious choice of how to respond. Say to yourself, *"How can I change this from a negative to a positive?"* Do it, engage the angel side of yourself, and change your behavior right then!

2. If you realize that a negative moment has occurred and you say something unsupportive like, *"I messed up. Stop!"* Take a color breath. Reinforce your success in a positive way. Say, *"Hooray! My Observer caught me in a negative moment. I learned from this experience."*

Recognizing that you had a negative moment is the first and most important step.

With either of these experiences, remember to acknowledge that you did well by recognizing negative behavior. Say, *"I AM proud of myself! I choose to make conscious choices. I AM growing physically, mentally, and spiritually every day."* Create your own reinforcement affirmations p. 249.

> ## *With your thoughts, you make the world.*
> –Buddha

Control the Mind, Eliminate Inner Demons

This section is a comprehensive discussion to eliminate inner demons. From what appears to be considerable detail, with a trained Observer, sometimes you get lucky and the process is almost instantaneous. In a few pages, I'll prove how fast my Observer eliminated one of my inner demons forever!

To eliminate your inner demons:

- Commit to YOU with Conscious Intention
- Be Kind to Yourself
- Recognize Behavioral Patterns
- Learn from My "Almost-Instantaneous" Example
- Source the Real Demon
- Recommit with an Oopsie-Strategy
- Live ColorAlchemy!

Commit to YOU with Conscious Intention

When demons are eliminated, you live in the moment and increase happiness. Commit to changing nonsupportive patterns into positive ones:

- Define productive thinking that promotes inner clarity
- Reveal false negative realities that your mind conditioned you to believe were true
- Solidify your plan of action so future responses and thoughts are positive
- Track and measure progress by observing your experiences

Right now, with all your colors and their attributes, make commitments to eliminate your demons, to train your Observer, and to perpetuate greater happiness.

To support your commitment, put on a Red shirt.

Breath and visualize yourself FULL of vitality, self-confidence, and courage!

- **Affirm that you are in complete control of your mind**
- **Know that your Observer is the conscious part of yourself that exists for the *Soul Purpose* to improve YOU**
- **Make a commitment for your Observer to acknowledge your mental process**
- **Commit to making conscious choices.**

You are blessed with the most
miraculous gift called

freedom of thought.

This is the genius of creativity.
Before there is creative form,
there is thought.

If your inner self didn't know,
that you can turn vision into reality,
the thought wouldn't have entered
your mind in the first place.

Commitment takes a little effort, and you can do it!

You have committed!
You are triumphant!

Promise to create good habits.

> ## You are practicing your two colorful minutes,
> ## YES!?

Pick a consistent time each day to review your commitment and to learn from your daily experience. Select a time when you won't be disturbed and you are relaxed (I use bathtime.) Deepen your commitment and clarify your thoughts by answering the following questions in your journal.

Journaling accelerates this insightful and transformational process. Journaling keeps the mind from wandering and focuses on the problem. For a complete explanation and benefits of journaling, p. 96.

- Did I honor my commitments?
- Did I make conscious choices?
- Was I kind to myself?
- Did I recognize behavioral patterns?
- How did I respond to stressful situations?
- Did I discover the root of the stress or negative behavior (the real demon)?
- Did I practice ColorAlchemy?

And:

- Did I experience a stressful situation today?
- What was it? Did I learn from experience?
- Did I use Color Breathing?
- Did I shift negative to positive?

If you answered *YES!*
Reinforce your success and be proud!
You had a triumphant day!

Yes to some and *no* to others?
Congratulate yourself on your accomplishments and recommit to your success for all *yes-answers* tomorrow.

If you answered *no,* be kind to yourself and go back to basics:

Recommit to a successful tomorrow!

Be Kind to Yourself

The key to honoring your commitment and success is to:

Promise to always be kind to yourself!

As you read the "Recognizing Behavior Patterns" and "Learn from My Almost-Instantaneous Example" in the following sections, pay close attention to how you may sabotage your efforts. Notice how the examples describe how I have belittled myself or called myself stupid (which is a perfect example of not being kind to yourself). When you say, *"I messed up"* or *"I AM such an idiot,"* that is unkind behavior, too.

Putting yourself down reinforces negative behavioral patterns. Your Observer is doing its job when it catches and stops you in a bad thought or reaction. The good news is that you are halfway there by recognizing you weren't being kind. Complete positivity reinforces good behavioral patterns and chisels away at the negative.

Make a conscious choice to be positive all the time. Even if you don't catch yourself before you *beat yourself up*, as soon as you recognize that you did it or that you are in a negative mode, stop yourself. Be nice. Say, *"I am human, and a smart one at that! I am so proud to have recognized my behavior."* Affirm in advance, **"Next time, I'll go the distance! Next time, I will not put myself down."** *Through conscious choice,* **"I commit to being 100% positive."** Move on.

You might slip. You probably will—I do. It is all right. Practicing mental kindness makes it easier for:

- Your Observer to come forward
- Disciplining yourself to make conscious choices
- Kindness to perpetuate itself
- Positive behavior to automatically replace negative behavior
- More moments of self-actualization
- Improving your life

Recognizing Behavioral Patterns

Good news: When the unconditioned mind slips into detrimental personal judgment, there is greater opportunity to reduce negative behavior.

Here is a silly pattern we all experience:

> You need something from another room. You enter the room and while standing in the right place, you completely forget what you wanted. You say to yourself, *"What did I come in here for?"*

> Automatically, you may react with such self-convincing, powerful words or thoughts: *"I AM so stupid! I AM such a dummy for forgetting what I came here for, especially after making a special trip!"*

Not nice! **Remember, reinforce with positive thoughts. Notice, the *I AM* that reinforces the negative, too. Be conscious!**

Make a conscious choice. Instead of belittling yourself, say, *"So what! I forgot! It happens!"* Retrace your thoughts and you will remember (especially with the Orange Tip I'll share with you on p. 91).

What if you misplaced your keys, forgot to pick up the laundry, or shattered a glass? Do these events really define stupidity? Never add power to similarly ugly thoughts or words that create unsupportive thoughts about yourself. *So what if you have a forgetful moment.*

Be Kind!

Create a colorful pause in your day.

Capture the magic of an inner rainbow.

The more you stop negativity with the simpler patterns, the easier it will be to remedy the challenging patterns.

Deeper and Challenging Patterns to Solve

Sometimes the naughty mind convinces us to give up before even trying. Perhaps the mind is programmed with such self-destructive thoughts as, *I can't accomplish it anyway. I am not good enough, smart enough, talented enough. I am too lazy, too old, too young, too fat,* and so forth.

Who says? On whose authority?
Your self-defeating, uncontrolled mind?

What is the source of why you think that you can't?

Here is a very personal example of sourcing a deep behavioral pattern. This brief but profound experience changed my life.

Learn from My *Almost-Instantaneous* Example

I live in a community where it is enjoyable to walk. Residents are typically friendly and greet each other. As I passed this fellow, I said hello. He didn't answer. I raised my voice. HELLOOO! After observing the experience, I admittedly recognized some anger in my spirit.

In seconds, my Observer and I had this dialogue. What was that about? Why are you so angry? What is WRONG with ME that he didn't reply? **Wait a minute!** *Is it possible that he didn't hear me? Was he preoccupied in his own thoughts? Perhaps he was just rude, but* **the questions about him were irrelevant! It was all about me! Things aren't always as they seem. Why did I respond with anger?**

The dialogue continued. Why did I take this personally? Why wasn't I worthy enough for him to reply? Ahhh, self-worth issues!? **The real demon!** *Do I have self-worth? Of course, I do! I have pride in my accomplishments: what a ridiculous notion to assume and reinforce negative judgment. How absurd it is to give away my power. I don't even know this guy. And, so what if I did?*

Based upon some deep-rooted and false perception that came from somewhere (Childhood? Past life? What difference does it really make?), I responded with preconditioned anger without any logical basis. How long was this demon living in my unconsciousness? How deep was the dis-ease?

In a seemingly insignificant moment, I discovered and resolved self-destructive behavior that would have continued had I left it unattended.

I AM so proud of myself to have recognized this inner demon. Its ugly head will never rise again without me seeing it. Each time I recognize it and quickly dismiss its negative energy, the self-destructive toxicity is reduced. Eventually, it will be gone, gone forever!

Source the Real Demon

The key to getting rid of your demons forever is to source the root issue.

Staying committed to your Observer helps you recognize when you:

- Call yourself names
- Belittle yourself
- React in negative autopilot
- Experience negative emotions: such as anger and frustration

These are not the root of the problem. As in my previous example, the root of my anger came from a false sense of not feeling worthy.

Source the real reason for self-sabotage. The habitual toxic response is perpetuated because it is so well practiced. These core issues are so deep within the psyche that we have come to believe that they are true, even though the negativity has no logical basis.

Remember, whatever triggered the **cause**, we (you and I) have no control. I *had no control over whether the man was going to speak to me. We have no control over inconsiderate drivers.*

We have no control over what anyone thinks or does, or the outcome of any circumstance. The only thing we have control over is the effect through our mind and conscious choices.

Through the power of mental control and conscious choice, when recognizing a negative moment (which includes all the times you are being unkind to yourself), Stop It. Dialogue with your Observer, as in my example. **Asking the right question(s) sources the problem, evaluates its validity, and reduces its power.** Journaling helps you stay focused on finding the source.

Use these questions and add your own to help source demons:

- Why am I hard on myself?
- Do I have self-defeating attitudes? What are they? Why?
- Is negative judgment influencing my thoughts?
- What is the source of my negativity?
- How can I make amends with this negativity?
- Are my thoughts real or a fabrication of my naughty mind?
- How can I turn this situation to generate positive results in everyone's best interest?

I was happy that because of my daily observations and ColorAlchemy, I was able to reveal my demon very quickly. Sometimes revelations take longer to recognize. **The freedom from mental torment and greater happiness is worth it.**

Consider yourself a *therapeutic detective*. Most of us can accomplish a lot of internal healing by controlling the mind and cultivating your Observer.

Do not give up! Do you need to recommit?

Incorporate ColorAlchemy

During any part of the process, add ColorAlchemy. With the following list, review the life qualities of each color. Which color(s) support healing your issue?

Red: Vitality, Courage, Security, Strength, Stamina
Orange: Happiness, Desire, Creativity, Emotion, Pleasure, Intimacy
Yellow: Personal Power, Dedication, Commitment, Drive, Ambition
Green: Love, Forgiveness, Joy, Compassion, Trust, Balance
Blue: Decision Making, Inner Truth, Communication, Clarity, Focus
Indigo: Intuition, Vision, Psychic Powers, Seeing Beyond
Violet: Peace, Bliss, Inner Knowing, Spiritual Love, Divinity, Inspiration

With the appropriate color(s), spend two minutes of Color Breathing to support your commitment. The next time a similar condition arises, your Observer will bring the color and its qualities forward to soften any negativity and enhance positive resolution. Eventually, you'll completely get rid of the demon!

Remember, repetition creates mental penetration. Strengthen your ColorAlchemy success with Colorful Affirmations:

With the Courage of Red, the Desire of Orange, and the Commitment of Yellow, may my inner self respond quickly with positive energy.

And, just in case you have any imperfect moments:

With the Forgiveness of Green, I support being kind to myself. With the Clarity of Blue, the Focus of Indigo, and the Inspiration of Violet, I quickly change my thinking to peaceful and loving thoughts.

Practice Your ColorAlchemy Triumphs To:

- Breath the Daily Color
- Be conscious of the colors around you
- Incorporate the energetic influences of color

Oopsie Strategies

If my mind is any indication that you'll be an immediate success at training your mind, I'd again say, *WE need practice*. If we have not prepared our mind before going into a stressful situation, it is likely to automatically revert into negative behavior.

For example, when I get into a car, I get stressed out. Knowing this in advance, I affirm, *Enjoy the ride. Don't let anything bother you*. It works! When *slippage* occurs, you are training your Observer to say *Oopsie* before or during an addictive, self-defeating response.

With an Oopsie, you already know to be kind to yourself. To change the negative into a positive, be proud of your improvement for catching yourself in the process! Take a Color Breath, and move on.

What if you have a double Oopsie? A double Oopsie is when you go to the closet, and 1) Oopsie you forget what you came there for and 2) double Oopsie, you belittled yourself: *"Man, I must have Alzheimer's!"*

Interestingly, my older, antiaging students always use this justification. Believe or give power to something with words and you'll create it. Remember to be careful what you think and speak. Make your words worthy of you.

Alzheimer's is a chemical imbalance. ColorAlchemy and training your mind strengthens memory. Memory loss, as part of the aging process, follows the same rules as muscle tone and flexibility: Use it or lose it!

Andrea, 70 years young at the time of this writing, will share Moving Rainbow Meditation on p. 209.

Recommit with an Oopsie Strategy

Commit to what you are going to do the next time a similar situation arises. Recommit now. Dialogue:

I AM in control!
I AM committed!

**Remember, be nice. It is all right not to be perfect.
Life's goal is to consistently improve.**

- Dialogue: *"I do not have Alzheimer's, I am not stupid,"* etc.
- I commit to further source the root of why I belittled myself.
- When unfavorable situations occur, I agree not to slip into an automated, self-defeating response.
- I commit to be present with my Observer and make conscious choices of how I respond.
- I commit to breathing my most needed color.
- I promise to be 100% positive.

*ColorAlchemy
Plan B candy!*

It doesn't matter how many times you recommit. The more you recommit, the greater your awareness, and the sooner you'll eliminate slippage, and, most important, get rid of your demons.

Living happily takes practice!

Live ColorAlchemy

Like watching your diet, being a good parent, developing muscular strength, or succeeding in business, training your mind takes persistence. Be conscious of your moment-to-moment experience. By removing negativity, you imprint positive patterns in your brain. Automatically, negative patterns are replaced with supportive ones.

Remember to engage your Observer before you enter into a stressful situation. *"I AM not going to allow the experience of bad drivers to push my buttons. I AM going to stay calm and relaxed."*

Practice *being calm and controlled* before going into **known** stressful situations so you'll be better prepared when **unexpected** stressful experiences occur.

Because your mind is the only thing that you have control over, it is important to recap the process.

1. Observe your mind when it recognizes:

- Negative thoughts about yourself or others
- An automatic, negative response
- Thinking about past or future thoughts
- Feeling trapped in replaying a scenario about something over which you have no control

During these observations:

Lovingly and gently say: *"Because I have control over my thoughts and reactions, I choose to serve my highest good. I AM successful in changing this negative thought or circumstance into one that is supportive."*

2. Develop good habits. Pick a time at the end of each day and review your successes and how you can improve what didn't work.

3. Change your thoughts. Dialogue with your observer. Journal your thoughts.

- What is/are my negative pattern(s)?
- What really happened?
- Do I really have any control over the situation?
  I only have control over my mind and reaction.
- What was I thinking and feeling to trigger my reaction?
- How does my anger, frustration, and/or negative response create a benefit?
- What is the true source of my thought or action?

- Is there some false and self-destructive judgment?
- How do I stop its continued repetition?
- How can I be kind, forgive myself, and transform the negative into a positive?
- How can I develop a plan to take affirmative action when similar conditions reoccur?
- I will commit to a favorable outcome the next time a similar situation is encountered.

As your observation skills improve, your inner dialogue improves. The revelations you discover about your core personality will create positive changes in your life.

4. Live ColorAlchemy!

5. Engage your Observer before going into stressful situations.

6. Develop the power of conscious intention.

> Consistently enhance the beneficial influence of color and deepen the absorption rate.

7. Count your blessings with positive and loving thoughts.

Colorfully embrace the magnificent, joyful person that you are.

Exercise & Journaling Practice

Spend a few quiet moments with yourself. Go to the deepest, most honest place within yourself. Find a repetitive negative *I AM* thought. Start a dialogue with that thought. Use some of the questions from the previous page or, better yet, ask questions that are more specific to your personal situation.

Practice this exercise every time you recognize a negative thought, response, or behavior.

Your Observer will reveal parts of yourself to transform your life and remove demons forever!

Physical
Color Alchemy

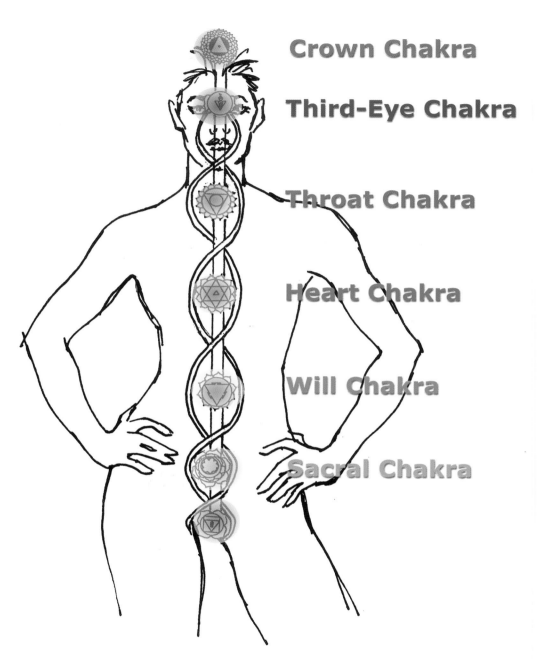

Crown Chakra

Third-Eye Chakra

Throat Chakra

Heart Chakra

Will Chakra

Sacral Chakra

Each chakra, its corresponding color,
day of the week, body locations and ailments,
diagnosis, and healing suggestions are detailed in
Daily ColorAlchemy Triumphs: Colors of Your Body, p. 111.

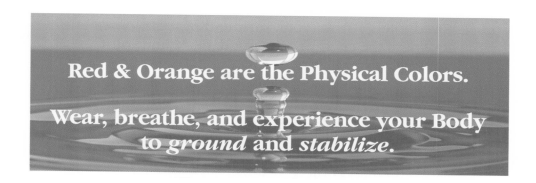

Red & Orange are the Physical Colors.

Wear, breathe, and experience your Body
to *ground* and *stabilize*.

So far, so good!? Are you experiencing the simplicity of ColorAlchemy and your inner rainbow? Are you wearing your colors and practicing two minutes of Color Breathing? Are you deepening your knowledge with the power of journaling?

Yes? Let's deepen your ColorAlchemy with the colors of the human body. In this chapter, you'll diagnose and strengthen life-quality weaknesses and improve mental, physical, and spiritual health through your body's chakra system and aura.

The Chakras: The Rainbow Body

In addition to the body's colorful-chemical composition, the chakra system is the *seven-color body*. The chakras are seven energy centers in the body that correspond to each of the seven spectral colors and follow the same vibrational, energetic sequence. Do you remember how Newton referred to the *refraction and dispersion* of light through a prism as the *seven-color body*. His description perfectly parallels the *duplicatable absorption and radiations* of your chakras.

The Root Chakra (at the base of the spine), with the slowest color-energy vibration has similar energetic qualities as Monday and the color Red. Following the spectral sequence, each chakra climbs the vibrational ladder up the body, ending with the Violet energies of Sunday, with its highest, spiritual-color vibration at the Crown Chakra (at the top of the head).

Chakras are energetic transmission stations in the body. They absorb colored energy from your surroundings and other people. They spiral the energy to the mind, body, and spirit.

They also radiate creative energy out into the universe like the spiral of a nautilus shell.

Chakras are attuned to the symbolism and sacred geometry inherent in nature and the body. In Sanskrit, the word chakra means "wheel" or "circle." Chakras continuously spin and renew their energy like the cycles of nature and the spiraling genetic energy of DNA, the building blocks of life.

Although the circle is the symbol of wholeness and eternity. The spiral is the momentum of energy as well as a symbol for personal and planetary evolution.

Although the body has hundreds of centers, the seven major chakras line up in the middle axis of the body along the spinal column. The chakras are the body's nurturing, spinning wheels of energy. Each chakra is located in a specific body area and supports organ function. Chakras maintain physical wellness and colorfully balance life's energetic qualities.

The Chakras Throughout History

Dating as far back as 3000 BCE, ancient Sumerians and Egyptians used the body's color energy for healing as well as for reaching spiritual enlightenment. Buddhist and Hindu traditions recognize that each organ vibrates to the same frequencies as each of the rainbow's colors.

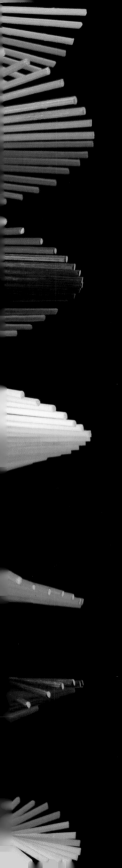

Spiritual tradition suggests that enlightened Buddhists and Hindu yogis are able to travel (astral projection) on light's invisible-color energy. It is also said that at the time of an enlightened Buddha's or yogi's death,

"They enable their bodies to be reabsorbed back into the light essences of the elements that created it. Their material bodies dissolve back into light and then disappear completely. This process is known as the rainbow **body** or the **body of light** because the dissolution is often accompanied by spontaneous manifestations of light and rainbows." [7]

You are connected to The Light

and the Source of Everything with your colorful body and spirit.

Because the body is *of the light*, when one chakra is not in sync with the others or tuned to its proper frequency, there is illness or mental disfunction. When each chakra is performing properly, the energy center is vibrating at the exact speed of its corresponding color. Weak chakras are enhanced by absorbing their needed energy through wearing color, practicing Color Breathing, and applying any ColorAlchemy Activators (such as shining colored light on the body, p. 192 and drinking color elixirs, p.197).

How Chakras work

High school science teaches that everything, regardless of shape, size, or solidity, consists of neutrons, protons, and electrons. Protons and electrons carry positive and negative charges. All natural interactions, as defined by the Chinese concept of yin and yang are scientifically broken down into the dance of positive and negative charges. This electric reaction creates vibration and movement in *everything*.

The body pulsates with electrical charges, too. Every cell carries a charge, creating an energy field or aura around the body. Through each chakra, this energy body is charged by absorbing color through the eyes and the skin. While the chakras do not actually exist in physical form like the heart, stomach, or kidneys, their vibration influences the health of each major gland and organ. chakras trigger hormone production that supports biochemical and endocrine systems.

Individual chakras vibrate or spin at a unique frequency, absorbing and radiating distinct types of energy. Their spin allows the absorption of only their right kind of color energy. Each chakra's distinctive energy parallels the life qualities of each spectral color. If a chakra is vibrating at its optimal level, it is exchanging life-affirming energy. If it is not, it attracts and imparts more of the same denser, life-restrictive energy.

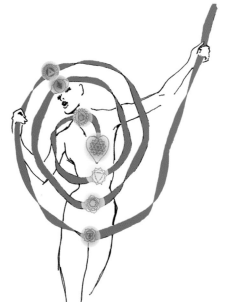

For example, if you are not grounded through the Root Chakra, without this solid foundation, the chakras above lose stability. If you are not receptive with the Crown Chakra, you may miss connection to your inner self and the sacred interconnectedness to all that exists.

The center of the chakra system is love, the heart of everything.

The Heart Chakra is the transmutation center for unconditional love.

Located in the chest, the Heart Chakra radiates spiraling energy that allows the lower, physical aspects of your being to be transformed into the spiritual aspects. The physical chakras (Root/Red, Sacral/Orange, and Will/Yellow) are transmuted through the heart center into the intuitive energies of the upper, emotional, and spiritual chakras (Throat/Blue, Third-Eye/Indigo, and Crown/Violet).

All chakras are connected through love. Survival of the Red/Root Chakra is no longer only related to the physical; it is connected to your spirituality. Conversely, the Green/Heart Chakra allows you to use Violet/Crown Chakra energy and pull it down into the physical world. This deeper, holistic understanding of chakra interconnectedness enhances all of the physical, emotional, and spiritual attributes.

Through chakra development, as with all *Living ColorAlchemy*, integrate all colorful-life qualities to be complete, balanced, and happy. With just minutes a day, be consistent with ColorAlchemy to deepen the effectiveness of color absorption and its beneficial influence.

Your Aura

The aura is the glow of the chakras. It is the colorful emanations of the rainbow body. It is the electromagnetic field around a body or any object. Scientific aura research dates as far back as 1911, and artists have rendered auras or halos in spiritual paintings throughout the ages.

In his book, *The Human Aura*, Dr. Walter J. Kilner first observed the colorful energy field around the body with a specially designed glass screen. Through the glass, he found that the aura extends as far as two feet from the body and has multiple layers.

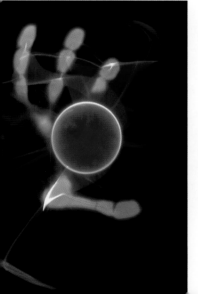

He discovered that these energy layers, just like the chakras, are transient and in constant flux with the conditions of the mind, body, and spirit as well as environmental conditions.

Aura research expanded in the 1940s when Russian electrician Seymon Kirlian developed a method of photographing auric fields. He and his wife, Valentina, experimented with photographing animate and inanimate objects. They discovered that most subjects emitted levels of visible energy based upon the *aliveness* of the object's electromagnetic field. Their fascinating studies revealed that energy emits from amputated limbs, which explains why people still feel sensations in missing areas and implies that the essence of who we are, our energy or soul, lives beyond physical form.

Modern aura machines continue to be developed for scientific research and for commercial use. In public, they are often found at psychic fairs and new-age expos. Some machines photograph the head or the entire body to indicate chakra strengths and weaknesses.

What do you think your aura looks like when you absorb toxicities or have chakra imbalances? What is your aura indicating as it radiates your life conditions?

Improving Your Chakras and Aura

Your inner rainbow is "the weather vane of the soul that relates to various aspects of our incompleteness. Colors emanating from a person are a vibrational status report on the body and mind. This is symptomatic of the influences at work through the body's systems." [8]

Your aura, the combination of the seven colors, and chakras create a complete package of personal energy. Depending on how each chakra is tuned, how they are in harmony with each other, and what color(s) they are radiating and/or absorbing from your surroundings and your emotional state, your aura illuminates the colors of the moment.

Create a ColorAlchemy moment.

Take a White Breath and visualize in a glow of perfect mind, body, and spiritual health. Ahhh!

Reading auras and evaluating the chakras provide insight into health issues, physical weakness or energy blockages, personality, intellectual strength, and level of spiritual development. Because they are always changing, an aura moment is frozen in time. An aura is a health indicator as well as a snapshot of mood, feelings, and disposition.

If all chakras were in perfect alignment, you would be a living saint or masterful guru and your aura would be white—the harmony of all spectral colors. You'll be happy to know that even the Dalai Lama says he is "still working at it" as he shines his delicious and most humble grin. In the same way that ColorAlchemy is an ongoing process and living life takes a lifetime, each chakra has life lessons to learn.

Four Components of ColorAlchemy Enhancement

Learn	**The individual Chakra:** • Color • Mind, body, and spiritual attributes • Physical locations and gland/endocrine systems • Associated ailments • Common addictions

Evaluate	**Diagnostic signs for each chakra through life-energy indicators:**
	• Aura
	• Overactive chakra attributes
	• Understimulated chakra attributes
	
	• *Matter* & *energy* chakra characteristics:
	  • Spiritual
	  • Emotional
	  • Physical

Release	**Let go of what doesn't serve your highest goals and best interests, use your:** • Journal • Observer • Mental ColorAlchemy commitments
Activate	**Balance and improve each chakra:** • *Matter* & *energy* enhancers

Learn the Yin/Yang of Matter and Energy

Here is the magnificent relevance of how everything sacred in life is interconnected and how to evaluate, activate, and improve the chakras with the only two components that exist in all of creation.

The concept of yin and yang, explained by Chinese theory, defines perfect balance with two equal forces that are united in a cosmic dance. All natural interactions are scientifically broken down into the dance of positive (yang) and negative (yin) charges. Light/dark, day/night, male/female, and energy/matter are the polarities of the spinning wheel of creation. Yin cannot exist without yang, matter cannot exist without energy: both exist in harmony with the other, because of the other.

Energy is the *mental and spiritual aspects of life* that combine with **matter**, the *physical form*, to create perfect universal balance.

Simply, **matter** is the physical stuff, and **energy** is the glue that holds the stuff together.

Scientifically: **Matter** is everything comprised in the table of the periodic elements: anything in physical form, from the smallest atom to planetary structure.

Energy is the magnetic, electrical, and/or spiritual force that holds matter in place.

Spectacular yin/yang sky

Matter is **Body ColorAlchemy and the** *Physical ColorAlchemy Activators* **experienced with the five senses.**

Physical ColorAlchemy Activators
(such as wearing your Daily Colors)
Integrating your chakras and aura

Energy is **Mental and Spiritual** *ColorAlchemy Activators* **experienced with the** Mind.

- Relaxing, Color Breaths and Visualization
- Cultivating your Observer
- Powers of intention, affirmation, and meditation
- Evolving spiritual consciousness

Learn

Evaluate

Release

Activate

Example of Chakra-Health Diagnosis

Evaluating the difference between energy and matter helps:

1. Diagnose life quality and chakra weakness based upon energy **(yin: spiritual & emotional) and/or** matter **(yang: Physical)** *symptoms.*

Red & Root Chakra Weakness

ENERGY	YIN: without Form	MATTER YANG: with Form
Spiritual	Emotional	Physical
You feel detached from the physical world and don't want to be involved with *real life*.	Financial, security, and not having *enough* fears are controlling your thoughts.	You don't feel like moving-- supreme couch potato. No motivation to lift a finger.

2. *Release* energies that do not serve you.

Use your journal, cultivated Observer, and Mental ColorAlchemy to let go of what is not in your highest goals and best interests with yin and yang energies.

YANG Energies Overactive Red	YIN Energies Under-stimulated Red
• impatient • aggressive • hyperactive • food addictions	• lack of energy • no enthusiasm • dull and lifeless

3. *Activate* with *matter and energy ColorAlchemy* enhancers to exponentially multiply effectiveness.

As you know, color comes from vibrational energy that materializes the physical world (matter). It is through the endless supply of these yin/yang forces that you alchemically channel healing vibrations.

In other words, add conscious **mental** and **spiritual** intention with **physical** *ColorAlchemy Activators.*

Physical ColorAlchemy (*matter*)		Mental/Spiritual ColorAlchemy (*energy*)
Chakras and Color	with	Visualization and Breathing
Healing Hands	with	Colored Rays
Blessing Body	with	Conscious Intention
Journaling	with	Cultivating Your Observer

Learn, Evaluate, Release, and Activate the Chakras

Learn

Read through the chakras, as detailed in the previous pages, to evaluate which you may help balance your energy and life.

Evaluate

Evaluate imbalance in yourself using the life qualities along with yin and yang energies of each chakra color as a guide. Are there any attributes that you want to further improve? Are some energies dominant or out of proportion?

Example: My Throat and Third-Eye Chakras are fairly strong, but with my overactive Will, I forget to relax. See if you can diagnose my chakra weakness. Go to the box at the end of this chapter to see if you diagnosed me correctly.

*Have FUN recognizing
color and chakra
aspects in yourself!*

Evaluate	Activate
• Is your (?) chakra in balance?	• Good! Just do your two-minute daily practice. What chakra(s) need attention?
• Is your (?) chakra overactive?	• Integrate more of the complementary color for the related chakra.
• Is your (?) chakra under-stimulated?	• Incorporate more *ColorAlchemy Activators* for related chakra.
• Do you experience any of the described spiritual, emotional, and/or physical feelings?	• Incorporate more *ColorAlchemy Activators* for the related chakra.
• Do you recognize (?) chakra blockages?	• Incorporate more *ColorAlchemy Activators* for the related chakra.
• Does your aura indicate: pure, light, or dark colors?	• Incorporate more *ColorAlchemy Activators* for the related chakra.

Bottom line:

- Which chakra(s) need enhancing to balance your energy and life qualities?

- Balance each individual chakra to improve the entire system.

- With the help of your Observer:

    - Release the energies that do not serve your highest good.
    - Recognize that you are in a *moment* that would be enhanced by a certain color.
    - Create a colorful mental pause.
    - With the right color(s) and Color Breathing, reduce toxic reactions to the stresses and problems of daily life. Ahhh!
    - Absorb your needed color for instantaneous relief and to attune to your highest purpose and ideals.

Improving Your Chakras

There is usually a blockage when:

- You do not like a color

- Visualizing a color is difficult

- Your concentration is off during Color Breathing

Mental ColorAlchemy
is the key to
instantaneous and
long-term mastery!

Review and Renew!
- What was working in the past may not be working today
- Imbalances may change over time based upon life priorities.

ColorAlchemy Healing

For holistic ColorAlchemy healing, absorb the vibrations of each ColorAlchemy Activator through:
- Matter (through your body)
- Energy (mental and spiritual focus)

Spirit is life essence, mind is the builder,
and the physicality of applied color is
your tangible support.

Living ColorAlchemy is the life-transforming result!

Heal yourself (and others) by recognizing what is needed.
Enjoy your favorite ColorAlchemy Activators.

I am happy to be an open book if you'll learn at my expense. Did you diagnose me properly? I bet you did just fine!

I would like greater inner peace (Violet/Crown Chakra) and more self-nurturing (Green/Heart Chakra). I am drawn to Green and Violet so they are easy for me to apply the ColorAlchemy Activators. Hummm, now that you are asking me to step up... I suppose I need to have more FUN! Wish I liked Orange better!

IMPORTANT! Remember, you are alive for the *soul purpose* of evolving into a more rounded and balanced person, and being the best you can be! Recognizing imbalance is an excellent thing, especially when you desire improvement and take action toward self-mastery! **Now, diagnose you!**

Of all of God's gifts, color is the holiest, the most divine, the most solemn.

—John Ruskin

Spiritual
Color Alchemy

Are you wearing your Daily Colors?

Yes? At the end of each week, you symbolically create the power of Divine Light within you by consciously connecting through your Daily Colors.

Indigo & Violet are the Spiritual Colors.

Wear, breathe, and experience them to *enhance consciousness.*

Spiritual ColorAlchemy

Color has been used for thousands of years to connect to the spiritual part of ourselves. In ancient Mesopotamia, Egypt, Greece, China, Tibet, the Native Americas, and medieval Europe, the symbolic use of color formed the building blocks of their spiritual worlds. Most civilizations integrated the profound, spiritual meaning of color into their lives through prayer, ritual, poetry, art, mythology, and clothing. When the ancients chose a colored ornament to wear, it was not a fashion statement. The intent was to communicate with the universal Divine Spirit.

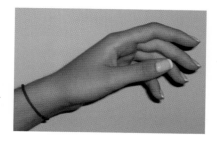

For example, the *red string* worn around the wrist for protection and as a blessing from God that is popularized with the renewed interest in Kabbalistic study is not an exclusive tradition. Inside every temple I visited in India, I was blessed with a red-string offering for the same purpose.

Wearing your colors is a physical reminder to consciously *Live ColorAlchemy*.

Colors of the Creator: The Consciousness of White Light

In *Living ColorAlchemy*, you learned that evolutionary scientists suggest that if something exists, *IT* is held together by consciousness. According to String Theory, consciousness is the cosmic glue that holds molecular structure together. Science and consciousness are connected through the fact that if *something* exists, *IT* is Reality. Reality is consciousness.

Consciousness is the creator of life. It is the source of all beingness. Universal consciousness is the big etheric computer that holds Cosmic Intelligence. Consciousness is the essence or spirit that exists within everything. Spirit is the energetic source that, according to worldwide spiritual traditions, is called by many names: God, Ein Sof, Universal Mind Substance, Great Spirit, and The Light. God said, *"Let there be light"*... and so there was light. Hildegard of Bingen, the visionary theologian (1098–1179) said:

The angels of color were created within the creation of the universe. God's first command brought into being the structural essential: Light. On the beams of this immaterial medium occur all divine manifestation.

The color that is experienced in any object is the part of light that is not absorbed by the object. Science also explains that objects do not have color. Is color the divine manifestation that Hildegard speaks of? This is what provides the perception of an object's color and even its existence.

We see because of our perceptions through The Light.

Creation comes through our mental, physical, and spiritual experience that allows us to see into the depths of our soul.

"Humankind's greatest goal is to overcome the cosmic illusion that all forms of life are separate and to rise above living within this separation. We need to expand ourselves and the universe as God's Absolute Nature-the-One, illuminated through the cosmic light. It is an expression of integration that is the essence of healing at the most fundamental level." [9]

Spiritual White Light

You already know that white light is the combination of all seven spectral colors and represents the source of conscious creation. White light is the creator of the universe that brings life to all that exists. White light brings spiritual energy into everything at the highest level.

Enjoy the wisdom of some of my favorite illuminated Masters who shed the light of *Spiritual ColorAlchemy* and can teach you better than I...

In *The Republic*, Plato writes:

"They came to a place where they could see from above a line of white light, straight as a column, extending right though the whole heaven and through the earth, in color resembling a rainbow, only brighter and purer ... and there, in the midst of the light, they saw the chains of heaven let down from above, for this light is the belt of heaven and holds together the circle of the universe." [10]

Plato is definitely describing the universe through his observations and our colorful world. (Is he also suggesting the existence of extraterrestrials? Intuitively, I think so.)

Sogyal Rinpoche:

"The essential nature of mind is a pure, pristine awareness that is at once intelligent, cognizant, radiant, and always awake. The light within is the Self and the heart of all religious truth that focuses on the sacred opportunity through which our spirit will evolve. It is truth, wisdom, and the love that exists within and that which we are all born with." [11]

Giuseppe Tucci:

"Man's vague intuition is viewed as a light that burns within him and which spreads out and is diffused. In this light is the whole personality that is concentrated and it develops around that light." [12]

Carl Jung:

"Acknowledging the probability that light and consciousness were connected in some basic way, Jung most likely described light as a symbolic representation of mystical expanses and emergence from physiological states of darkness." [13]

Edgar Cayce:

"The colors of the rainbow are radiations from the spiritual realm that form vibratory emanations of color, or light. Colors are the shadows of the Creator's movement, the essence of the physical world, because matter is only spirit or energy condensed in a form which we call matter." [14]

You already know that each color is a vibration with individual life-enhancing qualities. ColorAlchemy absorbs each color's vibration into the body's energy field and trains it how to receive maximum, holistic benefit.

"A vibration is spirit moving according to the idea of presenting purpose. Spirit prompts us to know our purpose. The light reaches us, reflecting things to our senses and allowing us to reflect upon them—both functions and vibrations. The physical light we receive is the shadow of the spiritual light of understanding emanating from God, yet within the shadow, the colors allow us to see." [15]

Absorb ColorAlchemy to add greater wisdom into your cells, to live heaven on earth...

and to be enlightened.

With the soul-light energy within, creatively express the wholeness of your true nature and realize your fullest potential.

Universal Light

Throughout the millennia and across cultures, white light and its spiritual association have been included in numerous religions, mythologies, and philosophies. White is associated with peace (like the white dove), perfection, and consciousness.

Kabbalists speak of:

- Light as another word for God
- Light force as the energetic intelligence of God
- Ein Sof as the condition in the spiritual world where the light represents the endless cycle of being in relationship with God

- You are:
  - The vessel to receive the light of the Boundless One
  - The vessel into which your soul energy is poured
  - **You are White Light**

A menorah filled with colored candles graces Hanukkah, the Festival of Light.

Christianity:

- Believes that white is the most symbolic color for the pure soul, integrity, light, and a holy life
- Uses white in their wardrobe during such sacred ceremonies as Baptism, First Holy Communion, Confirmation, and marriage
- Believes white is the color of the saints

- "In darkness we are separated from God—a condition of the benighted minds of the sinful-while the righteous see the light" as spoken by Jesus to Nicodemus in John chapter 3.

Hindus honor white as the highest symbol of:

- Pure consciousness

- The light and manifestation

- The light described in the Bhagavad Gita is as "Krishna manifests in a radiance equal to that of a thousand suns illuminating the universe"

Powders used during Holi

Tibetan monasteries fly flags of Blue (sky/space), White (water), Red (fire), Green (air), and Yellow (earth). Mantras or prayers written on the flags bless those who pass with good fortune for becoming enlightened.

Buddhists and Hindus also write prayers on colored silk and tie them to sacred trees and temples. I practiced this *Spiritual ColorAlchemy* ritual throughout my travels. *I wish I had tied a ribbon with prayers of returning to celebrate Holi.*

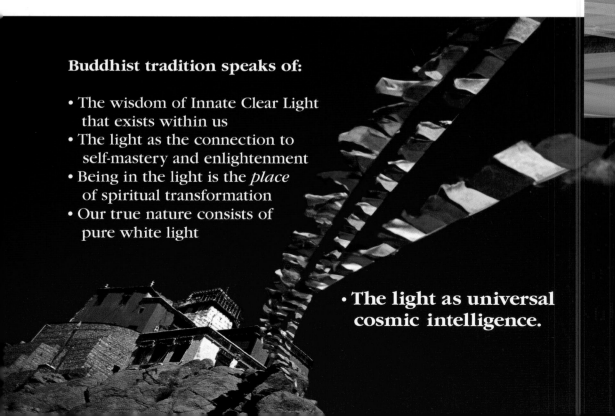

Buddhist tradition speaks of:

- The wisdom of Innate Clear Light that exists within us
- The light as the connection to self-mastery and enlightenment
- Being in the light is the *place* of spiritual transformation
- Our true nature consists of pure white light

- **The light as universal cosmic intelligence.**

Holi is the spring festival in India. Ancient origins celebrate triumph of *good over evil.*

Young and old hug each other in the streets and drench each other with color. Everything and everybody is covered, head to toe, in rainbow celebration.

I loved my pilgrimage to India and look forward to celebrating Holi on my return.

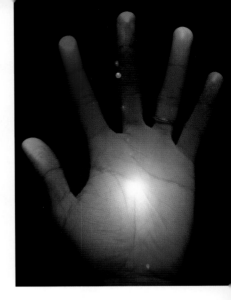

Capturing a rainbow is a glimpse into the Divine.

Living in the moment is living your divinity.

Wearing White

- Brides traditionally wear white in the Unites States as the color of virginity and purity.
- Goddesses in Celtic, Greek, Druid, and Roman traditions wear white during ceremonies.
- Hollywood traditionally dresses the hero in white.
- Medical personnel wear white to signify cleanliness and good health.

Spiritual Rainbows

When we experience rainbows, we are inspired. Its beauty invokes a magnificent, powerful, and wondrous majesty. In most spiritual traditions, capturing a rainbow has a divine quality because it is universally symbolized as the bridge between heaven and earth.

There is a Sanskrit term that translates as the Rainbow Bridge, which means "that which acts or works between." According to the Native American myth of Spider Woman, the rainbow web links us all to a central source of creation. Her web bridges the physical and spiritual realms to tie all of humankind together. Synchronistically, the bridge in your body is the Heart Chakra that keeps you grounded and connects you to your divine self.

Rainbows are beyond our realm, or are they?

Somewhere over the rainbow?

Its fleeting magic is something that we can never touch no matter how hard we try, or can we?

Experience your rainbow through ColorAlchemy!

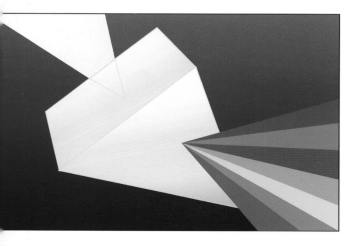

Sir Isaac Newton, the father of colorful science, took his experiment one step further.

When he put a second prism in the path of the seven colors diffused from the first prism, the rainbow was converted back into pure white light.

Rainbows are part of us and everything that exists.
The divinity of the rainbow is the colors of the divine within each of us.

Spiritual ColorAlchemy

When you absorb each
of the seven colors,
their holistic quality is combined
and converted into
spiritual white light.

Pause your day at any time to
capture a spiritual rainbow.

Rainbows and their colors illuminate our mind, body, and spirit,
they:

• Allow us to see
• Are the colors of heaven and earth
• Symbolically connect heaven and earth
• Scientifically and metaphysically connect us to the source of creation
• Are a metaphor for our impermanence
  (The cycle of life in Buddhist and Hindu traditions)
• Are scientifically and energetically an integral part of our bodies

Seven: Days, Rainbow Colors, Spiritual Energies & Chakras

As you already know through science, light is composed of seven energetic
frequencies. The number seven is said to be lucky because so many
scientific, philosophic, and spiritual collections are in groups of seven:
the seven phases of the moon, the seven musical notes, the seven planets
("original planets" of the ancient world), the seven graces, the seven
virtues and, biblically, the seven days of creation, the seven trumpets,
the seven plagues, the seven seas, and many more. The universal
numerology of seven as it integrates with the human spirit is endless.

Enjoy some universal *ColorAlchemy* traditions using the sacred seven:

Buddhists believe that the seven colors of the rainbow are related to the seven planets and the seven regions on earth.

As do contemporary color therapists, Buddhists use the seven colored rays of light directed toward the body (as we do in ColorAlchemy Activators) for healing physical ailments and integrating the mind and spirit.

The Buddhist Sogyal Rinpoche says that "when we integrate our mind and spirit, clarity is multiplied by seven,"[16] that's another reason why *Mental ColorAlchemy* is so important.

In Christianity, the seven colors are linked to the seven sacraments and the bow (as in rain-bow).

In the New Testament, the number for God is seven. Seven is the number of *the Creator: the seven colors of divine light*.

Interestingly, on another "Christianity Color Alchemical" numerology note, the symbol of the Trinity is conceptually created through the elements. When one end of the rainbow touches the earth and passes through the air to the other end, it rests on the water, which symbolizes our connection to heaven and earth though science and spirit, the mind, body, and spirit trinity.

The chakras: Many cultures integrate the Hindu practice of using the seven rainbow colors in association with areas of the body known as the chakras. In *Body ColorAlchemy*, you learned about the holistic, mind-body-spiritual energies of the Chakras and how they follow the same colorful, scientific, and vibrational sequence as the rainbow.

We are all connected through the magic of our universal colors.

It is time to set the intention for your colorful transformation. When practicing ColorAlchemy, you don't need a specific location, but it is recommended that you start by creating a safe and sacred space in which to practice.

This space could be in the living room, dining room, or bedroom, or anywhere that you will be undisturbed for a few minutes. It is also recommended that you sit facing one of your best Feng Shui directions (available on JamiLin.com with my compliments) and that you have blessed the space.

Have you made a colorful commitment? Schedule a few minutes to practice every day. Be consistent so you can develop your relationship with yourself, your Observer, and your colorful world. The more you practice, the more you will be able to practice anytime and anywhere.

Living ColorAlchemy exists within you. Your internal sacred space can be created in your external world whenever you call upon it and at a moment's notice.

Buddhist masters teach that when a person is conscious and completely present in action, past and future distraction dissolve. As described in *Mental ColorAlchemy*, the present is where to find happiness.

In the inspiring colorful words of Dudjom Rinpoche...

If you are walking,
walk toward the open space of truth.

Today holds the colorful energies.

When walking, when you see the color,
breathe in the life qualities and be conscious of
how they support and fill your spirit. [17]

Live ColorAlchemy anywhere and everywhere!

You are a colorful person with a colorful life.

Use color to balance and meet all life's needs
with the life qualities of color.

You have the colorful power within you to Be Divine.

**Be present in
your divinity.**

**Invoke your divine right
to be HAPPY by loving
the colors around you.**

Daily
Color Alchemy
Triumphs

Color Alchemy

7 Days 7 Colors
7 Triumphs

Colors of Your
Mind

Vitality Creativity Power
Love Focus Intuition Bliss

Happiness is found through the mind
the common denominator of physical and spiritual wholeness,

"For where the mind is, there is the treasure.
It sees neither through the soul nor through the spirit,
but the mind, which is between the two, which sees the vision ...
the inner self is composed of soul, spirit, and mind, and
visions are seen and understood in the mind." [18]

—Gospel of Mary of Magdala
from the lost Gnostic-Christian Scripture fragments

<<<<<<<< **Red** >>>>>>

> Stimulates energy and vitality
> Builds strength, security, and willpower
> Provides grounding and stability
> Stimulates blood and circulation
> Generates ambition
> Helps with a demanding day
> Focuses attention
> Transforms past issues and blockages

Red energy is raw and primal. It is the color of instinct and has pioneering energy. Red is excitement, passion, and the zest for life. Red is power and activity. It is the perfect color to use when you are feeling good but need extra get-up-and-go. Incorporate Red when deadlines are looming and you need a kick-start or motivation. (Red is a good coffee substitute!) Red is powerful for extra confidence and determination as well as for stimulating a response, creating affirmative action, taking charge, and being in control.

Feeling sexy? Red is passion. Red encourages being impulsive. (Think twice before being spontaneous.) It is said that men enjoy women when they wear Red.

Red means heat. Wearing Red has been known to keep you physically warmer than another color and may even prevent you from catching a cold. Think about how this makes sense. Try wearing a Red sweater on the next chilly day. Red warms your spirits when *feeling Blue* and reduces depression.

Red also has negative life qualities. Red signals danger and war. If you are a *Red Person*, too much Red may burn you up. Be careful using Red if you have a tendency to get aggravated quickly, if you are short-tempered, or if you have aggressive tendencies. Red's heat is not good for people who have high blood pressure. Try softer Red variations such as pink, magenta, or maroon.

Tip: Always consider language and colloquialisms as hints to colorful understanding. Example: *Thinking or seeing Red* describes anger and frustration.

Color Breathing: Close your eyes. For the next nine breaths, visualize the color Red coming in through your nose with slow and deep inhalations. As you inhale, imagine *Red Breath*, fill your entire body with *Vitality, Courage, and Self-Confidence*.

Repeat this process for your next eight breaths. (The average person breathes fifteen breaths a minute. Even with your breath slow and concentrated, this exercise will take no longer than two minutes!)

Wear something Red today to absorb the Daily Color. However, if today's plans are contrary to the Daily Color's energy, wearing a lot of the Daily Color may not be in your best interest. For example, if you are going to the hospital to visit an ill friend, instead of Red's vitality, you would be more nurturing and better received if you wore Green, Blue, Indigo, or Violet. Use your intuition with ColorAlchemy to make appropriate color decisions.

Every time you focus on your Red shirt, or accessory, and/or any time you experience the color Red, take a breath and fill your body with *Strength and Stamina*. Color dressing reminds you to practice Color Breathing several times during the day.

Complete your "Red moment" with thoughts of how lucky you are to be alive (which only takes a few more seconds). Before going to sleep, always take a few Color Breaths and your dreams will be more colorful. You will awake more refreshed to greet the new day.

The more you practice, the faster you experience the benefits of ColorAlchemy!

Make Color Breathing a ritual.

Add a few visualization suggestions to your Color Breathing:

Red Visualizations:
- Brilliant sunsets
- Poppy blossoms
- Dancing flames of a Red-hot log fire
- Fire engines racing to the rescue
- Gorgeous Red lips
- The perfect Red rose

Red Expressions:

- Painting the town Red
- Seeing Red
- Red-blooded male (or female)
- Red-letter day
- Red cent

<<<<<<< **Congratulations!** >>>>>>

You've completed today's Two ColorAlchemy Minutes.

That is how easy ColorAlchemy is to practice!

General ColorAlchemy Suggestions

The more you practice, the faster you will reap ColorAlchemy benefits.

Remember to:

- Be consistent with ColorAlchemy.
- Be aware of the colors around you.
- Pay attention to how your body and mind react to color.
- Stay present with your Observer.
- Incorporate sincere intentions for everyone's highest and best interest.
- Always wear something in the Daily Color and an item in the color you need.
- Practice Color Breathing several items a day.

Breathing is the most important event in the universe. The breath is the pulse of life. Its ebb and flow is the energetic source of all that is and connects everything on the molecular level.

Breathing does so much more than merely keep you alive through providing oxygen to the body in exchange for carbon dioxide. Breathing nourishes mental and spiritual energies. When you focus on your breath (as the disciplined mind-awakening technique used in many spiritual traditions) breathing helps train your mind by clearing away unwanted thoughts.

Unless you have been trained as a singer or a professional athlete, most of us do not breathe properly. We take short, shallow breaths, never allowing the breath of life to fill ever cell and fiber of the body. As we age, lung muscles get older, too. Unless we exercise them with proper breathing, the breath becomes increasingly more shallow. With ever-weakening breathing, the cells in our body are not fully nourished and they progressively lose function.

Steps for Proper Breathing:

For ColorAlchemy and all meditative practices, sit or lay down without crossing your legs or arms. *Crossing* is analogous to a kink in a hose that will not allow water (or breath) to flow smoothly. You can Color Breathe any time or any place, while standing (at the bank, in a checkout line, etc.), by just following the easy steps.

With each inhalation and exhalation, visualize nurturing air coming in and going out of your body as if your breath were a circle of energy. Without holding your breath, imagine the first half of the circle during the inhalation, with the circle returning to its starting point with your exhalation.

Inhale: Breathe in through your nose:

1. Fill your lungs/chest.
2. Fill your abdomen (upper belly).
3. Fill your lower belly (contrary to your mother saying to keep it sucked in).

By completely filling your entire respiratory system to capacity, fresh oxygen squeezes out any stagnant air and toxins trapped in the cells.

Exhale: Many breathing and meditation experts suggest that breathing out through your nose is best. My experience suggests that mouth exhalations help you breathe more fully.

Breathe out through your mouth and empty the oxygen in the opposite order that it came in:

1. Empty the air in your lower belly.
2. Empty the air in your abdomen (upper belly).
3. Empty the air in your lungs/chest.

With each full breath, visualize every cell and fiber in your body saturated with nurturing and healing energy.

Suggestion: Each time you start Color Breathing, count the seconds of your inhalation and exhalation. This is especially effective for the first few breaths. With every new session, try to extend the count and improve breathing capacity without straining. The longer the inhalation and exhalation cycle, the more your cells are nourished and the more toxins are released. The more rhythmic and consistent your breath, the more you will also be able to control conscious thought and explore your unconscious mind.

The breath of life benefits everything!

Body:
- Invigorates when tired or sluggish
- Slows a racing heart
- Reduces blood pressure
- Sustains muscle wellness.

Mind:
- Aids clarity and concentration
- Reduces mental stress
- Releases anxiety and panic
- Nurtures calmness
- Promotes sleep

Spirit:
- Creates quiet within
- Develops inner peace
- Taps into the universal breath of life
- Connects to divinity
- Expands psychic abilities

Practice proper breathing as much as possible.

Because your breath is the source of life and "always there," it is the only resource for healing and personal development available to you at an instant. Pay attention to the world around you. Call on Color Breathing whenever you feel stressed or need the qualities of a certain color. You may want to keep a journal to deepen your experience.

Enjoy Dudjom Rinpoche's wonderful words:

"Today holds colorful energies. When walking, when you see the color, be conscious, breathe in the attributes and how they fill your spirit." [19]

Adding Visualization to Color Breathing

In *Mental ColorAlchemy*, we talked about the only thing that we have control over: the mind. Through mental conditioning, when you visualize a color you absorb it and its attributes more fully. This empowers you all day, and the energies are more powerful the next time that same color is needed. Incorporate this simple exercise to increase the benefits of Color Breathing. It is easy and doesn't require any additional time.

As **Tuesday is an Orange Day**, today has the perfect energy to add imagery and visualization. Why? You already know: Orange is the day of creativity.

Let's start with an easy visualization and get your creative juices flowing.

In your mind's eye, see your body as a clear glass vase. Visualize your *body vase* as exactly the same size and shape as your body. Your body vase has arms, legs, torso, and head: It looks just like you.

Visualize Orange (or the Daily Color) coming into your body with your breath as a colored ray. Picture the ray as smoke rising from a freshly blown-out candle. Imagine it gently flowing into your nose with *Fun-Loving, Spicy, and Creative* Orange energy.

> When you practice this exercise on other days, use the Daily Color and its attributes. You may want to have a list of the attributes in front of you until they become second nature.

As you breathe in the colored ray, visualize the energy filling your body vase, starting with your head. When your head is full of colored energy, continue filling your body down your neck, your shoulders, chest, and so on, one part at a time. From the top down, fill your entire body, as if you were filling a vase with colored smoke.

As you feel the color within and throughout you, know that the life qualities of the color are filling you at the same time. You are now one with the color and all of its positive qualities.

While I enjoy the purity of the previous *just-using-color* visualization, you can also add visual imagery. You may find that visualizing associations of the Daily Color will enhance Color Breathing. Every Daily Color this week includes visualization ideas to get started.

Tip: It has been three days since you have been working with color. Start using your intuition to determine the attributes of color. Close your eyes and bring any color into focus. When you concentrate on the color, pay attention to your associations with that color and how your body responds.

◄◄◄◄◄◄◄ Orange ►►►►►►

> Brings more joy into your life
> Removes inhibitions and limitations
> Generates creativity and ingenuity
> Balances sensual intimacy with yourself, others, and the world
> Promotes sociable behavior and friendliness
> Alleviates depression, pessimism, and fatigue

Orange is the happy color and adds spice to life. Orange is joy and youth. Orange has antidepressant qualities and enhances well-being. Orange exudes spontaneity, optimism, and enthusiasm. While Orange is not as *hot* as Red, its gentle warmth is less aggressive yet it stimulates and excites. Orange is celebration and fun. It adds sparkle to your life. Like Red, Orange removes inhibitions.

Orange is the color for making friends. It is congenial and good-natured. Use Orange when working on projects requiring creative energy and cooperation. Orange generates free expression and the sharing of new ideas.

Orange even helps you to remember. The next time there is something you do not want to forget, see *IT* in an Orange bubble in your mind and say, *I will remember* _____, and you will!

If you are an *Orange Person*, too much Orange may be too stimulating. Experiment with variations of Orange such as peach or salmon. It is best not to dress your bed in Orange linen or to wear Orange nightclothes. With so much creativity, you may have trouble getting restful sleep.

◄◄◄◄◄◄◄ Today's Two ColorAlchemy Minutes ►►►►►►

Color Breathing: Fill your body with *Happiness and Desire* for nine, slow and deep Orange breaths.

Wearing Orange: Every time you focus on your Orange shirt or accessory, and/or any time you experience Orange, take an Orange breath full of *Emotion, Creativity, and Pleasure.*

tuesday

Intuitive Activators: If you are going to a business meeting requiring professionalism (inappropriate for being emotional), consider Red or Yellow.

Use your intuition to receive maximum benefit with ColorAlchemy and to make appropriate color decisions.

Habitual Gratitude: Complete your "Orange moment" with thoughts of how lucky you are to be alive.

The more you practice, the faster you'll experience the benefits of ColorAlchemy!

Orange Visualizations:

- Buddhist monks
- Marmalade on golden-brown toast
- Goldfish shimmering through water
- Fragrant tangerines in a beautiful bowl
- Jack-o'-lanterns, pumpkins, and fall vegetables
- Fresh-squeezed orange juice
- Tiger lilies, daylilies, and marigolds

Orange Expressions:

- The spice of life

Visualization example: As you do your Color Breathing, visualize sipping fresh-squeezed orange juice. As you drink "Orange," fill yourself with its sweet nectar and delicious taste. See yourself completely happy and joyful (with Orange attributes). If you have visualizations that you relate to better, use them. Be creative: it is your visualization.

<<<<<<< Congratulations! >>>>>>
You've completed today's Two ColorAlchemy Minutes..

What are the colors of the objects that you see around you? What are their pleasant associations? Example: When you encounter a bowl of Oranges, recreate its form and color in your vision. What do they smell like? What does the skin of an Orange feel like? How do they make you feel?

Test your observation skills and make mental notes.
Be aware and give consciousness to your experience.

Increases self esteem
Releases mental stress
Energizes the digestive system
Brings imbalances back into harmony
Aids clarity and focus
Improves comprehension
Enables clearer perception
Boosts determination and confidence
Stimulates interest and curiosity
Enhances perception and understanding

Yellow is optimistic, radiant, and playful. Yellow energy is best symbolized as a ray of sunshine. It says wake up! Yellow radiates optimism and a sunny disposition. Yellow is a signal for cheer and good will.

Yellow relieves boredom, impatience, and the winter Blues without the harshness associated with Red or Orange. Yellow people are usually quick-witted, smart, and have command over what they want and where they are going.

Yellow is a great color to sharpen the mind by providing an inner spark when mentally fatigued. Yellow stimulates awareness and curiosity. Its impulsive energy confidently blurts out the right answer almost before the mind engages. Yellow stimulates metabolism and may help you lose weight when dieting.

If you are a *Yellow Person*, too much Yellow may engage intellect so much that it outweighs intuition and feelings. Be careful of Yellow when you do everything by the book that you've lost sight of your creativity. Yellow may also be too stimulating if you are naturally a *hot person*.

Did you figure out the warm and cool colors? Red, Orange, and Yellow are warm colors. Blue, Indigo, and Violet are the cool colors. Green is the color of the heart and universal balancer that bridges the two.

Engage all the colors of the rainbow to balance the perfection of mind, body, and spirit.

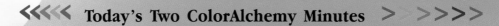

Color Breathing: — Fill your entire body with *Personal Power, Dedication, and Commitment* for nine, slow and deep Yellow breaths.

Wearing Yellow: — Every time you focus on your Yellow shirt or accessory, and/or any time you experience Yellow, take a Yellow breath full of *Ambition and Dedication*.

Intuitive Activators: — Remember, if today's plans are contrary to the Daily Color's energy, wearing the Daily Color may not be in your best interest. For example, if you are going to marriage counseling to heal friction between you and your loved one, the willfulness of Yellow would not be the best choice. Calming colors like Green (for love and compassion) or Blue (for clarity) would be more supportive.

Habitual Gratitude: — Always complete your "Yellow moment" with thoughts of how lucky you are to be alive, and count your blessings (which only takes a few more seconds).

The more you practice, the faster you experience the benefits of ColorAlchemy!

Make Color Breathing a ritual.

Remember, because your breath is the source of life and always there, it is the only resource for healing and personal development available to you at an instant. Observe your reactions to the world around you. Call on Color Breathing whenever you feel stressed or need the life qualities of a certain color.

Add a few visualization suggestions to your Color Breathing:

Yellow Visualizations:

- Lighthouse signaling across the water
- Pollen grains on a flower stamen
- Rays of sunlight dancing through the trees or clouds
- Smiling field of sunflowers
- A cheerful bowl of lemons
- Daffodils signaling springtime

Yellow Expressions:

- Golden mean (and perfect mathematical proportions of phi)
- Yellow-bellied
- Mellow yellow
- A lightbulb going off when an idea comes to mind
- Yellow streak

‹‹‹‹‹‹‹ Congratulations! ›››››
You've completed today's Two ColorAlchemy Minutes.

Tip: It has been three days since you have been working with color. Start using your intuition to determine the attributes of color. Close your eyes and bring any color into focus. When you concentrate on the color, pay attention to your associations with that color and how your body responds.

Daily Habits

Yellow-Wednesday, the day of Personal Power, is a great day to commit to good ColorAlchemy habits!

The importance of consistent, daily ColorAlchemy is worth repeating. Because it only takes twenty-one days to create a habit, practicing Color Breathing two minutes each morning and evening will reward you. Consistency will allow you to immediately experience the benefits whenever they are needed.

Remember, the only thing that you really have control over is the mind. Just like a computer, the brain gives back what you put into it.

To recap, Color Breathing is the first step in training your mind to:
- Change negative thinking into positive thought patterns
- Reduce stress and soften a demanding moment
- Connect mind, body, and spirit
- Call on whatever color is needed on demand
- Develop intuition
- Develop greater inner peace and outward joy.

With ColorAlchemy on the brain, within seconds of needing the qualities of a certain color, your thoughts automatically focus on the needed color. Immediately, the situation that was once stressful will become lighter and you will have absorbed the color's attributes.

Journaling

A journal is different than a diary. It is the sacred space where you have the freedom to write about your feelings and express your innermost thoughts. Often called brain-writing, journaling creates a written record of your experience and provides deeper insights into your ColorAlchemy and life.

There is something magical about writing on paper with a pen or a pencil as compared to typing on a computer. There is a connection between your thoughts and your hand. Writing by hand helps your mind stay focused and processes thoughts that you may have never thought of before.

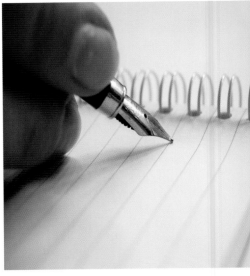

Journaling is a fancy word for writing your thoughts.

Why Journal?

The reason why it is often difficult to maintain mental focus is because of the naughty, monkey mind. When deep-rooted thoughts arise that your mind would prefer to avoid because of uncomfortable or painful associations, the undisciplined mind sabotages the potential for insight by *changing the subject.*

Unless your Observer is well trained, familiar thoughts automatically pop into your mind before you even realize they have arrived. Unfortunately, the more comfortable the automatic thought, the more potential it is for becoming your reality. Negative, self-defeating thoughts create failure. Positive thoughts create success. That is why working with your Observer is so important. When negativity occurs (and our untrained mind is more likely to replay negative thoughts), your Observer needs to acknowledge the familiar automation and change the thought to a positive one.

When you write on paper, it is easier to keep your mind from wandering. With the mind-hand connection, focus deepens and the secrets of your soul unfold.

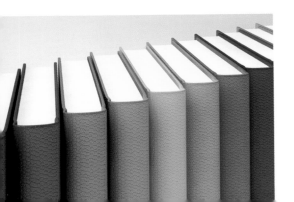

A journal is for your eyes only.
Do not hold back.

The more freedom you allow yourself to express your inner thoughts without restriction, the greater your personal insight will be.

Journaling is about
the lessons you learn about you.

You don't need to be a good writer. You don't even need to know how to spell. Journaling is not about the presentation or what the end product looks like.

Journaling:
- Helps you be more honest with yourself
- Develops mind control by transferring mental chatter to paper
- Improves clarity of thought
- Helps clear away self-defeating mental issues
- Reignites dreams and goals
- Helps channel and connect to your inner self

The more you journal, the more you will:
- Find it to be a retreat from your busy life
- Connect with thoughts that may not otherwise be heard
- Discover profound things about yourself and your mental process
- Find that thoughts and insights almost write themselves
- Stay connected to the truth of who you really are
- Have a record that reflects your soul
- Deepen your ColorAlchemy experience

While there is no substitute for journaling your thoughts, doodling is another creative way of expressing yourself. Doodling allows the unconscious to communicate in symbols. Symbols have universal as well as personal meanings. Like journaling, doodling unlocks your unconscious mind. Doodling frees your mind when you are mentally stuck or as a preliminary exercise before journaling. In fact, creative drawing is so important that I teach you about mandalas (p. 187) in *ColorAlchemy Activators*.

When doodling or journaling, select a piece of colored construction paper. You may choose the Daily Color or a particular color that supports your energy. With colored pencils or pens, journal or doodle with no expectations. You'll be surprised how quickly you'll enjoy the experience and receive profound insight.

Journal and Doodle Suggestions:

- I like using a loose-leaf binder so I can add pages by the date and add drawings or other collectibles that I pick up on my ColorAlchemy journey.

- Allow yourself 5 to 10 minutes every day.

I enjoy journaling at the end of the day to access my daily experience. To learn from less-successful moments, I journal about what color qualities would have turned the negative into a positive. I script a success story to ensure results the next time a similar situation arises.

• Select a special space to journal so you won't be disturbed.

My favorite location is the bathtub, even though my journal gets a bit soggy. The bathtub is the place where my unconscious reveals creative ideas and personal insights because my body and mind are completely relaxed.

Light a candle in the Daily Color or turn on a lamp with a colored lightbulb. If your special spot is a favorite chair, drape yourself with a colored piece of fabric.

• When ready to journal, take a few deep breaths.

Fill your body with Divine Light, and say a quick blessing (refer to p. 102). If there is something on your mind, support your thoughts by Color Breathing in the related color before journaling.

If you don't know how to begin journaling, start with these questions:

- How does each color make you feel?
- How does each color influence your mind, body, and spirit?
- What pushed your buttons today?
- What color was associated with that "button-push" energy?
- What color could help balance the situation?
- What color could make you feel better?

• With your blessed materials (p. 101), write with an open mind and clear intention. As thoughts begin to form, visualize your thoughts flowing on a gentle river. You will be amazed at what your inner self can reveal.

• Write for as long as your inspiration carries you.

• When you have stopped *streaming*, say a little thank-you prayer for the time, the freedom of self-expression, and the gained knowledge.

When you journal regularly, you'll realize how beneficial and pleasurable it is. Journal whenever inspiration arises. Carry folded paper and a few favorite colored pens so you won't miss an opportunity to learn from your journal. Always include the date to track your thoughts and to chronologically add your journal entries.

<<<<<<< Green >>>>>>

> Creates greater joy
> Enhances inner peace through acceptance and self-love
> Provides overall balance and integration of energies
> Harmonizes mental and physical life qualities
> Relaxes muscles, nerves, and thoughts
> Provides feelings of renewal, peace, and harmony
> Balances your whole being with unconditional love

Green is the color of Mother Earth; it feels familiar and comfortable. Green is easy and gracious like a gentle stroll in the woods and the smell of a freshly mowed lawn. In nature, Green arrives as winter turns into spring, ushering in the renewal of fresh beginnings. In this context, Green signifies "being green" as lacking experience, but I love that expression. It is youthful innocence without preconceptions, allowing creative seeds to sprout into great trees of loving wisdom. **Be blessed with curiosity and wonder—that is what keeps us young.** *Remember that!*

The color Green is of unconditional love and the color of the heart. It is the nurturing interactions between mother and child.

Green is the great balancer. As the trees bud in spring, Green balances the seasons' cold and warm temperatures. Green is the bridge (or balancer) between cold and warm colors. Green is the mental, physical, and spiritual place where heaven and earth meet, where heaven can be lived on earth. The color Green is a loving metaphor for compassion and generosity. Green is calming and serene. It soothes muscles and aids in relaxation. Light a Green candle during your next bubble bath.

If you are a *Green Person*, too much Green may give you tendencies to "never say no" to your personal detriment. You may genuinely love others, but at your own self-sacrifice. This generosity can easily deplete physical and emotional energy. When this happens, use Yellow to help you stand your ground and strengthen your inner desires.

<<<<<<< Today's Two ColorAlchemy Minutes >>>>>>

Color Breathing: Fill your entire body with *Love and Forgiveness* for nine, slow and deep Green breaths.

thursday

Wearing Green:	You can never go wrong with wearing Green: the rainbow balancer. Green is the color of the heart that ties the physical, emotional, and spiritual together.
Intuitive Activators:	Always consider your schedule to determine the best color to wear today (and always). There may be a more appropriate color(s) to wear on the outside, but still wear some Green on the "inside." Remember, incorporate intuition with ColorAlchemy. This is only your fourth day, and I bet you are already doing great!
Habitual Gratitude:	Complete your "Green moment" with thoughts of how lucky you are to be alive, and count your blessings (which only takes a few more seconds).

Remember, the more you practice,
the faster you experience the benefits of ColorAlchemy!

Add a few visualization suggestions to your Color Breathing:

Green Visualizations:

- Freshly mowed grass
- Leaves shimmering on a gentle breeze
- Golf course with morning dew
- Sparkling emeralds
- Dollar bills (U.S. currency)

Green Expressions:

- To give the green light
- Green-green grass of home
- Green thumb
- Green-eyed monster
- Green with envy
- Green with youth
- Greenbacks
- Greenhorn

≪ ≪ Congratulations! ≫ ≫≫≫
You've completed today's Two ColorAlchemy Minutes.

Blessing Your ColorAlchemy
Journal & Materials

There is only one more thing to do, and today is an excellent day to do it! Green vibrates with the color of the heart because it is the balancer between the physical and the emotional worlds.

Thursday is a perfect day to bless your materials. (If you don't have all your materials, get them by next Green-Thursday. I'll remind you.)

ColorAlchemy is a sacred and universal process for improving the quality of your life. Just as special as the light of the sun warms your body and allows you to experience the light of God, your ColorAlchemy journal and materials need to be sacred and special, too. Blessing your materials is a short ritual that makes them special. When you infuse blessings into an object, it holds and vibrates with Divine Light.

Suggestions: Pay attention to this blessing.
You can also use the following for all
Colorful Activators.

Blessing Your Space is done the same way you bless your materials. In step 7, with sacred energy flowing through your hands, hold them toward the direction of the space that you want to bless.

If you are blessing an entire room or your house, walk into each area and sweep your hands across each area while holding your blessing visualization.

*Start collecting
ColorAlchemy Activators!*

Blessing

1. Select a time and *blessed* place where you will not be disturbed for about 10 minutes. Set the stage with your favorite "meditative-mood" accessories. You may want to prepare the space with quiet music and/or light a few candles.

2. With your ColorAlchemy journal and materials (and any other objects you wish to bless) in front of you, sit in a comfortable position (on the floor or in a chair) with your back straight. Make sure that your materials are close enough that you can touch them.

3. Take a few deep breaths to relax and calm your spirit. Breathe deeply, all the way down into your belly. Breathe Green into your body and fill it with balancing and loving energy.

   When blessing other objects, consider Color Breathing with the Daily Color or the appropriate color of what the object represents. Dismiss all negative thoughts from your mind and release any tension in your body.

4. Gently touch the materials with the palms of your hands. Make as much loving contact with them as possible.

5. In your mind's eye, imagine the top of your head as a funnel to receive the Light of God.

6. With your spiritual eye or Third-Eye Chakra (located in between your eyes in the center of your forehead), visualize the Light as Christ, Buddha, Quan Yin, Isis, Lakshmi, or any spiritual being who has special significance to you.

   You can also visualize taking a breath of White Light as an energy beam that fills your body.

7. As the sacred light comes in through the top of your head and fills your body, see the energy flow down your arms, through your palms, and into your materials. Hold the visualization that you are infusing your materials with *all that is sacred*. You are impregnating and energizing the molecular structure of the materials with the Light of God.

8. Upon completion, return the Light and sacred helpers to heaven. Thank them for their participation. Remind them of how appreciative you are that they are always "on call" whenever you need them.

9. Finish by saying your favorite blessing nine times. The number nine holds the highest vibration because you cannot add another number without adding another digit. Interestingly, any number added to the number nine reduces back to itself. For instance: $9 + 4 = 13$ and $1 + 3 = 4$ again. The number nine is magical!

Blessing Suggestion (and my personal favorite):

Om Ma Ni Pad Me Hum

OM purifies the negative actions of the body.
AH purifies speech, and *HUM* cleanses the mind.

Buddhists say that chanting this prayer releases negative karma.

When I am having trouble sleeping because my mind is racing, I repeat this prayer to myself with rhythmic Color Breathing and all I remember is waking up in the morning.

Beautiful translations of this Sanskrit, Tibetan Buddhist prayer:

1. I am One with Nature. I am One with God.

2. The Jewel in the Lotus is Unfolding.

The Jewel is YOU,
as the sacred Jewel that you are.

The lotus is the symbol for enlightenment. A lotus flower blossoms even though it grows in swamp water. This signifies that as humans, with all of our terrestrial imperfections, we can learn their lessons and rise above them.

In *Colors of Your Body* (week #2), remember to notice the traditional lotus graphic for each chakra. As each chakra grows its spiritual sequence, more petals get added: from the Root Chakra, with its four petals to the ten-thousand-petaled Crown Chakra.

Whenever a Buddhist deity is in graphic or sculptural form, notice how he sits, "as the jewel," in the center of a lotus. *I thought you'd like to know, I have a lotus tattoo as a permanent symbol, in our world of impermanence, to remind myself that I too*

The ColorAlchemy of Yin/Yang

According to Chinese yin/yang theory, two equally-weighted forces in opposition create perfect harmony and balance. In ColorAlchemy, the two polarities are the yin colors and the yang colors. The two polarities have two ColorAlchemy polarities. As you remember from *Body ColorAlchemy*, you 1: Evaluate and Activate ColorAlchemy with 2: Matter (yang) and Energy (yin).

Warm and Cool Colors of the Rainbow Bridge

As you learned in *Living ColorAlchemy*, the reason why you see different colors is because of the frequency of color waves. Red, Orange, and Yellow, the colors with low frequency, are yang colors or warm colors because they excite, add vitality, strengthen, and activate. Blue, Indigo, and Violet are the cool colors. They have higher vibrational energies and are yin colors because they are sedative and increase inner awareness.

You also know that the rainbow contains all seven spectral colors. Notice that Green is located in the middle between the yin and yang colors. Green and the Heart Chakra, is like yin/yang itself: the supreme balancer.

Adding the Complementary Colors

Each color has an opposite, its yin or yang complement, based on its spectral sequence on the color wheel. Color theory suggests that if you were painting and you wanted a darker color, instead of adding black (which muddies the color and dulls the vibration) you deepen the color with a touch of its complement.

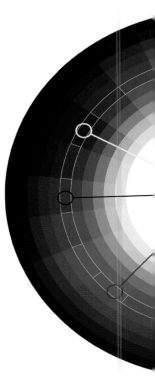

The same concept applies to Complementary-Color Breathing. When a chakra is dominant or overactive, reduce its power and unbalanced influence by breathing the complementary color.

When breathing a needed color for chakra enhancement and/or life support, breathe out the complementary color during the exhalation.

Use this color wheel (or the simper ones on p. 117 or p. 255) to find a color's direct opposite.

Complementary-Color Breathing detoxifies and purifies the energy in the body and simultaneously adds greater life-quality balance. In *Colors of Your Body*, deepen visualization by focusing on each chakra's location, color, and attributes as you exhale the mental image of the related complementary color.

<<<<<<< Blue >>>>>>

Regenerates, sedates, and calms the whole body
Reduces resistance and anxieties
Enhances communication and organization skills
Stimulates inner confidence
Relaxes the mind and the nervous system
Alleviates sleeping problems
Mellows hyperactivity and hypertension
Connects you to holistic thought
Increases wisdom and clarity
Generates greater trust within yourself

While Yellow is the color of the intellectual mind, Blue is instinctual and intuitive. Blue connects to our inner clarity so we can know ourselves better.

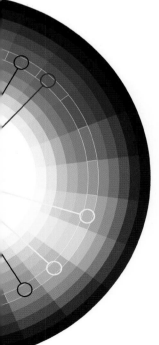

As an earth color, Blue is symbolic of the wide-open space of the sky and the ocean which traditionally are use to describe the expansive, unlimited mind.

Blue helps focus and offers self-realization. Blue is the first of the higher-vibrational frequencies that connects to our spiritual being. Blue instills truth and promotes loyalty, sensitivity, responsibility, inner wisdom, and trustworthiness. It is the color of communication and speaking your truth. A *Blue Person* would not hesitate to speak up against injustice even at his or her own emotional expense. Blue is kind and understanding.

Physically, Blue is calming and relaxing. The next time you are having trouble sleeping, practice breathing Blue. When you keep your mind focused on your breath, you'll be asleep in no time.

If you are a *Blue Person*, too much Blue may promote *the blues*. While contemplating the inner workings of your mind is enlightening, too much Blue may keep you in your own thoughts and out of touch with the real world. If Blue is creating depression or making you unrealistically tired, consider using Red, Orange, or Yellow to warm your spirits.

friday

Friday has great energy to deepen breathing and visualization.

Color Breathing: Fill your entire body with *Communication and Personal Clarity* for nine, slow and deep Blue breaths.

Wearing Blue: Every time you focus on your Blue shirt or accessory, and/or any time you experience Blue, take a Blue breath full of *Decisiveness and Clear Thought*.

Intuitive Activators: If today's plans are contrary to Blue's energy, wear a supporting color. Wearing Blue when *feeling blue* adds insult to injury. Red, Orange, or Yellow will support Vitality, Creativity, and Personal Power to help you out of the funk.

Habitual Gratitude: Don't forget to complete your "Blue moment" with thoughts of how lucky you are to be alive—so lucky and so blessed!

Integrate: Take at least one Inner Truth energizing breath every time you see the color Blue and you are on your way!

Add a few visualization suggestions to your Color Breathing:

Blue Visualizations:
- Brilliant blue water shimmering in the sunlight
- Bluebell flowers
- Lapis lazuli outlining the eyes in King Tut's mask
- Bright, cloudless sky. You know that beautiful color!

Blue Expressions:
- Bluebird of happiness
- Mr. Bluebird on my shoulder
- Once in a blue moon
- Out of the blue
- Feeling blue
- Blue-blooded

<<<<<<< Indigo >>>>>>

> Unites outer and inner being
> Raises inner consciousness and intuitive knowledge
> Increases mental alertness for powerful meditations
> Reduces stress
> Establishes inner peace and composure
> Expands intuition, clairvoyance, and dream recollection
> Lowers blood pressure and balances hormones
> Regulates hyperactivity

Indigo is known as the humanistic color because it influences the desire to be of service to others. Indigo enhances intuitive intelligence and visionary insight. It represents the subconscious and allows access to universal knowledge. Indigo expands personal consciousness symbolized by the infinite, blue-black sky. Its calm, peacefulness, and expansiveness provides a glimpse into the deep mysteries of life. By awaking to the vast collective unconscious of Indigo, psychic abilities are enhanced and spiritual levels are heightened.

Indigo is also associated with dreams and the unconscious mind. When you and your loved one sleep on Indigo sheets, intimacy is deepened through a spiritual bond. Incorporate Indigo into your bedroom to help with insomnia. Because of its sedative nature, it is best not to work with Indigo when you need to be mentally alert or use heavy machinery.

If you are an *Indigo Person*, too much Indigo may be dreamy and you may live in thoughts of the past or future. Living in fantasyland may distract your capacity to stay grounded and to perform real-life necessities. When working with Indigo, make sure it is balanced with a warm color (Red, Orange, or Yellow) to avoid depression or negative psychic experiences.

<<<<<<< Today's Two Color Alchemy Minutes >>>>>>

Color Breathing: Fill your entire body with *Intuition and Vision* for nine, slow and deep Indigo breaths.

Wearing Indigo: Every time you focus on your denim shirt or Indigo accessory, and/or any time you experience Indigo, take at least one Indigo breath full of *Seeing beyond the Seen and Psychic Power*.

saturday

Intuition & Vision: Psychic Powers • Focus • Seeing Beyond   107

Intuitive Activators:	To be mentally sharp and focused, Blue is a *cool* alternative to Indigo. When you need to be physically strong, Red, Orange, or Yellow is better.
Habitual Gratitude:	Complete your "Indigo moment" with thoughts of how lucky you are to be alive, and count your blessings.

The more you practice, the faster you experience the benefits of ColorAlchemy!

Here are a few visualization suggestions:

Indigo Visualizations:

- Midnight sky sparkling with the light of a million stars
- Ink from a squid baffling its prey
- Your favorite blue jeans
- The color behind your eyelids

Indigo Expressions:

- Burn the midnight oil
- Deeper than indigo
- Indigo nights

<<<<<<< Congratulations! >>>>>>

You've completed today's Two ColorAlchemy Minutes

‹‹‹‹‹‹‹ Violet ›››››

> Heightens spiritual connection
> Strengthens link with cosmic energy
> Connects identity to divinity
> Expands spiritual values
> Nourishes creativity and artistic talent
> Soothes, heals, and calms the nervous system
> Purifies thoughts and feelings for greater inspiration
> Connects to spiritual self for guidance and wisdom
> Increases inner strength
> Awakens deeper meditation
> Focuses concentration on your inner world

The color Violet is the highest of energetic vibrations. Violet is the color closest to God and to your spiritual self. It takes the life qualities of Indigo one colorful step further for complete universal understanding and connection to the collective unconscious. Violet is divine inspiration through wisdom for the benefit of all life. Violet is liberation.

While Orange is creativity in bloom, Violet is inspirational creativity at its deepest level. This creativity helps define your higher purpose, spiritual values, and compassion. When in a Violet-meditative state, it is said that you are capable of experiencing God with the earthly senses.

While Green is the *earthly balancer*, Violet is the *heavenly balancer*. Violet provides insight to open mental blocks, integrates the left and right hemispheres of the brain, and combines your feminine and masculine sides. Violet perpetuates states of grace and brings dreams into reality.

If you are a *Violet Person*, too much may swing your lofty ideals to a place that I call your ass-hol-i-ness. (I made that up and enjoy its perfect description.) That condition is where humility is forgotten and replaced with an overinflated ego. Be careful if haughty arrogance and ego take the place of spiritual understanding.

‹‹‹‹‹‹‹ Today's Two ColorAlchemy Minutes ›››››

Color Breathing: Fill your entire body with *Peace, Inner Knowing, and Spiritual Love* for nine, slow and deep Violet breaths.

Wearing Violet:	Every time you focus on your Violet shirt or accessory, and/or any time you experience Violet, take a Violet breath full of *Divinity, Inspiration, and Bliss.*
Intuitive Activators:	Take at least one *Peaceful* breath every time you see the color Violet, and you are on your way!
	You are becoming a pro at wearing your colors, yes? I still recommend that you wear something in the Daily Color (if only in your undies—and I do that Activator daily!) because at the end of each week, you'll align with your inner rainbow for spectral, mental, physical, and spiritual balance.
Habitual Gratitude:	Complete your "Violet moment" with thoughts of how lucky you are to be alive, and count your blessings.

Are you experiencing the benefits of ColorAlchemy?

Have you made Color Breathing a ritual? Remember to take a few Color Breaths before going to sleep so your dreams will be more colorful. You will awake more refreshed and excited to greet the new day.

Add a few visualization suggestions to your Color Breathing:

Violet Visualizations:

- Wisteria or lavender flowers
- Lightening against a deep purple sky
- Vivid streaks of violet in a sunset
- A huge eggplant
- Regal violet robes of a king
- A bowl of luscious purple grapes

Violet Expressions:

- Born to be purple
- Shrinking violet
- Purple with rage

<<<<<< **Congratulations!** >>>>>>
You've completed today's Two ColorAlchemy Minutes.

Color Alchemy

7 Days   7 Colors
7 Triumphs

Colors of Your
Body

Vitality Creativity Power
Love Focus Intuition Bliss

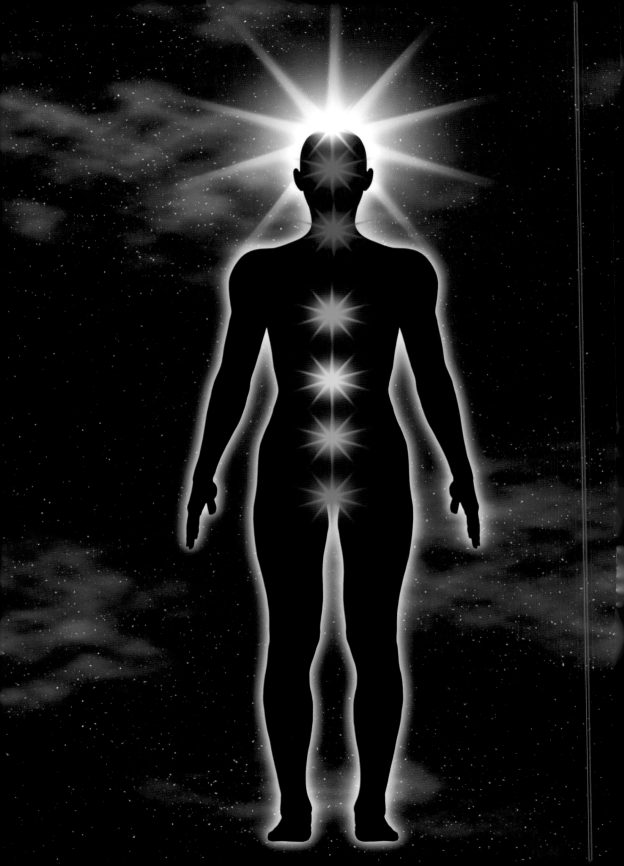

Connects you to the physical world
Defines BE-ing and acceptance of BE-ing

Serves as the foundation for every other life function

Provides energy of survival instincts and physical energy
Promotes balance and stability

The first chakra is located at the base of the spine at the perineum. It is the grounding chakra because it is closest to the earth. It is the foundation that keeps you connected to Mother Earth and all her resources. The Root Chakra is the link to your terrestrial source of energy and vibrates to the color Red.

Survival, making your own way in the world, and completing projects are Root Chakra energies. Money and providing for life's basic needs are within the first chakra's influence. This energy center provides for basic needs and safety along with a stable base on which to build your life.

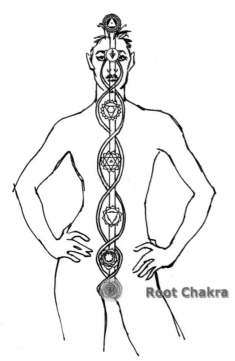

Root Chakra

You receive everything you need to survive from the stability of the earth. Unfortunately, issues of scarcity and greed are human weaknesses created by our sabotaging minds. This chakra develops confidence in knowing that you will be taken care of: that you'll always have *enough*. Because the Root Chakra is connected to the earth, when you tap into its energies with your Observer, it provides trust in knowing that you have everything you need.

Someone who has continuous health problems or is living day to day, concerned about where his or her next meal or paycheck is coming from has unresolved Root Chakra issues. This question cannot be resolved simply by getting a better paying job. Fear and financial insecurity are pervasive in our culture and reside in the lower Chakras.

Physical Vitality: Courage • Security • Strength • Stamina   113

Trouble visualizing Red during meditation or Color Breathing is an indication that the attributes of the Root Chakra are weak. It suggests that a person may be unrealistic and more *in the clouds* than stable, secure, and rooted in physical reality.

The Root Chakra increases connection to the earth and strengthens the life force that helps you live in the physical world. It charges and protects the entire lower body.

Survival & Grounding

Key Concepts:
Stillness, stability, money, safety, space boundaries, security, foundation, grounding, individuality, journey, life experience, projection

Balanced Root Chakra:
Alertness with bright energy
Present and aware, in the moment
Gets the task done
Male energy
Secure and stable

Body Areas:
Centered on the spinal column at its base
All solid and structural parts of the body: bones and spine, teeth, nails, arms, legs & feet, anus, prostrate adrenal glands, and immune system

Associated Ailments:
Weight issues-obesity, anorexia nervosa, bulimia; hemorrhoids, constipation, sciatica, arthritis, knee problems

Common Addictions:
Alcohol, sex, compulsive cleaning

The lotus is the symbol of mental, physical, and spiritual growth and the *unfolding of the chakras* in evolutionary sequence. The traditional lotus graphic for each chakra is included on its respective *Color of the Body* page. Notice how the petals grow from four petals with the Root Chakra to the fully-opened, evolved, ten-thousand-petaled Crown Chakra.

Visualize this traditional lotus graphic of the Root Chakra during your Color Breathing and chakra meditation with the Root Chakra to the fully-opened, evolved, ten-thousand-petaled Crown Chakra.

Remember your
Mental ColorAlchemy

Learn
Evaluate
Release
Activate

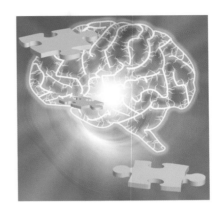

Evaluate:

Red & Root Chakra Weakness

ENERGY	YIN: without Form	MATTER YANG: with Form
Spiritual	**Emotional**	**Physical**
You feel detached from the physical world and don't want to be involved with *real life*.	Financial, security, and not having *enough* fears are controlling your thoughts.	You don't feel like moving-- supreme couch potato. No motivation to lift a finger.

Red Aura Indicators: (learn about auras on p. 153)

Pure: Excited, pioneering, confident, outgoing, radiant
Light: Nervous, impulsive, immature, frenetic personality
Dark: Volatile temper, over dominate ego
All: Nervous tendencies

Release:

YANG Energies Overactive: use Green	YIN Energies Under-stimulated: use Red
• impatient • aggressive • hyperactive • food addictions	• lack of energy • no enthusiasm • dull and lifeless

Learn and Activate:

Too much Red and/or overstimulated Root Chakra people are obsessed with material objects. They often are attracted to violence and sexual addictions. They may lose control of a healthy relationship to sex.

Activate with Green Complementary-Color Breathing (p. 104): Breathe in Green and focus on your Heart Chakra for balance, love, sense of renewal, and compassion. Visualize that toxins and negativity are being released as you breathe out Red.

Too little Red and/or underdeveloped Root Chakra people lack energy and common sense. They have a tendency to be unstable and avoid responsibility. They are insecure and fearful. They feel like everyone is out to get them.

Activate: Use Red when you meet a demanding day, or when you feel drained of energy and strength. The color Red provides the power from the earth and gives energy on all levels. It connects us to our physical body. Start everything with the life vitality of Red.

Use the endless supply of colors around you as a trigger for integrating your *mental, physical*, and *spiritual ColorAlchemy*.

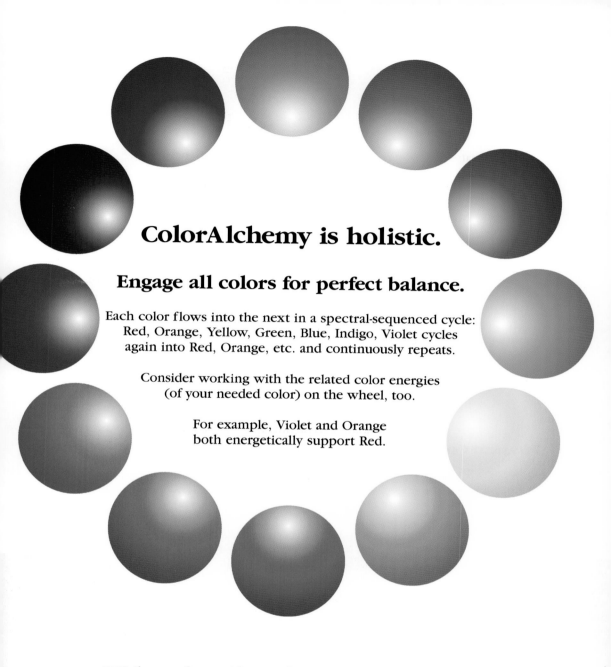

ColorAlchemy is holistic.

Engage all colors for perfect balance.

Each color flows into the next in a spectral-sequenced cycle:
Red, Orange, Yellow, Green, Blue, Indigo, Violet cycles
again into Red, Orange, etc. and continuously repeats.

Consider working with the related color energies
(of your needed color) on the wheel, too.

For example, Violet and Orange
both energetically support Red.

**With each Daily ColorAlchemy Triumph,
visualize that each chakra absorbs and benefits
with its transformational color and attributes.**

Balance and Improve the Root Chakra with Red *Energy* and Red *Matter*

Experience Red and you'll automatically feel its heat. Red warms cold areas to reduce pain. It increases blood and circulation and aids with depression. Because of its powerful and stimulating influence, it is best not to use Red very long if you become agitated, aggressive, or anxious or have high blood pressure.

Mental ColorAlchemy (*Energy*) Activators—Anytime, Anywhere:

Red Breath Meditation: (p. 88) Close your eyes. For the next nine breaths several times during the day, visualize Red coming in through your nose with your slow and deep inhalations. Release toxins and negativity with Green exhalations.

Fill your body with a Red Ray. (p. 147) Visualize the full concentration of pure Red Energy coming in through the top of your head and funneled into your hands.

Several times a day, pause and benefit with an energizing Red breath of *Courage and Strength*

*Physi*cal ColorAlchemy (*Matt*er) Activators—So Easy, So Fun

Wear a Red shirt or accessory today. Every time you glance at your Red item and/or any time you experience Red, pause. Energize your mind, body, and spirit with Vitality and Energy.

Use Red Healing Hands (p. 124) to channel *Energy and Vitality* into your Root Chakra. Red helps burn through cancer. Red dries a watery nose (colds) and open wounds. With conscious intention, imagine a healing Red Ray of *Courage, Vitality, and Strength* flowing through your palms as you gently touch your Root Chakra. Nourish your adrenal glands and visualize your nervous system as strong and stable.

Personally, I enjoy them all and celebrate them through the simplicity of my daily routine: drinking elixirs at the gym, storing daily vitamins in teeny colored boxes, spraying myself and the house with essential oils, sipping afternoon green tea, and of course, during bathtime sanctuary.

Spiritual ColorAlchemy (*Energy & Matter*) Activators—Divine

Monday is especially good to do some Chakra Dancing or Moving Mediations. (p. 208).

All ColorAlchemy Activators triumphantly transform your life!

Source of sexual energy, creativity, and emotional stability

The center of emotions and feelings
Balances giving and receiving with friends and lovers

It is the procreative center for all that you create
Stimulates desire and emotions

The second chakra is located in the lower abdomen, specifically in the genital or womb area. It vibrates to the color Orange and its primary energy is procreation. The Sacral Chakra is the center of sexuality, emotions, intimacy, desire, and pleasure. This chakra transforms sexual energy into creation and desires into reality. It enhances the immune system and increases ambition.

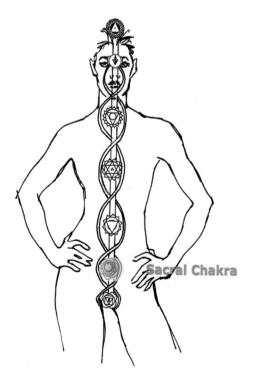

Sacral Chakra

The Sacral Chakra is polarity, duality, and movement. The Chinese philosophy of yin/yang teaches that the universe and reality are based on dualism (light/dark, day/night, female/male) from which ongoing creation is generated. Duality is why Complementary-Color Breathing is so effective.

This polarity refers to relationships and the concept of opposites attracting to create a whole. You experience *your polarity* as a reflection in a mirror. What you seek in others is what may be lacking in yourself.

Without dualism, you may never seek what may be missing and lose out on vital life experience. You make yourself whole through finding "the opposite" and integrating that energy into your being. Marriage, sexuality, and friendships are the celebration of this concept as the joining of opposites become one.

tuesday

Emotions & Creativity: Happiness • Desire • Pleasure • Intimacy

From the union of opposites a greater creation is born.

This union has everything to do with your choices to create life experience. When you absorb the limitless abundance of the earth through your first chakra and the color Red, you are able to create through your second chakra. Notice how the energy of the chakras build on each other. Remember that all mental, physical, and spiritual systems are holistically connected.

Desire is the foundation of creation.

The Sacral Chakra is the center of feeling. Because Western society (unfortunately) prioritizes reason over feeling, often true feelings remain dormant in the Sacral Chakra without being released. When this energy gets stuck, it stagnates and is unable to generate or create. Feeling is also the best intuitive resource (and ties into Indigo and the Third-Eye Chakra) for all ColorAlchemy and life.

When you truly feel, you are capable of creating what you really want.

Create the life of your dreams: FEEL what is really important to determine how to spend your time and energy. These feelings must be yours, not the recycled or regurgitated thoughts of others. Integrate the energy of the Throat Chakra and Blue to add clarity to your thoughts and to trust your feelings. When you release the need for social approval restricted by *reason over feeling*, you create your true desires.

Trouble visualizing Orange during meditation or Color Breathing is an indication that the attributes of the Sacral Chakra are weak. It suggests that a person may have emotional problems, sexual guilt, and/or insecurities about body image.

Desire, Pleasure & Creation

Key Concepts:	Feelings, empathy, emotional needs, boundaries, intimacy, socialization, emotions, partnership, relationships
Balanced Sacral Chakra:	Joy, Feels like dancing Male energy, creates lift-off, playful movement energy
Body Areas:	Centered on the spinal column, front to back and side to side in the genital area, pelvis, reproductive organs, large intestine, lower abdomen, spleen, and lower back
Associated Ailments:	Impotence, frigidity, uterine, bladder or kidney problems, lower back pain
Common Addictions:	Sugar, food, alcohol, sex

Evaluate:

Orange & Sacral Chakra Weakness

ENERGY	YIN: without Form	MATTER YANG: with Form
Spiritual	**Emotional**	**Physical**
Nothing brings you joy. Everything is a chore or an obligation. Nothing is fun. You are *running on automatic*.	You are not joyful and happy. You are depressed and emotionally lethargic. You are insecure of what people think about you. You forget how to have fun.	You don't like touching or hugging. You don't enjoy being at home or you don't enjoy meals with family or friends. You always look frumpy.

Orange Aura Indicators:

Pure: Thoughtful, considerate, self control, healthy sexual attitudes
Light: Lazy, indifferent
Dark: Lack of ambition, repressed sexually, addictions, kidney ailments
All: Generates creativity

Release:

YANG Energies
Overactive: use Blue

- arrogant
- proud
- sexual dominance
- sexual addictions

YIN Energies
Under-stimulated: use Orange

- introverted
- not-good-enough feelings
- holds grudges
- ashamed of body

Visualize the traditional lotus graphic of the Sacral Chakra during your Color Breathing and chakra meditation.

Learn and Activate:

Too much Orange and/or overstimulated Sacral Chakra people act with demanding energy: I, me, mine! They only do what they want to do, when they want to do it. They may overindulge in terrestrial pleasure: drink, food, and sex. To much or too little Orange can create an addictive personality.

Activate with Indigo Complementary-Color Breathing: Breathe in Indigo and focus on your Third-Eye Chakra for visualization ability, intuitive power, and developing leadership skills. Visualize that toxins and negativity are being released as you breathe out Orange.

Too little Orange and/or underdeveloped Sacral Chakra people have a tendency to be insecure, dishonest and irresponsible. They turn their attention inward and may be depressed and unmotivated.

Activate: Use Orange to bring joy to the workday and strengthen your appetite for life! Orange is the best emotional stimulant. Orange connects you to the senses, helps to remove inhibitions, and creates independence and a desire for social interaction.

<<<<< < Today's Two ColorAlchemy Minutes > >>>>

Balance and Improve the Sacral Chakra with Orange *Energy* and Orange *Matter*

Experience Orange and you'll automatically know its joy and playfulness. Softer than Red, Orange has a gentle, enthusiastic energy that is a great pick-me-up color. It increases the immune system and increases sexual desire. Orange helps digestive problems and kidney disease. Similar to Red, too much Orange can cause agitation, anxiety, and aggressive behavior.

Mental ColorAlchemy (*Energy*) Activators—Anytime, Anywhere:

Orange Breath Meditation: Close your eyes. For the next nine breaths several times during the day, visualize Orange coming in through your nose with your slow and deep inhalations. Release toxins and negativity with Blue or Indigo exhalations.

Fill your body with an Orange Ray. Visualize the full concentration of pure Orange Energy coming in through the top of your head and funneled into your hands.

Several times a day, pause and benefit with an energizing Orange breath of Happiness and Desire

Physical ColorAlchemy *(Matter)* Activators—So Easy, So Fun

Wear an Orange shirt or accessory today. Every time you glance at your Green item and/or any time you experience Orange, pause. Energize your mind, body, and spirit with *Pleasure* and *Delight*.

Use Orange Healing Hands to channel *Emotion* and *Creativity* into your Sacral Chakra. Orange Healing Hands are the ultimate antidepressant. With conscious intention, imagine a healing Orange Ray of *Youth, Joy,* and *Zest* flowing through your palms as you gently touch your Sacral Chakra. Nourish your glands and endocrine system. These systems govern the ovaries, and through the spleen, help convert food into energy. Visualize balancing your emotions along with nurturing (your respective) male or female sexual systems.

Spiritual ColorAlchemy *(Energy & Matter)* Activators—Divine

If you moved your divinity on the outside with movement yesterday, feel spiritual energy on the inside. Tone your musical instrument, p. 212 and feel the vibration of your sound through every cell and fiber of your body.

All ColorAlchemy Activators triumphantly transform your life!

Reminder: Your environment is an extension of your body, as room and board support the security of Red Energy. Orange-Tuesday is a great day to look around your home and office. Clear some clutter, practice Feng Shui and/or add any *ColorAlchemy Activators* to your home and/or office (p. 164).

ColorAlchemy is holistic. Practice some ColorAlchemy with the respective color and its attributes each day so you will triumphantly integrate all the colors of happiness at the end of each week.

<<<<<<< Congratulations! >>>>>>
You've completed today's Two ColorAlchemy Minutes.

Healing Hands

Healing Hands is exactly as the name suggests. It combines the physical (matter: your hands) with love and mental, conscious intention (energy). With Healing Hands you improve the health of an area by transmitting healing energy through your hands to a weak part of the body.

Mothers instinctively practice healing hands (or healing lips) when they kiss the skinned knee of their fallen child. Within seconds, Mom radiates love and the child stops crying when he absorbs the mental, physical, and spiritual nurturing.

While there are people who are born with great healing ability, the more you practice healing hands, the more skilled you become. In fact, the first time I practiced healing hands, I didn't even know I was doing it.

> *While designing a client's office, he mentioned he had a life-changing disease. Somehow, I knew (with the vision of my Third-Eye Chakra) that I could project healing energy into his body. With his permission, it felt right to put my hands on his place of illness. Intuitively, the knowledge that inherently exists in each of us, with visualization and conscious intention, we both could actually feel currents of energy radiating out of my hands as if pulsing in rhythm with his heartbeat. Through the experience, he learned how to practice healing hands on himself, and combined with Western and Chinese medicine, he is now in better health.*

After that experience, I learned that there are many traditions of healing hands, and to my knowledge, Reiki and Light Touch are the most widely practiced and are considered very effective techniques. Since I have priorities to learn other things, I practice my *intuitive technique* because it seems to be enough. As needed, I experience instant energy and, depending on the circumstance, on-the-spot, in-the-spot relief. It doesn't matter to me whether or not healing hands provide immediate pain relief or psychological healing (as with Mom's kiss); I love that it is so simple and effective.

Healing Hands can be used for any reason, on any part of the body, and at any time. You can even use healing hands on your pets. Touch is love and comfort. Healing Hands add specific therapeutic energy and nourishment. Apply Healing Hands for:

Comfort and pain reduction: Do you have a pain in your neck from too much computer-ing? Did you do too many crunches and your stomach is sore? Did you bruise a hip or smash a toe bumping into the table? Were you on your feet all day?

Serious health issues: Do you have a recurring ailment? Are you preparing for surgery? Did you recently have surgery?

Use Healing Hands for spiritual, emotional, and physical chakra balancing along with improving life qualities. *Refer to each chakra for diagnostic indicators and suggestions.*

Balances inner strength and conviction with
the rest of the chakras

Command center for our physical world that provides
the impetus to wake up and greet each day

Balances aggression with command

The third chakra is in the navel area. Its color or vibratory frequency is Yellow. The Will Chakra governs personal will, self-esteem, self-confidence, and self-respect. It helps develop a deep sense of inner strength and the personal power to create the life of your choosing.

The Will Chakra is the main focal point of personal energy. It is your *gut reaction* that never steers you wrong. To not have personal power means you may be dominated and misdirected. The third chakra is best when aligned with Divine Will (and the Violet energy of the Crown Chakra).

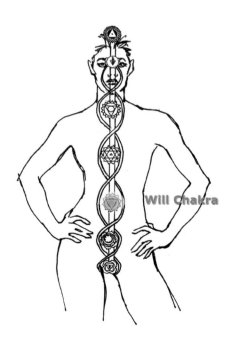

Will Chakra

Power requires responsibility for the decisions that you make. The Will Chakra and Yellow aid with mental clarity on the physical plane (as the Throat Chakra and Blue adds mental clarity on the mental plane). Both help distinguish between right and wrong. They reveal what is appropriate and help break debilitating social patterns that keep you limited by an occupation, relationship, and/or activities that no longer serve you. The Will Chakra helps you stand up and speak the truth from your Throat Chakra.

This is not to say that it is easy to divine your will. Trust your gut and use your Third-Eye Chakra and Indigo to *see beyond what is seen,* even if your vision seems to go against what you have been taught, and you will walk your divine path.

wednesday

Confidence & Intellect: Power • Commitment • Ambition 125

If you have low self-esteem and think yourself unworthy or undeserving, you give away your power to someone else, which weakens you. Use your power to create your fullest capability and receive support from your Root Chakra and creativity from the Sacral Chakra. Notice how the energy of the chakras build on each other. Remember, all mental, physical, and spiritual systems are holistically connected.

Tap into your will power to consciously improve your life.

Trouble visualizing Yellow during meditation or Color Breathing is an indication that the attributes of the Will Chakra are weak. It suggests that a person may be angry, insecure, and/or feel like a victim.

Will & Power

Key Concepts:	Energy, transformation, logic, laughter, joy, anger, balancing control over self vs. others, personal capacity, confidence
Balanced Will Chakra:	Secure Relaxed judgement Male energy Stands strong with muscles ready to take action
Body Areas:	Centered on the spinal column, front to back and side to side at the solar plexus and abdomen, middle and lower back, liver, spleen, pancreas, stomach and small intestines, digestive system gall bladder, nervous system, adrenal glands
Ailments:	Ulcers, diabetes, hypoglycemia, intestinal problems, indigestion, liver problems, hepatitis, adrenal dysfunction, arthritis
Common Addictions:	Food, caffeine, bread, detail freak, compulsive cleaning

Visualize this traditional lotus graphic of the Will Chakra during your Color Breathing and chakra meditation.

Evaluate:

Yellow & Will Chakra Weakness

ENERGY	YIN: without Form	MATTER YANG: with Form
Spiritual	**Emotional**	**Physical**
Others have control over you or you are easily manipulated. Little things *set you off*, such as people talking too loudly on cell phones.	You have to fight for every little thing. You need to be in the center of attention for emotional fulfillment. You value other's ideas more than your own.	Simple issues become mountains instead of molehills. You are unable to detach from physical possessions that no longer serve you. Great color for Feng Shui de-cluttering!

Release:

Yellow Aura Indicators:

Pure: Learns easily, happy person, confident
Light: Timid, inferiority complex, indecisive, weak-willed
Dark: Overinflated ego, obsessed with power, extreme confidence
All: Feels like sunshine, good health and wellness

Learn and Activate:

Too much Yellow and/or overestimated Will Chakra people have a tendency to be workaholics, judgmental, manipulative, and domineering. Yellow people want everything their way.

Activate with Violet Complementary-Color Breathing: Breathe in Violet and focus on your Crown Chakra for connection to your inner divinity and spirit. Visualize that toxins and negativity are being released as you breathe out Yellow.

Too little Yellow and/or underdeveloped Will Chakra individuals may over-criticize and be critical of everything. They may be limited in their thinking and follow rules unconditionally without any personal assessment as to whether the rules have merit.

Activate: Breathe Yellow to clarify thoughts, increase awareness, and stimulate interest and curiosity. Yellow energy is related to the ability to perceive and understand. The Yellow energy connects you to your mental self.

⫷⫷⫷⫷⫷⫷ Today's Two ColorAlchemy Minutes ⫸⫸⫸⫸⫸⫸

Balance and Improve the Will Chakra with Yellow *Energy* and Yellow *Matter*

Experience Yellow and you'll clear mental fog to help you think on your feet. Yellow is a good antidepressant that will keep spirits high. Yellow aids with skin problems and dermatitis. Because it is a warm color (like Red and Orange), Yellow may be exhausting and overstimulating if used too much or if you have a *hot personality*.

Mental ColorAlchemy (*Energy*) Activators—Anytime, Anywhere:

Yellow Breath Meditation: Close your eyes. For the next nine breaths several times during the day, visualize Yellow coming in through your nose with your slow and deep inhalations. Release toxins and negativity with Violet exhalations.

Fill your body with a Yellow Ray. Visualize the full concentration of pure Yellow Energy coming in through the top of your head and funneled into your hands.

Several times a day, pause and benefit with
an energizing Yellow breath of Power and Dedication.

Physical ColorAlchemy (*Matter*) Activators—So Easy, So Fun

Wear a Yellow shirt or accessory today. Every time you glance at your Yellow item and/or any time you experience Yellow, pause. Energize your mind, body, and spirit with *Command* and *Ambition*.

Use Yellow Healing Hands to channel *Confidence* into your Will Chakra. Yellow Healing Hands are the power generators. With conscious intention, imagine a healing Yellow Ray of *Intellectual Focus* and *Commitment* flowing through your palms as you gently touch your solar plexus. Support your pancreas and adrenal glands. Adrenaline helps you express yourself with confidence. Visualize nurturing your stomach as well as small and large intestines.

Spiritual ColorAlchemy (*Energy & Matter*) Activators—Divine

Use Yellow's mental power to *BETA Scan* (p. 224) core issues that restrict your inner self. Evaluate and release energy to fully expand your positive, full potential.

All ColorAlchemy Activators triumphantly transform your life!

Reminder: Yellow-Wednesday is a wonderful day to journal (p. 96), as it helps command your thoughts and cut through mental blockages. If you can't make time to journal today, make a commitment to yourself and plan ahead. Schedule some time to journal with the personal truth of Blue-Thursday's clarity of thought.

It takes twenty-one days to make a habit. Commit to your ColorAlchemy Activators and have fun with them. You'll have great ColorAlchemy habits in no time, and you'll experience instantaneous shifts from negative to positive and transformational long-term results!

<<<<<< Congratulations! >>>>>>
You've completed today's Two ColorAlchemy Minutes.

Healing Hands Suggestions

Visualization: Instead of seeing the actual stomach and miles of intestines (for example), imagine the entire Will Chakra area healthy and glowing in pure Yellow light (or in the specific color of the chakra you are working on).

Colored Rays: Depending on what area you are healing, add the related color to your Healing Hands. Intuitively determine how long to maintain the healing hands and mental connection.

If working on yourself, pay attention to how you and the area feels. Five minutes of concentrated energy may be enough.

If working with a loved one, talk to him. Make decisions together on how long to hold the mental and physical healing. Have the person visualize receiving your loving Healing Hand energy. Make sure he visualizes the location glowing in the appropriate color and getting stronger and more healthy.

129

Healing Hands

1. With a quiet and focused mind, ask your Observer (and/or your higher self, angels, guides, etc.): *Is it in everyone's best interest to perform Healing Hands at this time?* If your intuition replies *yes*, you will do a fine job.

2. If you are offering healing hands to a loved one, ask for permission to touch him or her. (Skip this step if you are practicing on yourself.)

3. With loving and nurturing thoughts pull the warm, Red, Orange, and Yellow colors up from the bottom of your feet to your Heart Chakra. With visualization, draw the cool, Blue, Indigo, and Violet colors down through the top of your head into your heart.

4. In your mind's eye, mix these colors with the Heart Chakra's Green to create the perfection of healing white light.

5. With love, visualize the light spiraling from your heart into your shoulders and down into your hands.

   The power of love radiates from the Heart Chakra, which is connected to smaller energy centers throughout the body (including the palms of the hands) through hundreds of subtle energetic channels, or what Chinese medicine calls meridians.

6. Gently touch the area to be nurtured. Visualize healing energy as a calm, steady stream of electricity or water flowing from your hands into the body. Picture the location engulfed in loving light and imagine what the entire area looks like when it is nourished and heathy.

◄◄◄◄◄◄ Green & Heart Chakra ►►►►►
Mental, Physical and Spiritual Balancing

> Balances the *earth-energy* lower chakras with
> the *heaven-energy* upper chakras
>
> Processes feelings and emotions by holding energy to give
> and receive love freely without fear or self-consciousness
>
> Patience, kindness, and compassion are centered in the heart
> to love the self and others. Provides peace and understanding

The fourth chakra vibrates to Green and is located at the heart. It is the center chakra, midway between the three physical chakras (Root, Sacral, and Will) below the heart and the three, upper esoteric chakras (Throat, Third-Eye, and Crown). The Heart Chakra, known as the rainbow bridge, resonates with unconditional love, trust, commitment, compassion, and hope. It helps recognize and heal the opposites within yourself: hatred, loneliness, anger, and bitterness.

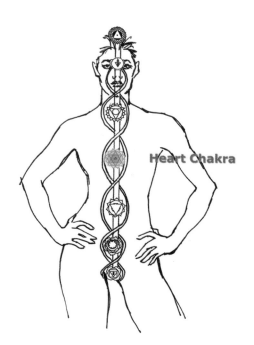

Heart Chakra

This spiral of love energy is not only balancing, but because love is the highest expression of all chakras, it also feeds the other chakras. Through the Heart Chakra, you give and receive unconditional love, share abundance, and radiate friendship, love, laughter, and joy.

The Heart Chakra is your body's energetic healing center. Heart energy is connected to energy centers in the palms of the hands through hundreds of subtle, energetic conduits that run throughout the body.

Using the Heart Chakra, healing goes further than the physical level, reaching the emotional and spiritual planes. Important ingredients for all levels of healing are forgiveness, compassion, and mercy.

thursday

Unconditional Love: Forgiveness • Trust • Compassion • Balance

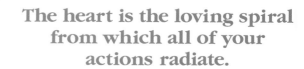

The heart is the loving spiral from which all of your actions radiate.

Forgiveness does not mean condoning what another person did, but it moves you past seeing yourself as a victim. Revenge is reactive. Forgiveness is proactive.

Forgiveness fuels your inner healing. Through Green and unconditional love, *one day the global WE* will forgive everyone and change the world!

When the Heart Chakra is open, you are able to spontaneously heal yourself and others.

Trouble visualizing Green during meditation or Color Breathing is an indication that the attributes of the Heart Chakra are weak. It suggests that a person may be lonely, sick, and/or out of sorts.

Love

Key Concepts: Caring, compassion, trust, giving and receiving, open to change, self love and beyond, forgiveness, love of family, children, heart of home, beauty, harmony, comfort, balance

Balanced Heart Chakra: Experiences freedom
Balances the chakras
Male and female energy
Stands soft, is flexible, and moves without effort

Visualize this traditional lotus graphic of the Heart Chakra during your Color Breathing and chakra meditation.

Body Areas:	Centered on the spinal column, front to back and side to side center of chest/heart, upper back, skin, circulatory system, arms and hands, thymus gland
Ailments:	Heart disorders: high blood pressure, heart disease, asthma, breast cancer
Common Addictions:	Cigarettes/nicotine, marijuana, etc.

Evaluate:

Green & Heart Chakra Weakness

ENERGY	YIN: without Form	MATTER YANG: with Form
Spiritual	Emotional	Physical
All aspects of life run together. There is no separation between work, children, alone time, play, and/or intimacy.	Your feelings and relationships are out of balance. You forget to love yourself and you always put yourself down.	You or your schedule is so out of whack that the love is missing when taking care of loved ones. Health and home is out of balance. Everything is *off* a little bit.

Green Aura Indicators:

Pure: Helpful, trusted, kind
Light: Deceitful, dishonest, brokenhearted
Dark: Self-sacrificing, martyr tendencies
All: Signifies that a person is a good healer

Release:

YANG Energies Overactive: use Green	YIN Energies Under-stimulated: use Green
• jealousy • anger • circulatory problems • martyr complex	• possessiveness • anxiety • neediness • can't give/receive love

It is best to support overactive yang Green with Green while focusing on self-love (even though Red is the complementary color).

Learn and Activate

Too much Green and/or overstimulated Heart Chakra people may be all over the place with uncontrolled emotions. They often want to be loved and nurtured without giving love and nurturing back.

> **Activate with Blue Complementary-Color Breathing:** Breathe in Blue and focus on your Root Chakra for increased Strength and Vitality. Visualize that toxins and negativity are being released as you breathe out Green.

Too little Green and/or underdeveloped Heart Chakra people lack emotion: they are stone-faced without any expression. They are so concerned with material things that they stop feeling.

> **Activate:** Wear Green along with practicing Color Breathing and Healing Hands. Helps relax muscles, nerves, and thoughts. Cleanses and balances energy, to give a feeling of renewal, peace, and harmony. Green connects us to unconditional love and is used for balancing our whole being.

≪≪≪≪ ◄ Today's Two ColorAlchemy Minutes ➤ ≫≫≫≫

Balance and Improve the Heart Chakra with Green *Energy* and Green *Matter*

Experience Green and you'll automatically feel happiness and comfort. Green is the energy of sharing, positive feelings, and nurturing. Green is the strongest color for healing because it balances emotions, stabilizes disproportional mental, physical, and spiritual energies, and provides a sense of calm. Green, the color of nature, helps growth and regeneration.

Mental ColorAlchemy (*Energy*) Activators—Anytime, Anywhere:

> **Green Breath Meditation:** Close your eyes. For the next nine breaths several times during the day, visualize Green coming in through your nose with your slow and deep inhalations. Release toxins and negativity with Red exhalations.

> **Fill your body with a Green Ray.** Visualize the full concentration of pure Green Energy coming in through the top of your head and funneled into your hands.

Several times a day, pause and benefit with an energizing Green breath of Love and Joy.

Physical ColorAlchemy *(Matter)* Activators—So Easy, So Fun

Wear a Green shirt or accessory today. Every time you glance at your Green item and/or any time you experience Green, pause. Energize your mind, body, and spirit with *Balance* and *Compassion*.

Use Green Healing Hands to channel *Love* and F*orgiveness* into your Heart Chakra. With conscious intention, imagine *Compassion, Forgiveness, Harmony,* and *Goodwill* flowing through your palms. Nourish your thymus gland by visualizing as many white blood cells as you need to immunize your body. Feel your healthy heart.

Spiritual ColorAlchemy *(Energy & Matter)* Activators—Divine

Thursday is the best day to practice adding Green to everything that you do because it holds the energy of the love color and the love chakra. Just in case this wasn't obvious, don't wait until Thursday to incorporate Green and LOVE! Use Thursday and its special, love-connecting energy to reinforce and deepen love to everything that you do, EVERY day.

There is never a better time than to pause your day and capture a colorful, loving moment. Absorb and radiate love through your rainbow bridge. Remember, the heart receives the ever-abundant, inexhaustible source of love and spirals it out to the rest of your body, through your hands, and to the rest of the world. Your heart is the bridge to exponentially project "the source of everything" to nourish your mind, body, and spirit as well as to ripple loving influence to everyone and everything you touch.

Reminder: I promised to remind you to Bless your Materials (p. 101). While you are in the blessing mood, bless your space, and body too with one of the Colors of your Spirit meditations, such as the Comic Orbit (p. 224).

We all shift in and out of different chakra weaknesses depending on life circumstances. Don't get stuck in thinking that you only need your *weakness color*. Use Green and the Heart Chakra to have patience with yourself. Integrate your needed color(s) to support your current circumstance.

Get into good ColorAlchemy habits during times that you aren't doing anything else, such as waiting for a Green light or standing in the grocery checkout.

With each colorful thought, breath, or meditation, visualize that your chakra is in perfect, vibrating health with color's purest tone. Set conscious intention to absorb the benefits of that color. Visualize that color being added to your *colorful portfolio* of divine white light. Savor your harmony and balance. *Live ColorAlchemy* in the peaceful light of love and abundance.

<<<<< < Congratulations! > >>>>>
You've completed today's Two ColorAlchemy Minutes.

As Above, So Below
Liquid-Light Meditation

This meditation is an excellent preparation for all breathing, visualizations, blessings or meditations where you want to engage spiraling heart energy. Use this meditation all the time as it takes longer to read than it does to actually do it.

Surprise! You already did it with yesterday's Healing Hands. Now, add the key to all chakra meditations: visualize each color merging into the others as if the colored energy were a liquid. Visualize *liquid light* filling every cell and fiber of your body. Exactly as the name suggests, all you do is combine the above/yin (or upper chakras/colors) with the below/yang (lower chakras/colors) and mix them with the Green, rainbow bridge of your Heart Chakra.

Take a few deep breaths to relax and calm your spirit. Breathe deeply, all the way down into your belly. Dismiss all negative thoughts from your mind and release any tension in your body.

With conscious intention, start with the *as below energies* for a grounded foundation. Bring the warm, *below colors* (Red, Orange, and Yellow) up from Mother Earth. Imagine Red molasses being absorbed through the soles of your feet.

As you continue, draw Red up your ankles, shins, knees, and thighs. The Red energy will progressively mutate into Orange molasses, as the color energetically fills your body. As the visualization moves up to your hips, the thick, nurturing liquid transforms into Yellow. Ultimately the energy flows into Green when it reaches your heart.

Gently touch every part of your body with loving Healing Hands during your visualization. With the below/yang part of your body completely filled with color, visualize your Heart Chakra expanded to its full loving capacity.

From heaven, incorporate energies from *as above*. Draw the cool colors (Violet, Indigo, and Blue) down from Father Sun. Imagine Violet molasses being absorbed through the top of your head. As you continue, move the energy down over your brow as the energy mixes with the colors of your chakras and progressively mutates into Indigo molasses as the color fills your head. As the visualization moves down to your throat, the thick, nurturing liquid transforms into Blue, and ultimately flows into Green when it reaches your heart.

With the yin and yang parts of your body completely filled with color, visualize love filling your body with the energies that came from *above* and *below*.

When complete, because you *borrowed* the energy, be respectful and quickly reverse the process to return the energy to its source. Finish with a quick statement of appreciation and gratitude to have access to the universal energies of Mother Earth and Father Sun.

<<<<<<< Blue & Throat Chakra >>>>>

Connects feelings and emotions into outward expression

The purpose is to know the deepest aspects
of the self through wise inner perceptions, and to
speak and walk each day with truth and integrity

Teaches you to learn the truth within yourself
and brings harmony to speech and voice

The fifth chakra radiates bright Blue and is located at the throat. It is the center of self-expression and speaking personal truth.

**The Throat Chakra is the energy center that
connects personal will (Yellow and the Will Chakra) with
divine will (Violet and the Crown Chakra).**

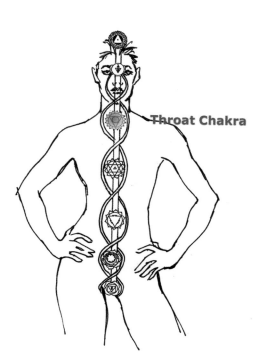

Throat Chakra

The first three chakras are physical energies and govern self-realization, helping you recognize who you are and what you are capable of. The Heart chakra inspires selfless love. The Throat Chakra allows you to surrender to your true nature. It is your voice to the world. The Throat Chakra allows you to communicate your special gifts to express your creativity (Orange and Sacral Chakra) and accomplish goals (Yellow and Will Chakra).

This is the energy center of choice. Personal power lies in your thoughts and actions. Every thought and action has repercussions so choices and their influence need to be considered carefully.

friday

Thoughtful & Holistic: Decisiveness • Clarity • Communication

Remember what you learned in Mental ColorAlchemy about releasing demons? The Throat Chakra and Blue can help with your freedom of choice.

The Throat Chakra deals with judgement and criticism. With negative thoughts, negative forms are created. When you criticize others, you fail to realize that they are a mirror of your own demons. By not speaking the truth, you deceive yourself and reduce true potential. Releasing your demons strengthens the Heart Chakra to grow more love and compassion.

Trouble visualizing Blue during meditation or Color Breathing is an indication that the attributes of the Throat Chakra are weak. It suggests that a person may be "bottled up" and is fearful of expressing him or herself.

Communication & Creativity

Key Concepts:	Listening, speaking up, release of judgement, service to others, expression of BE-ing
Balanced Throat Chakra:	Freshness like a clear sky Relaxed and comfortable, female energy
Body Areas:	Adam's apple, lungs, vocal chords, throat, jaw, neck, mouth, neck, shoulders, thyroid and parathyroid
Ailments:	Throat/mouth ailments, sore throat, stiff neck, colds, lung problems, thyroid problems
Common Addictions:	Smoking, nasal inhalant, runner's high

Evaluate: Blue & Throat Chakra Weakness

ENERGY	YIN: without Form	MATTER YANG: with Form
Spiritual	**Emotional**	**Physical**
You value others' ideas more than your own. You don't recognize your own truth or have your expressive voice. *What needs saying?* Unresolved feelings.	You get frustrated by not being able to communicate or know how to respond to a situation. Others are confused by what you are *really* saying.	You are rushing around so much--you can't think clearly. You have no time to breathe. You are feeling sick with a sore throat or cold, especially when stressed!

Visualize this traditional lotus graphic of the Throat Chakra during your Color Breathing and chakra meditation.

Blue Aura Indicators:

Pure: Diligent, focused, dedicated
Light: Lack of emotional depth
Dark: Moody, tendencies for depression
All: Unselfish, thoughtful, spiritual seeker

Release:

YANG Energies Overactive: use Orange	**YIN Energies** Under-stimulated: use Blue
· frustration · talking constantly, saying nothing · fanatical	· shy · fear of change · don't stick up for self · moody

Learn and Activate:

Too much Blue and/or overestimated Throat Chakra people talk all the time. They have a tendency to be manipulative, as their desire for power and fame may take control over their consciousness.

> **Activate: Orange Complementary-Color Breathing:** Breathe in Orange and focus on your Sacral Chakra for joy, fun, and spontaneity. Visualize that toxins and negativity are being released as you breathe out Indigo or Blue.

Too little Blue and/or underdeveloped Throat Chakra people talk so softly that others have to strain to hear them. They are afraid of expressing themselves because of a poor self-image.

> **Activate:** Use Blue to mentally relax. It has a pacifying effect on the nervous system and brings great relaxation. Ideal for sleep problems and hyperactive children. Connects to holistic thought and gives you wisdom and clarity, enhancing communication and speech.

Today's Two ColorAlchemy Minutes

Balance and Improve the Throat Chakra with Blue *Energy* and Blue *Matter*

Experience Blue and you'll soothe the mind. Blue's cooling energy has been recognized as an anti-inflammatory, helps reduce fevers, and slows bleeding. It eases most respiratory ailments, including flu and congestion. Blue (and Indigo) calms frazzled nerves. Be careful if you are a *Blue person* or have tendencies of being cold. Too much Blue may leave you colder and/or stimulate depression.

Mental ColorAlchemy (*Energy*) Activators—Anytime, Anywhere:

Blue Breath Meditation: Close your eyes. For the next nine breaths several times during the day, visualize Blue coming in through your nose with your slow and deep inhalations. Release toxins and negativity with Orange exhalations.

Fill your body with a Blue Ray. Visualize the full concentration of pure Blue Energy coming in through the top of your head and funneled into your hands.

Several times a day, pause and benefit with an energizing Blue breath of Decisive and Clear Thought.

*Physi*cal ColorAlche*my (M*atter) Activators—So Easy, So Fun

Wear a Blue shirt or accessory today. Every time you glance at your Blue item and/or any time you experience Blue, pause. Energize your mind, body, and spirit with *Thoughtfulness*.

Use Blue Healing Hands to channel *Communication* into your Throat Chakra. Blue Healing Hands are the power generators. With conscious intention, imagine a healing Blue Ray of Communication and Personal *Clarity* flowing through your palms as you gently touch your throat. Nourish your thyroid to regulate the metabolic process and how food and air are transformed into energy. Visualize stimulating enough hormones to control metabolism and the growth of new cells as well as your healthy throat.

Spiritual ColorAlchemy (*Energy & Matter*) Activators—Divine

Rituals (p. 236) add spiritual consciousness to all aspects of life. Color Breathing is a ritual that immediately deepens awareness, even during a mundane routine, such as brushing your teeth. Grow ColorAlchemy consciousness with more *momentary pauses* to *separate the ordinary* and expand connection to universal realms.

All ColorAlchemy Activators triumphantly transform your life!

Reminder: If you haven't been journaling regularly, empower yourself with today's clarity of thought and ability to speak your truth.

Journaling Exercise:

Track your experience. While no one can quantitatively measure the beneficial influence of personal growth, as you continue to cultivate your Observer, journaling helps you recognize how much easier your life is going.

Document your personal *stories* of how you controlled your automated and preconditioned negative responses or what you learned when you had an Oopsie.

Keep your eyes open for special sales on *ColorAlchemy Activators*—find great inexpensive items that you can creatively add to your triumphs! Play with all the variations of the spectral colors and have fun discovering which look the best on you!

≪≪≪≪≪ Congratulations! ≫≫≫≫≫
You've completed today's Two ColorAlchemy Minutes.

Blessing Your Body

Blessing your body is a short ritual that adds greater effectiveness to Healing Hands whenever you are the giver or the receiver. Your blessing stimulates each chakra to vibrate and glow with life quality and its healing purpose. Radiating in unison, the light of your rainbow aura strengthens to provide more healing power.

1. Select a time and place where you will not be disturbed for about 10 minutes. Set the stage with your favorite "meditative-mood" accessories. You may want to prepare the space with quiet music and/or light a few candles.

2. Take a few deep breaths to relax and calm your spirit. Breathe deeply, all the way down into your belly. Dismiss all negative thoughts from your mind and release any tension in your body.

3. Gently touch your heart with the palms of your hands. Make as much loving contact with it as possible.

4. Fill your body with the *As Above, So Below, Liquid-Light Meditation,* (p. 136).

5. Imagine the top of your head as a funnel to receive the light of God.

6. With your Third-Eye Chakra, visualize the light filling your body. If it is helpful, imagine the light as Christ, Buddha, Quan Yin, Isis, or any spiritual being who has special significance to you.

7. As the sacred light comes in through the top of your head and fills your body, see the energy flow down your arms, through your palms, into your heart, and fill every cell and fiber of your body. Hold the visualization that you are infusing your body with *all-that-is sacred*. You are impregnating and energizing the molecular structure of your body with the light of God.

8. Upon completion, return the light and your special helper deities to heaven. Thank them for their participation. Remind them of how appreciative you are that they are always *on call* whenever you need them.

9. Finish by saying your favorite prayer (such as *Om Ma Ni Pad Me Hum,* (p. 103) nine times.

> Connects to the deeper source of knowledge
>
> Inner knowing is revealed from vision *beyond ourselves*
>
> Mystical *universal data* expands to provide deep insight
>
> Promotes understanding harmony and knowing your BE-ing

The sixth chakra vibrates to Indigo and is situated at the brow in the center of the forehead. This is the visionary chakra that propels ideas out into the world. The Third-Eye Chakra is where ideas, which seem to come out of nowhere, are integrated to become usable in the physical world. The Third-Eye Chakra and Indigo work in tandem with Orange and the Sacral Chakra to create reality out of vision.

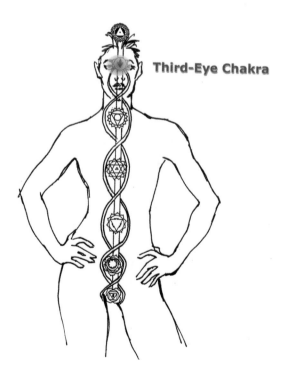

Third-Eye Chakra

The Third-Eye Chakra is the gate of perception through which you see, hear, feel, and experience events that have no rational explanation. You see without eyes and you hear without ears. In this chakra, the clarity of Blue and the Throat Chakra transform into Indigo's divine truth. This chakra makes synchronicity and universal trust more available.

Through greater awareness, seemingly magical events grow with greater frequency, and events and people seem to coincide at exactly the right time.

By acting spontaneously with intuitive information, you enhance decisions and actions. The Third-Eye Chakra allows you to tap the collective unconscious or the huge data bank of information that your rational mind has no other way of accessing. It is the transmitter of conscious intention.

saturday

Intuition & Vision: Psychic Powers • Focus • Seeing Beyond

Life-changing situations such as the death of a loved one, an unexpected loss of a job, or an illness may have plunged you into a depression where personal power alone has not been enough. It is during these times of crisis that you learn to understand and tap into this divine consciousness.

Through the Third-Eye Chakra, visualize the kind of life you would like to live. As learned in *Mental ColorAlchemy*, **Thoughts Create**. Give visual form to your desire and fill them with the energy of creation through the Third Eye. This chakra manifests your ColorAlchemy desires, *sees* what you want to create, and brings thought into form.

Tap into the force that is larger than yourself and simultaneously is a part of you. Acting with conscious intention magnifies all possibility, cultivating inner peace and well-being.

Trouble visualizing Indigo during meditation or Color Breathing is an indication that the attributes of the Third-Eye Chakra are weak. It suggests that a person may be having trouble moving forward in life or visualizing the future.

Seeing & Intuition

Key Concepts:	Awareness, clairvoyance, psychic powers, inner vision, self-cultivation, consciousness
Balanced Third-Eye Chakra:	Peace, relaxation and openness. Female energy Comfortable without restriction or self-consciousness
Body Areas:	Center of the forehead above eyes, face, eyes, ears, nose, sinus, brain, nervous system, pituitary gland
Ailments:	Headaches, nightmares, eyestrain, blurred vision

Evaluate: Indigo & Third-Eye Chakra Weakness

ENERGY	YIN: without Form	MATTER YANG: with Form
Spiritual	Emotional	Physical
You are resentful you have no time for yourself. You feel guilty and/or indulgent when you take time to revitalize yourself. You lack direction and no vision for the future.	You are angry most of the time and you are uncomfortable with your feelings. You are indifferent to everything and/or are numb to your feelings.	You make no time for home or eating properly. Your house is a mess, clothes are spilling out of the hamper, and dishes are piled in the sink.

*Visualize this traditional lotus graphic
of the Third-Eye Chakra during your
Color Breathing and chakra meditation.*

Indigo Aura Indicators:

Pure: In service to mankind,
benevolent understanding, awakening

All: Higher purpose, reaching higher spiritual levels,
soul identity

Release:

YANG Energies Overactive: use Orange	YIN Energies Under-stimulated: use Indigo
· bad dreams · too dreamy · not grounded in reality · flaky	· absentminded · mentally confused · fuzzy head · can't concentrate

Learn and Activate:

Too much Indigo and/or overstimulated Third-Eye Chakra people live in their minds and are ungrounded in physical reality. Often they have anxiety attacks and are delusional. They have trouble fulfilling basic personal needs.

Activate with Orange Complementary-Color Breathing: Breathe in Orange and focus on your Sacral Chakra for joy, fun, and spontaneity. Visualize that toxins and negativity are being released as you breathe out Indigo or Blue.

Too little Indigo and/or underdeveloped Third-Eye Chakra people are rigid in mental discipline but seem to still live in a dreamy way. They either turn off their intuition or completely disregard it.

Activate: Breathe Indigo to connect to your unconscious self and provide the experience of being part of the whole. Indigo strengthens intuition, imagination, and psychic powers, and increases dream activity.

Balance and Improve the Third-Eye Chakra with Indigo *Energy* and Indigo *Matter*

Experience Indigo to cool and calm respiratory systems. It reduces swelling and has an anesthetic influence. It reduces bleeding and calms an overactive thyroid. Indigo (like Blue) has a sedative effect. It tones and tightens skin, shrinks tumors, and reduces swelling. Too much Indigo causes dreaminess and disconnection to reality.

Mental ColorAlchemy (*Energy*) Activators—Anytime, Anywhere:

Indigo Breath Meditation: Close your eyes. For the next nine breaths several times during the day, visualize Indigo coming in through your nose with your slow and deep inhalations. Release toxins and negativity with Orange exhalations.

Fill your body with an Indigo Ray. Visualize the full concentration of pure Indigo Energy coming in through the top of your head and funneled into your hands.

Several times a day, pause and benefit with an energizing Indigo breath of Intuition and Vision.

*Physi*cal ColorAlche*my* (*Ma*tter) Activators—So Easy, So Fun

Wear an Indigo shirt or accessory today. Every time you glance at your Indigo item and/or any time you experience Indigo, pause. Energize your mind, body, and spirit with your *Psychic Powers* and *Intuition*.

Use Indigo Healing Hands to channel *Vision* into your Third-Eye Chakra. Indigo Healing Hands are the power generators With conscious intention, imagine a healing Indigo Ray of *Otherworldly Knowing* and *Healing* flowing through your palms as you gently touch your Third-Eye Chakra. Nourish your pineal gland and visualize creating the perfect amount of melatonin in the bloodstream and stimulating higher consciousness.

Spiritual ColorAlchemy (*Energy & Matter*) Activators—Divine

Deepen your S*piritual ColorAlchemy.* Enjoy my favorite meditations such as Buddha's Mind, Body, and Speech, (p. 243), Crystal Rainbow, (p. 244), and Cosmic Orbit, (p. 244).

Reminder: The more you practice, the faster ColorAlchemy uplifts your consciousness on a moment-to-moment basis. Complete your energizing pause with thoughts of how lucky you are to be alive, and count your blessings.

‹ ‹‹‹‹‹ Congratulations! › › ›››
You've completed today's Two ColorAlchemy Minutes.

Color Rays & Healing

Using Colored Rays (also referred to as Solar-Ray Therapy) deepens the therapeutic influence of healing hands. It is a visualization technique that can be traced to ancient Egyptian color healing.

Contemporary healers use this technique along with using colored light (as you will too in Colorful Applications) to strengthen physical areas and/or emotional conditions. It is as easy as Healing Hands except that you add color to the process.

Please refer to Healing Hands steps 1 through 3 on p. 130 and add Colored Rays starting with step 4.

4.   In your mind's eye, mix these colors with the Heart Chakra's Green to create the perfection of healing white light.

   Imagine the white light in your mind as it provides the purest source of healing: *the light of God.*

   Remember: "Colors are from the fundamental forces of vibration as they apply to the material forces manifested by the physical world. It is through these forces that healing comes to us from the Divine—the source of universal supply. It is through these forces that we may channel healing vibrations to ourselves and others." [19]

   With your ColorAlchemy knowledge, the following Color Ray guide, and your intuition, select the color and vibration that will support the weakened body area or emotional condition.

   Without separating the white light into its seven colorful components, *color-ize it* with the needed color. To help with your Colored Ray visualization, think of water in a colored glass. The nurturing aspect of water hasn't changed, but it becomes more powerful because the vibration of the healing color is added.

5.   Visualize the specific Colored Ray of light spiraling from your heart into your shoulders and down into your hands.

6.   Gently touch each area to be nurtured. Visualize the Colored Ray of healing energy as a calm, steady stream of colored electricity or water flowing from your hands into the body. Picture the location engulfed in loving, colored light and imagine that the entire area is heathy and glowing with the color(s) most suited for healing.

7.   Intuitively determine how long you should maintain the healing-hands and mental connection. For tips for working on yourself and others, refer to p. 129.

Color Ray Guide

ColorAlchemy is not a book on improving specific physical ailments with color. *Let There Be Light* by Dinsha P. Ghadiali (the grandad of color healing) and *Color Medicine* by Charles Klotche provide extensive, color combinations to use with hundreds of disorders. For our purposes, the best rule of thumb is to incorporate the color(s) of either the physical location(s) and the related chakra , and/or the color of the associated life qualities that need enhancement. *Is this chart second nature to you yet?*

Ray	Chakra	Life Qualities
First Ray	Root Chakra	Vitality, Courage, Security, Self-Confidence, Strength, Stamina
Second Ray	Sacral Chakra	Happiness, Desire, Creativity, Emotion, Pleasure, Intimacy
Third Ray	Will Chakra	Personal Power, Dedication, Commitment, Drive, Ambition
Fourth Ray	Heart Chakra	Love, Forgiveness, Compassion, Trust, Balance, Renewal, Growth
Fifth Ray	Throat Chakra	Decisiveness, Truth within Self, Communication, Focus, Clarity behind Illusion
Sixth Ray	Third-Eye Chakra	Intuition, Vision, Psychic Powers, Seeing Beyond
Seventh Ray	Crown Chakra	Peace, Bliss, Inner Knowing, Spiritual Love, Divinity, Inspiration

Color healers also use the rays below for energetic and spiritual healing. They are known as the Soul-Spirit colors. They are located above the body and extend into the auric field. Starting with the Eighth Ray above the Crown Chakra, each ray progressively is higher up to the Twelfth Ray which extends to the top of a person's aura. The *top* of an aura depends upon the person's spiritual connection. The more evolved or illuminated a person is, the higher his/her aura will extend toward God. **Play & Experiment!**

Ray	Color	Spiritual-Life Qualities
Eighth Ray	Seafoam Green Magenta	Projects goodness in the world Highest vision and intuition
Ninth Ray	Turquoise	Connects spirit, soul & personality
Tenth Ray	**Pearl White**	**Illumination**
Eleventh Ray	Peach & Rose	Love and purity of the heart Source of everything
Twelfth Ray	Gold	Spiritual wisdom and compassion Color of God - Universal Life Force

Connects you to the divine forces of the universe

Captures the *world beyond words* and spiritual intelligence

Links you with cosmic essence and pure loving consciousness

Helps you overcome self limitations. It is your pure BE-ing

The seventh chakra is at the crown of your head and vibrates with the color Violet. This is the transcendental and spiritual center. Just as Red and the Root Chakra ground the energy of Mother Earth, the Crown Chakra is the connection to Father Sun and the energy of the cosmos.

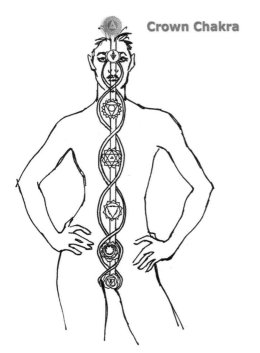

Crown Chakra

All that seems incomprehensible, all the concepts that appear to be bigger and grander than yourself, are accessible through the Crown Chakra. It is the sacred link to God, your divine essence, and the energy of creation. Through this chakra you experience your *Spiritual ColorAlchemy* with selflessness, humanitarianism, faith, grace, spirituality, and divine bliss.

Grow toward en-LIGHT-en-ment to experience spiritual wholeness through the Crown Chakra.

The Crown Chakra is the gate of consciousness. It is the universal connection to the Divine that fills you with knowing who you are and the purpose of your existence. When you are born into your colorful body, your energy takes physical form and becomes matter, but this is not the essence of who you are.

sunday

Spiritual Divinity: Peace • Bliss • Inner Knowing • Inspiration   149

Living is the transitory state where you (hopefully) learn why you are alive and what you are capable of. You are given the opportunity to share your gifts with the world. When you tap into your spiritual consciousness or divine essence, you integrate the lessons of all seven chakras and colors to meet new and unfathomable experiences. You align with the colors of God and experience all the energies of your inner rainbow.

Trouble visualizing Violet during meditation or Color Breathing is an indication that the attributes of the Crown Chakra are weak. It suggests that a person may be negative and has lost all sense of hope.

Understanding

Key Concepts:	Inner knowing, oneness, connection, empowerment, selfless service, spiritual love, divinity, bliss, attainment, completion, spiritual awareness, calm
Balanced Crown Chakra:	Enhances self-respect and dignity Spiritual feelings, no concerns and worries Transcends maleness and femaleness Desire to touch heaven
Body areas:	Top and center of the head, Central nervous system, brain, skull, pituitary gland
Ailments:	Depression, alienation, boredom, apathy

Evaluate: Violet & Crown Chakra Weakness

ENERGY	YIN: without Form	MATTER YANG: with Form
Spiritual	**Emotional**	**Physical**
You can't release negative emotional experiences and you are lethargic and depressed. You can't find any joy or satisfaction in anything. You feel lost, hopeless, and abandoned.	You are consumed with trying to be perfect and have fear-of-failure issues. You procrastinate or get depressed due to performance anxiety.	You are uncomfortable in your home and/or feel like you can't stand being in your own skin. You feel that no place is sacred or special.

*Visualize this traditional lotus graphic o
f the Crown Chakra during your
Color Breathing and chakra meditation.*

Violet Aura Indicators:

Pure: Makes things happen, highly evolved
Light: Fear of the inner mysteries
Dark: Overbearing, indicates stomach problems
All: Seeker of spiritual wisdom

Release:

YANG Energies
Overactive: use Yellow

- uncontrolled ego
- your *ass-holi-ness*
- lost in space
- can't function in the world

YIN Energies
Under-stimulated: use Violet

- negativity
- hopelessness
- depression
- despair

Learn and Activate:

Too much Violet and/or overstimulated Crown Chakra people are attached to the spirit world and disconnected to the physical world. This energy not only keeps them from functioning in the world, but it may also create fear, confusion, and lack of orientation.

Activate with Yellow Complementary-Color Breathing: Breathe in Yellow and focus on your Will Chakra for increasing objectivity and mental intellect. Visualize that toxins and negativity are being released as you breathe out Violet.

Too little Violet and/or underdeveloped Crown Chakra people have a tendency to feel inner emptiness and that life has no purpose. People may be self-centered as they live in extremes to fill their disconnection. They are a poor judge of character or investments and are usually left disappointed.

Activate: Use Violet to purify thoughts and feelings for inspiration in all undertakings. Violet energy connects you to your spiritual self, bringing guidance, wisdom, and inner strength. Violet enhances artistic talent and creativity.

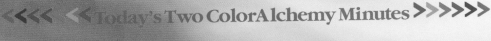

Balance and Improve the Crown Chakra with Violet *Energy* and Violet *Matter*

Experience Violet to bring awareness to spiritual beliefs, focus on higher purposes, and create forward movement in life. Violet helps reduce hunger, relaxes muscles. Violet calms internal body systems including the metabolism. It helps purify the blood and maintains mineral balance. Violet (like Indigo) has a sedative influence, but too much may be too "out of this world" and create disorientation.

Mental ColorAlchemy (*Energy*) Activators—Anytime, Anywhere:

Violet Breath Meditation: Close your eyes. For the next nine breaths several times during the day, visualize Violet coming in through your nose with your slow and deep inhalations. Release toxins and negativity with Yellow exhalations.

Fill your body with a Violet Ray. Visualize the full concentration of pure Violet Energy coming in through the top of your head and funneled into your hands.

Several times a day, pause and benefit with an energizing Violet breath of Peace and Divinity.

Physical ColorAlchemy (*Matter*) Activators—So Easy, So Fun

Wear a Violet shirt or accessory today. Every time you glance at your Violet item and/or any time you experience Violet, pause. Energize your mind, body, and spirit with *Bliss, Inner Knowing, Connection*, and *Spiritual Love*.

Use Violet Healing Hands to channel *Divinity* into your Crown Chakra. Violet Healing Hands are the power generators. With conscious intention, imagine a healing Violet Ray of *Inspiration* and *Spirituality* flowing through your palms as you gently touch the top of your head.

Nourish your pituitary gland. Visualize creating the perfect amount of hormones to influence bone structure, sexual maturity, general metabolism, and connection to universal wisdom. Your Crown Chakra is the most important receptor of light and spiritual energy.

Spiritual ColorAlchemy (*Energy & Matter*) Activators—Divine

Recognizing that you passed an Initiation (p. 250) is divine bliss. Consistent success is the key to mental, physical, and spiritual happiness.

Reading Auras

Diagnosing your aura is an excellent way to indicate your chakra health and the wellness of their relating attributes. The same way your doctor keeps a file to indicate health changes, you should journal aura results to track your chakras and life improvement.

The technique in seeing auras is easy even though it may take some practice. Seeing auras depends on your natural ability, how receptive you are to seeing them, and how much you trust what you see (that's the challenging part!).

I did an experiment with a class to see how many people could see auras. Twenty percent saw them immediately. Fifty percent thought they saw color radiations by the end of the hour.

How to Read an Aura

If you don't have access to an aura machine at a new age or physic fair, the best way to discover your aura is with an *aura buddy*. Find a trusted friend who is open and receptive to mutually share the aura experience. Take turns, relax, and have fun. Select a time that you will not be disturbed.

Location: Select a room that has soft natural light. Find a wall that's not bright white or too dark. You'll need a blank space on the wall large enough to stand or sit with no obstructions (art, light switches, etc.) several feet on either side of you. Make sure that there is no direct light or shadows on the wall. The light source (a window or a lamp with a full-spectrum bulb) is best on the opposite side of the room. If you cannot find a wall large enough, pin a smooth piece of fabric, such as a light-colored sheet, on a bookcase.

Have your friend sit or stand with her back three to four inches away from the wall. Sit directly in front of your friend, leaving about five or six feet between you. Get comfortable and take slow, rhythmic breaths. Relax your body and mind as if in a semi-meditative state.

When relaxed, look at your friend as if you were looking through her. Look beyond her without focusing or straining your eyes. Closing your eyes halfway may help bring the aura into focus.

If you need to rest your eyes, just close them for a few minutes before trying again. Remember, seeing auras and trusting what you see takes practice, so be patient with yourself.

As you start to see auras, you may notice a thin blue/gray-white ring just beyond the body. As you see this, hold that gaze and trust your eyes to differentiate subtle color changes between locations and multiple layers of the aura.

If you have trouble seeing your friend's aura, have her try *making your aura bigger.* Ask your friend to meditate and fill her body with light as if it were a balloon packed to capacity and then extend the light beyond her body.

In addition to knowing that you can see auras, here is another exciting point:

The more conscious intention and focus on your light, the more light is spread to others through you.

Diagnosing Auras

Each chakra description has *Aura Indicators* that describes color variations. Generally:

- When the corresponding color is glowing in its right chakra location, the area is healthy and receptive.
- The purer the spectral color and the more colors that are represented, the more the chakras are in balance.
- The brighter and more a color influences the entire aura, the more its overactivity may dominate and overshadow other chakras.
- A gray aura or gray spot indicates that the body, area, or related emotions are depleted and are in desperate need of nurturing. It may identify depression and/ or imminent sickness. Take care of your mind, body, and/or spiritual needs.
- A black aura or dark spot suggests that there are serious health issues in that area or that a person has dark motives. (While I know anyone reading this book is of the light, when you are good at reading auras, avoid people with dark emanations.)

After diagnosing aura conditions, refer back to the
Four Components of Chakra/Aura Enhancement (p. 59)
and absorb your favorite *ColorAlchemy Activators.*

You've had a very full and exciting ColorAlchemy week. You have breathed and absorbed the entire rainbow. You have aligned with the colors of God within your body and ColorAlchemy gets even better!

Color Alchemy

7 Days 7 Colors
7 Triumphs

Colorful

Activators

Vitality Creativity Power
Love Focus Intuition Bliss

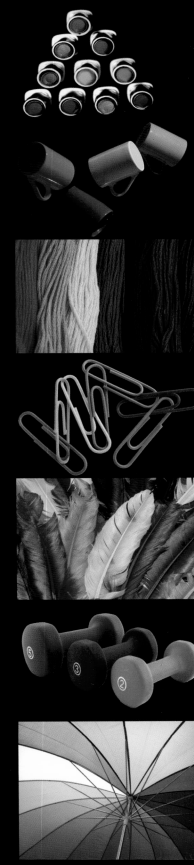

ColorAlchemy Essential Oils & Gems

Color	Life Qualities	Gemstones	Essential Oils
Monday	Vitality, Courage, Strength, Stamina	ruby, red tiger eye, bloodstone, garnet	vetiver, ginger, patchouli, black pepper, cinnamon
Tuesday	Happiness, Desire, Creativity, Emotion, Pleasure, Intimacy	moonstone, carnelian, tourmaline, copper (mineral)	geranium, grapefruit, ylang-ylang, sandalwood, orange
Wednesday	Personal Power, Dedication, Commitment, Drive, Ambition	citrine, amber, gold topaz, tiger eye	cedarwood, bergamot, cypress, rosemary, lemon, lemon grass, grapefruit, fennel
Thursday	Love, Forgiveness, Compassion, Trust, Balance	emerald, aventurine, jade, malachite, peridot, rose quartz, kunzite	Roman chamomile, lavender, orange, ylang-ylang, sandalwood, rose
Friday	Decisiveness, Truth within Self, Communication, Clarity	aquamarine, turquoise, sapphire, lapis lazuli, sodalite, blue agate	lemon, peppermint, myrtle, pine, lavender, lime, thyme, clary sage
Saturday	Intuition, Vision, Focus, Psychic Powers	lapis lazuli, sodalite, indigo sapphire, opal, tanzanite, dark-blue agate	lemon, juniper, peppermint, eucalyptus, rosemary, basil, myrrh, patchouli
Sunday	Peace, Bliss, Inspiration Spiritual Love, Divinity	amethyst, quartz crystal, alexandrite, opal, sapphire, tanzanite	Roman chamomile, frankincense, jasmine, sandalwood, clary sage, lotus, myrrh

Pure essential oils should never be applied directly to the skin. Always blend them into a carrier oil or purified water. Some essential oils should not be used during pregnancy.

Wear and/or incorporate RED when you need to:
Balance Green energy
Feel strong and powerful
Express confidence and energy
Stand out in a crowd or be seen
Strengthen physical ability or your sexuality

Energy & Antioxidant Foods:
radishes, cherries, red pepper, tomatoes, beets,
watermelon, meat, cayenne pepper, strawberries,
pink grapefruit, red apples, red pears, red wine (YEAH!),
pomegranates, cranberries

Red foods create vitality, energy, and stimulate blood flow.

Health Benefits: Helps prevent heart disease
as well as prostate, colon, and rectal cancer

Healing Stones: Ruby, red tiger eye, bloodstone, garnet

Essential Oils: Vetiver, ginger, patchouli,
black pepper, cinnamon

<<<<<<< **Happy Red-Monday: Your Momentum Day!** >>>>>>

The ColorAlchemy Activators are the most ColorAlchemy fun!
Get ready for easy and quick ways to:
- Strengthen weakness
- Further absorb your needed color(s)
- Release toxins created by tension and stress
- Continue to balance and evolve your rainbow body

Now that you are developing your skills at improving your chakras and life
qualities with diagnosing colorful weakness,

By the end of each week, you are also absorbing:
- The entire rainbow
- The colors of God
- **All the attributes of human balance**

Use ColorAlchemy Activators

1. With the Daily Color:
    a. Two minutes: upon awakening, before bed, and periodically during the day with Color Breathing and visualization
    b. Wearing the Daily Color.

2. With the color most needed, based upon:
    a. Energetic weakness or imbalance
    b. Energetic boost for daily task(s) or event(s)
    c. Going to your closet and let the vibration of a color choose you. The color to wear will *jump out at you*. It will be the right one to support your day, even though you may not know it at the time.

ColorAlchemy *On the Body*

Clothing on the body is the most influential ColorAlchemy Activator:

• You absorb the color physically (matter) through the skin.

   From scientific research and *Feeling Color through the Skin* (p. 196), a sightless or blindfolded person experiences different reactions when exposed to different colors.

• You respond emotionally and physiologically (energy) through receiving color through the eyes.

   Ninety percent of the color you see triggers the brain to respond (consciously or unconsciously) with what you have trained it. With ColorAlchemy training, you receive the color's attributes by simply glancing down at the colors you are wearing. So simple!

• *Wearables* are so easy and easily changeable! Develop a ColorAlchemy wardrobe.

Be on the lookout for clothing that fits your lifestyle with color variations that you are drawn to. It is easier to discover a great treasure on sale than to have to find something that you need.

Gentlemen: Don't think you are left out here! My husband has silk shirts in every rainbow color (that he buys on sale!). If you still wear a tie, wearing the Daily Color is easy. Ties look great, even worn loosely with jeans. Collect T-shirts, baseball caps, socks, and of course, underwear! Carry or wear colorful bandanas. **Be creative!**

• Wear color for protection and combine the attributes with your personal power (energy) to shield you during difficult or stressful times. The colors that you traditionally wear say a lot about you.

Expand your wardrobe palette to increase energetic awareness and energy. Reevaluate color dislikes: what are they saying about what you need to learn? **The stronger your color intolerance, the more you may be rebelling from the important lessons the color has to teach you.**

With any color you have an aversion to, use it to diagnose energy imbalances (or confirm what you already know but wouldn't necessarily admit to yourself).

• Wear color combinations of needed colors. *Use scarves totie outfits together*.

• Colored underwear is your little secret.

When you put on the Daily Color, remember to inhale three Color Breaths while visualizing all its attributes coming in on the appropriate Color Ray.

Wear the Daily Color or your most needed color *on the top*. Your shirt is the most important colorful piece of clothing. It covers your Heart Chakra, which you know is the source of your love energy. It is the area that you see most often, so remember to take a Color Breath and to absorb the color from your surroundings. It is also the vibration of what you project to others, even if they only receive your loving ColorAlchemy on a subconscious level.

Personal accessories don't have to be fancy, but you do have to enjoy wearing them to remind you to absorb ColorAlchemy energy.

Jewelry: Fancy, not fancy, or even make your own!

Scarves: Start a collection! Find one in every color to dress anything up. Scarves are so versatile—wear them around the neck, waist, head, hatband, and more.

We all are fragile in some way. I've had respiratory problems my whole life. It makes sense, since you already know blue isn't my favorite, but at the onset of a cold, even if it is 90°F outside, a blue silk scarf goes right around my neck.

At the first sign of any physical ailment, wear or treat the area (see Color Toning p. 192 and aromatherapy p. 176) with the corresponding color for vibrational healing.

Shawls: If you see the rainbow colors in a product and they are a really good price, buy them. I recently bought seven pashmina-quality scarves for seven dollars each!

Just think of all the possibilities:

• Drape the back of your office or
   meditation chair to wrap your body
• Make a rainbow room divider .
   Stretch scarves on a wood frame.
• Create a rainbow on your wall;
   push pins will go directly into drywall
• Sew them together and make a TV
   snuggly for cold nights.
• Of course, wear them. **Be Creative!**

And speaking of creativity, go for it! Life is too short!

Nail polish: It is so much fun to have funky feet! My toes are usually painted in all seven rainbow colors, a different on color each toe in spectral progression. Every time I look down (I never wear shoes), I smile and enjoy ColorAlchemy *happy feet.*

Personal Items

As you find ColorAlchemy items when shopping, consider all the fun ways to incorporate them.

I found clear, plastic, colored boxes in all sizes. Sitting like sparkling jewels on the shelf, they caught my eye right away. I bought two sets.

I have a set of Daily Color boxes for my vitamins. I always remember to take them now because they look so inviting. *As the vitamins are swallowed with the Daily Color Elixir p. 197, I visualize they are floating in a colored sea of nurturing, healing support that fills and strengthens my body.*

I glued a set together in spectral order and made a lipstick holder because each box was a perfect size. It looks great on my makeup table. *Every time I pull out a lipstick (not in the Daily Color), I create a brief, life-enhancing ColorAlchemy pause. Notice how as I do the physical task (matter), instead of allowing my mind random thoughts, I consistently train my Mental ColorAlchemy (energy) to exponentially reinforce the moment. And it doesn't take a second longer!*

Eyeglasses: There are several manufactures that make glasses with vibrational colored lenses. Wearing colored lenses for 10 to 15 minutes a day is a great way to absorb the full energy of color. Color drawn in through the eyes directly improves our overall state of being.

Remember: Take a color breath and visualize the color of your clothing or accessory radiating through your body while concentrating on the related chakra. Whenever you need a color charge, focus on the color you are wearing. Visualize the chakra pulsing its pure color beaming throughout your body.

ColorAlchemy *In the Body*: Colorful Food

I love to eat. Invincible and in great health, I have never been interested in nutrition until the onset and fear of wrinkles. As I conveniently choose to forget where the kitchen and grocery store are located, my husband Joel took over those responsibilities. We are both happy that he takes great joy in sharing his healthy creations. With the way to my heart and satisfied belly, I am thrilled to be delegated to clean up.

Commit to taking a deep and invigorating Orange breath before getting out of bed tomorrow.

161

I learned ColorAlchemy nutrition with two fascinating observations.

I was Feng Shui-ing Lowes Hotel on South (Miami) Beach and working with the executive chef. In addition to maximizing the interiors to support the comfort of guests and performance of the staff, we worked on the *Feng Shui of food*.

Each dish was more beautiful and delicious than the next. They were designed with the five Chinese colors in mind. Each gastronomic delight included something green/columnar, red/pointy, yellow/flat, white/circular, and blue/wavy. Although I ate way beyond satisfaction, I felt healthy and invigorated.

While teaching Feng Shui at a Destination Manager's convention, my experience was quite the opposite. Tex-Mex was the fare. While the food could have included the brilliant colors of Mexico such as corn and green, red, and orange peppers, lunch was gray. It included gray-vegetable pate squeezed out of a pastry bag (use your visualization skills to know what it looked like), dead bird with brown sauce, and white corn. Everyone was tired after lunch, as the food lacked energy.

Sir Winston Churchill described the meal better than I could.

> *I cannot pretend to be impartial about the color.*
> *I rejoice with the brilliant ones,*
> *and I am genuinely sorry for the poor browns.*

If you don't want to think about nutrition, make it simple: Just eat colorful foods!

Colorful food is alive and feeds the body with energy.

There is so much more to learn about the specific antioxidants in food and how they help support good health and reduce aging. Please refer to Dr. Nicholas Perricone's books and Dr. David Heber's book, *What Color is your Diet*. Experiment with the Colorful Foods in each Daily Color header box. No doubt that food is medicine to energize, to maintain good health, and to lift the spirit.

Bottom line: Colorful food choices are so easy, Eat:
- Colorful, fresh, and organic (without pesticides or steroids)
- Nothing white (sugar or flour)
- No processed or prepackaged foods
- Live food: don't kill the nutrition by putting it in the microwave

Enjoy the ColorAlchemy of your colorful plate as you enjoy better health and more radiant skin. Remember a *Mental ColorAlchemy* (energy) reinforcement.

With the first bite of each colored food, visualize colorful nutrients exploding in your mouth like fireworks. Imagine each sparking nutrient is guided to the area of your body where it is most needed.

Wear and/or incorporate ORANGE when you need to:

Balance Blue and Indigo energy
Be creative and motivated
Free your spirit from being too rigid
Have people be drawn to you
Feel happy and have fun

Energy & Antioxidant Foods:

oranges, pumpkins, apricots, peaches, mangoes, melons, carrots, yams, mandarins, orange pepper, acorn squash, golden beets, persimmons, sweet potatoes, winter squash, mixed vegetable juice, kumquats, nectarines, tangerines, papayas, peaches

Orange foods generate optimism, reduce disappointment, and strengthens the immune system.

Health Benefits: Boosts the immune system and inhibits cholesterol; reduces cancer growth helps prevent lung disease, heart disease, and birth defects; improves communication between cells; reduces cancer from spreading

Healing Stones: Moonstone, carnelian, tourmaline, copper

Essential Oils: Geranium, grapefruit, ylang-ylang,

>>>>>>>Happy Orange Tuesday: Creativity Day! >>>>>>

With a blessed Orange marker or pencil, color the next four Tuesdays on your calendar. Set the conscious intention to be reminded to:

Create! *Tuesday is not too late, you still have momentum with Orange*

Spend a few purposeful minutes thinking with new creativity.
Have FUN!

Emotions & Creativity: Happiness • Desire • Pleasure • Intimacy   163

Creative ColorAlchemy: Use Tuesday to create new ideas that I haven't thought of! **Be Creative in Life:**

with Family: What brings relationships closer?
with Love: How can you deepen intimacy?
with Work: Design a better mousetrap!
with YOU: Create a better YOU!

ColorAlchemy Around the Body: Colors in the House

ColorAlchemy does not compete or conflict with Feng Shui, as they have two distinctive influences. Feng Shui's Heaven, Earth, and Man energies are *speaking* and influencing you at all times, whether you are conscious of them or not.

ColorAlchemy includes *Mental ColorAlchemy* with conscious intention, observation, evaluation, learning from your internal process (by cultivating your Observer), awareness, and celebrating the Daily Color to make its benefits exponentially effective and, ultimately, automatic.

Speaking of ColorAlchemy awareness:

Take a stress-reducing, ColorAlchemy pause now.

Train yourself when you see the Daily Color to periodically pause and colorfully nourish yourself during the day!

Reinforce rainbow balance with a minute Orange (color) breath. With the inhalations, visualize an Orange Ray filling every cell and fiber of your body. Release toxins with a Blue or Indigo Ray exhalation.

Integrate ColorAlchemy (and Feng Shui): Everywhere!
The key is to keep the colors changing based upon your need or the Daily Color.

Important Feng Shui note! There is a huge difference between strategically placing a decorative ColorAlchemy item (or a collection of seven) and clutter. Even though I am giving you all the ideas that I can think of (and personally use), please make sure that positioning is purposeful and that accessories are not cluttered.

Suggestion: Position one ColorAlchemy item on a buffet top, leaving the other six readily accessible in the top drawer *waiting for its day. Change them daily to bring consciousness to your Daily Color.*

Flowers: Bring nature's color inside. In Feng Shui, fresh flowers are also symbolic of new beginnings. Make sure you get rid of them as soon as they start to die, as they have lost their life force.

Silk flowers will work but because they aren't alive, they may have a tendency to become permanent (and that is all right if placed in a good Feng Shui location). Make sure silk flowers are kept free of dust so they don't collect stagnant, dusty energy.

Silk-flower idea: Go to a silk-flower store and buy one flower in each spectral color. Find a clear glass vase to hold all seven flowers and a clear glass bud vase. Make sure the two vases look decoratively nice together. Place both in an area that catches your eye every day. As you take a grand breath of the Daily Color, just switch the daily flower in the bud vase.

Colored candle holders or candles: So easy!

Use colored lights in a torchere: While the therapeutic influence isn't as powerful as healing with Color Toning, ambient colored light shifts the energy and feeling of a room. It is excellent for practicing any *Mental ColorAlchemy* such as Color Breathing, Color Meditation, or any *Color of Your Spirit* in a room filled with colored light.

The simplest way to get that effect is to get a torchere, which directs light onto the ceiling. Either use colored light bulbs or white, full-spectrum bulbs with theatrical gels (also used in our homemade, light-therapy lamp, p. 192).

In the Kitchen/Dining Room:

- Enjoy your coffee or tea in a Daily Color mug.
- Drink your eight glasses of water in clear, colored glasses. Use them to make elixirs too, p. 197
- Use colored napkins and place mats.

Aren't these great for a ColorAlchemy BBQ or picnic?

Find all sorts of colored household items everywhere you go! Buy 'em when you see them and figure out how to incorporate them into your everyday life when you get home.

In the Bathroom: Seven dollars for seven colors! Fifty bucks and I had a set of ColorAlchemy towels. If I feel drained in a certain color, I'll select the colored towel that I need.

Feel color on your skin (p. 196). Absorb the towel's colorful attributes as it absorbs the water on the body and do your Color Breathing at the same time.

Use towels for ColorAlchemy in other ways, too.

Take a colored towel into the bathtub with you and lay it on your chest. It is very relaxing and nurturing. Try it!

Colorize your meditation or office chair by sitting on a colored towel or draping it around the back.

In the Bedroom: Sheets: While they are too expensive and labor-intensive to change every day, if you want to greatly enhance the energies of color, there is no better way to absorb color than to sleep completely wrapped in your needed color.

Eye pillows make a great ColorAlchemy substitute for the impracticality of changing bedding every day. These are so comfortable to place on your eyes when you are having trouble sleeping or if a room isn't dark enough. Place some drops of lavender or your favorite relaxing essential oil on the opposite side of the pillow for the fragrance to help you sleep. Use your eye pillows if you lie down to meditate or to relax the eyes. If you cannot find eye pillows for purchase, make your own. They make great gifts.

Accessories: Endless possibilities.

Fill a bowl with decorative ornaments or hang a mobile that catches the light.

Office ColorAlchemy

Organize projects with different colored file folders, legal pads, pens, and/or sticky notes. I always use different colors to take notes and to highlight or underline.

Get a playful pencil cup especially for your blessed, colored pens. Use the colors to note events and to-do's in your calendar based upon the energy.

To-Do's
Priority
Fun Event
Confidence
Family Affair
Private Time: Think/Journal
Massage
Prayer/Mediation

In addition to colorfully organizing my calendar, I have fun with this highly effective and helpful organization. On my desk is one stack of *to-do's-of-the-day* folders. For every day, I have two weeks of clear, colored folders in Daily Color order. To stay organized, on the folder I have written the times of recurring daily events.

A paper clip on each folder allows notes to say secure. Depending on urgency and priority, papers can be clipped inside or outside. Because the folders are clear, I can see the related papers placed inside. Each morning, the Daily Colored folder is at the top of the pile, I greet the color and to-do's with reinforcing *Mental ColorAlchemy* such as: *With the thoughtfulness of Blue, I deepen my communication skills and gain greater clarity through teaching* (I teach on Thursdays). At the end of each day, the top folder goes to the bottom of the stack and any left over items get moved to the next folder.

Remember to select a *Mental* or *Spiritual ColorAlchemy* reinforcement as you incorporate your *Around the Body* activators.

What are your chakra and color weakness? Is the weakness based upon spiritual, emotional, and/or physical indicators?

What colors did you use? What did you discover with Color Breathing and visualization? Did you perform Healing Hands? Where and why did you select that area? Did you have pain before starting? How quickly did you feel relief?

Was the weakness more in balance on the days that followed the healing? How many times, for how long, and how often do you incorporate ColorAlchemy? How can you integrate it more?

What happened during a recent stressful situation? Did you pause and create a ColorAlchemy moment? Did you change negative to positive with Color Breathing? Did you dialogue with your Observer? What did you discover about your *Mental ColorAlchemy*? What did you learn about you?

As you write and achieve understanding, always be sensitive to your reaction(s) to the color(s). To expand how you benefit, consider:

If you have a Red personality, when you wore red, did you get too fired up? Did your heart start to race and/or did you become aggressive (instead of assertive)? Does a softer-Red variation such as magenta (which you remember is a Soul-Spirit color) motivate with less heat, and does it have an enlightening influence? Journal why Red may be too hot and why magenta could be better.

Magenta may be a better spiritual color than Violet if you are dreamy and your head is often in the clouds. If you have a Blue personality, because all yang colors support motivation, what color is more effective for you: Red, Orange, or Yellow?

Even though each color has consistent and generic attributes, you respond differently based upon your personality and the conditions of personal experience. Discover who you are and how you personally benefit from the focus of journaling your thoughts.

Understanding personal color nuances allows you to duplicate the benefits. Adjust your colors and/or variations according to your personal goals to serve your highest interest, balance your energy, and make conscious holistic choices.

Wear and/or incorporate YELLOW when you need to:

Balance Violet energy
Stimulate your metal abilities and be sharp
Tell yourself and others what you can do
and how well you can do it
Prevent being depressed and feeling blue
Express how smart you are

Energy & Antioxidant Foods:

lemon, pineapple, bananas, olive oil, eggs, passion fruit, yellow peppers, grapefruit, corn, avocado, grapefruit, collard greens, cucumber, guavas, starfruit

Yellow foods generate a brightness of character and zest for life and helps eliminate toxins.

Health Benefits:

Boosts the immune system and inhibits cholesterol, reduces cancer growth, helps prevent cataracts and macular regeneration, improves communication between cells, helps fight spreading cancer, protects against clogging of carotid arteries

Healing Stones: Citrine, amber, gold topaz, tiger eye

Essential Oils: Atlas cedarwood, bergamot, cypress, frankincense, rosemary, lemon, lemon grass, grapefruit, fennel

<<<<<<< Happy Yellow-Wednesday >>>>>>

Before we get into today's ColorAlchemy Activators, go outside and feel the sun's spectral rays warming your skin. If the day is cold or gray, still get some fresh air and find a place to protect you from the elements for a moment. With your improving visualization skills, soak in the radiance of *the light*. Know that you are complete, filled with confidence and zest, and greet the day with enthusiastic energy.

Hello world, I am ready to share my light.

Confidence & Intellect: Power • Commitment • Ambition   169

wednesday

Nothing would exist without the energy of the sun's light. Gemstones and essential oils (derived from plants) are created in the light. Respectively, they are frozen or liquid light, both nurtured, and of, Mother Earth.

As with incorporating ColorAlchemy into your clothes and home, it is easy to include working with stones and fragrance. They too can be used *On the Body* and *Around the Body*. I benefit from working with stones and essential oils daily, several times a day.

Absorb Mother Earth's gift of frozen and liquid light.

The purest essence energy of the Heaven-Earth world coalesces into rock.
—Kong Chuan

Frozen Light: Gemstones

Ancient philosophers personified rocks as the bones of the earth. "Bones are the framework that sustains corporeal structure, they may be regarded as a fitting emblem of the spirit—the divine formation which supports the composite of mind, body, and soul." [20] Since rocks come from the *Earth Mother of all creatures*, ancient myths describe how rocks scattered on the earth evolved into an entire race of human beings. Many other universal myths reveal the power of stones as talismanic jewels and describe how they are imbedded in magical rings. Stones are a testimony to existence through the stability of the Rock of Ages. "The rock of refuge is the psychological cornerstone of terrestrial life. And "the philosopher's stone is likened to the magic jewel whose touch transmutes base substances into priceless gems like itself." [21]

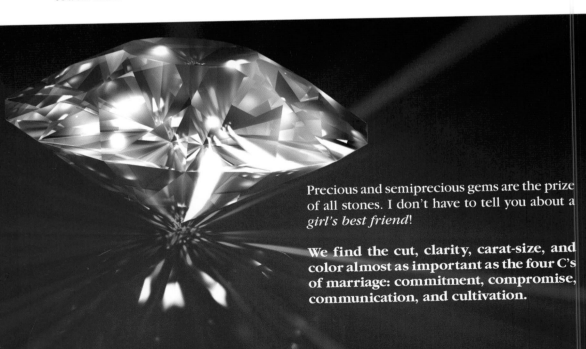

Precious and semiprecious gems are the prize of all stones. I don't have to tell you about a *girl's best friend*!

We find the cut, clarity, carat-size, and color almost as important as the four C's of marriage: commitment, compromise, communication, and cultivation.

Gemstones are the most tangible form of color. Their power is highly concentrated, as they have been soaking up the vibration of light for as long as the gem has been created into the form of matter.

"Gems and stones are solid versions of color in crystalline structure. Each element, each stone, and each vibration of stone has its own atomic movement, held together by the units of energy that in the universe are concentrated in that particular activity. Hence they come under varied activities according to their color, vibration, and emanation." [22]

Crystals are energy transmitters. Depending on the frequency of the specific stone, they are used in modern technology and are the basis for transmitting energy for radio and television. All semiconductors and microchip processors have a form of crystal technology, hence the name of *Computer Land*: Silicon Valley.

Because color is the source of creation, its elements, infused with light, define a stone's unique and individual color. Each gem radiates its specific life-enhancing vibration. "Partaking of the astral virtues of their source, these elements neutralize certain unbalanced forms of celestial activity and contribute to the well-being of man." [23]

"Jewels are used in healing to adjust the inner light of the subtle body. Gems are believed to be mines of radiation containing the power of the seven aspects of light, the cosmic energy as manifested from the diamond-like void into rainbow light. The seven-fold spectrum of light in the rainbow represents the basic energies, forces, and qualities of the manifest world." [24]

We are so blessed to *Live ColorAlchemy*!

It is documented that a king "extended his life with the aid of seven magical rings. Each of these seven rings was set with a gem symbolic of one of the ruling planets of the week. By changing the rings, the king projected himself against sickness by the intervention of the planetary influences." [25]

All gemstones have unique, healing, and energizing properties. For example, according to Buddhists, "Sapphires will open barred doors and dwellings (for the spirit of man); it produces a desire for prayer, and brings with it more peace than any gem." [26] Isn't it fascinating that sapphires are Indigo and they hold the frozen energy and attributes of prayer, vision, and meditation?

Each stone listed on the Daily Color headers enhances your ColorAlchemy according to its color and unique vibrational energy.

Stones

- Balance and tune the chakras and your aura
- Remove blockages

- Enhance the mind by:
  - Defining feelings and emotions
  - Stimulating metal process and Observer cultivation
  - Promoting calm
  - Reducing stress and anxiety
  - Enhancing visualization

- Enhance the body by:
  - Increasing energy
  - Providing healing

- Enhance spirit by:
  - Inspiring meditation, focus, and clarity
  - Working as a conduit for lucid and educational dreams.

With the stone and life-quality list to enhance a specific need, select a stone with the related color and attribute.

There is so much more to learn about the specific energies and applications of stones. If you are drawn to working with stones, read some of the many available books and explore each of their unique qualities before purchasing specific stones that you want to work with. Particularly useful is the book, *Love Is in the Earth: A Kaleidoscope of Crystals,* by Melody and Julianne Guilbaut.

For example, there are four Yellow stones listed in today's header: citrine, amber, gold topaz, tiger eye. In addition to their Yellow energy, they each have specific, energy vibrations. Consider which Yellow stone(s) are best for your purpose. When shopping for your stone favorites, trust your instincts: select the one that feels the best in your hands or *calls to you*.

Cleanse and Bless Your Stones

Before using your stones, cleanse them by quickly dipping them in salt water. (For fragile or porous stones, or if you have any doubt of their qualities, be safe and cleanse stones in distilled water only.) Rinse and dry them in the sun to allow the light to recharge them. (Do not leave stones out in the sun for more than twenty-four hours, as they may be altered with too much light.) It is a good practice to cleanse your stones periodically in this manner.

Pay attention to your stones; if they become dull or cloudy, they will *tell you* when it is time for cleansing. Additionally, if you use your stones to release heavy energies, they need regular cleansing. Be aware of what your stones *say to you*, and trust your intuition.

Your stones will be ready to use after blessing them with your energy.

Prepare for the blessing as discussed previously.
During your Stone Blessing, individually:

- Hold each stone in your hand with conscious intention.

- Visualize the appropriate Colored Ray infusing the stone with the power of Healing Hands.

- Charging each stone with your energy, imagine:
  - All the specific attributes of the stone and color are captured by the stone.
  - Each time you use the stone, the attributes are exponentially magnified and given back to you.

If your stones are not being displayed when not in use, find a special container for them. A clear glass box or crystal bowl is perfect; as you may have thought, stones do not like to be kept in the dark.

Using Stones

- Wear them as jewelry: pendants, beaded necklaces, or bracelets.
- Carry them in your pocket. Don't have a pocket?
  Place a small stone in your bra.
- Hold stones in your hand to absorb their energies.
  Hold them during meditation.
- As in the Buddhist tradition, use a stone mala or prayer beads to count how many times a mantra or prayer is said.
- Feature them as decorative objects.
- Place them on your body for healing or enhancing the chakras.
- Place them in close proximity during blessing to help charge other materials.
- What are your creative ideas?

I lay these flat stones on the body during chakra healings and ColorAlchemy facials.

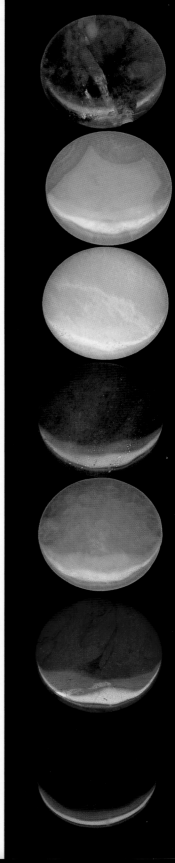

Using Stones:

- *In the Body*: in Daily Elixirs (p. 198)
  - Collect a set of seven-smaller stones for Sunday's lesson.

- *On the Body*:
  - Extra bathtime charge: make a full-body elixir by placing stones in the tub. Water is a conductor and enhances stone energy. Make sure your gems are big enough so you don't lose them down the drain.
  - I wear chakra pendants daily, each with its respectively colored stone. I blessed them as protective and energizing talismans.
  - I sleep with one under my pillow.

Here is am interesting story illustrating how to collect stones. At a gem show, I was drawn to a translucent, white (the color of the spectrum) stone. I loved its striated crystalline structure and bought the selenite. Intuitively, I placed it under my pillow. One night as I was having trouble sleeping, I reached for the stone and said to myself, *sleep now, the stone will help you*. I went right to sleep. As the days and weeks followed, when I couldn't sleep, I would touch the stone.

With such great consistent results, it was time to learn about selenite. A few of its attributes are: Provides clarity of mind, expands self awareness, provides insight into truth, cuts through the unconscious for awareness clarity, and integrates the conscious and mystical selves. Related astrological sign: Taurus (my rising sign) and vibrates to 8 (wow: in Feng Shui we are celebrating the great energy of Period Eight through 2023!). Three bucks: a wondrous deal!

Trust your intuition.
Need intuitive assistance? Practice Indigo breathing!

Get ready, ColorAlchemy and essential oils are coming up tomorrow.

You'll be able to bless your stones with aromatherapy the same way that Jacob (from the Bible) *anointed his stony pillow with oil.*

Commit to taking a deep and invigorating Green breath before getting out of bed tomorrow.

Wear and/or incorporate GREEN when you need to:
Balance Red energy
Find peace within yourself and others
Connect to nature
Feel loving and full of love
Birth new endeavors
Ease a heartache or broken heart

Energy & Antioxidant Foods:
green peppers, broccoli, cucumber, green salad, peas, artichokes, brussel sprouts, collard greens, green apples, green beans, honeydew melons, kiwi, bok choy, mustard greens, romaine, spinach, zucchini, green cabbage, kale, chard, watercress

Green and chlorophyll foods increase physical stamina (think Popeye and spinach), help alleviate uncertainty, and are great for the entire system: eat your veggies!

Health Benefits:
Helps prevent cataracts and macular degeneration, improves communication between cells, helps fight spreading cancer, protects against clogging of carotid arteries, protects against prostrate cancer, enhances breakdown and excretion of liver carcinogens

Healing Stones: Emerald, aventurine, jade, malachite, peridot, rose quartz, kunzite

Essential Oils: Roman chamomile, lavender, orange, ylang-ylang, sandalwood, rose

≪≪≪≪≪≪ Happy Green-Thursday ≫≫≫≫≫

They say that Wednesday is hump day—the middle of the work week—suggesting that the week is half over. ***Why live half empty instead of half full?***

Unconditional Love: Forgiveness • Trust • Compassion • Balance   175

From this day forth, live half full, ready to greet the *other half* with the magic of Green-Thursday: the connecter between your physical and spiritual worlds.

Happy *Rainbow-Bridge, Love* Day!

Liquid Light: Essential Oils

You are already meditating with the energy of liquid light, now benefit with the delicious-smelling, liquid light from plants. Essential oil is concentrated plant energy nurtured with *the light* of the sun. Fragrance is a fast track to *Live ColorAlchemy* because it is the quickest of all the senses to create a response in the brain. Using essential oils provides immediate influence. When oils enter the body through the skin or respiratory system, they instantaneously move through the muscle tissue and into the bloodstream.

Essential oils are treasures of the senses and enhance mental, physical, spiritual well-being. While each essential oil has unique and holistic medicinal properties, they all:

- Smell good!
- Deepen consciousness and awareness.
- Are enjoyable and easy to use.

- **Benefit the Mind, Body, and Spirit. Essential oils:**
    - Open and balance the chakras
    - Influence the body's systems: circulatory, respiratory, digestive, immune, and nervous systems
    - Benefit various body systems depending on the oil's unique chemical composition
    - Essential oils may be: analgesic, antidepressant, stimulant, anti-inflammatory, antiviral, deodorizing, and sedating
    - Stimulate imagination, emotion, and memories
    - Evoke images and reinforce positive thinking, and so much more!

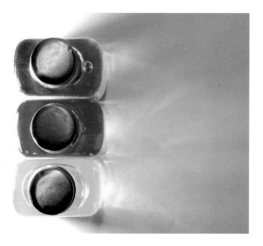

Essential oils are antimicrobial and antibacterial to reduce airborne toxins (great for personal protection on an airplane) and reduce EMFs (toxic emissions from electrical equipment leading to geopathic stress).

Look for colored bottles to protect your oils and to see how beautiful they look on your table or when sparkling with light.

Appreciate a few mental, physical, and spiritual benefits of the first essential oil for your collection,

Lavender:

On the Body:
- Rub it on your skin to promote healing a cut or to take the itch out of an insect bite.
- Rub it on your forehead to reduce a headache.
- Place a few drops in the tub to relax sore muscles.

With the Mind:
- Take a whiff to relax and reduce anxiety.

Through the Spirit:
- Place drops on your pillow to encourage sound sleep.

Fragrant History

Integrating the holistic benefits of essential oils dates back more than six thousand years. Ancient civilizations used oils for perfume, in religious ceremonies, for accelerating spiritual enlightenment, and in medicinal healing. Science validated that ancient Egyptians used oils in purification rituals and mummification. It is also said that oils helped maintain Cleopatra's exquisite beauty.

Did you know that lavender and other essential oils produce collagen and promote a more youthful appearance when applied directly on the skin? I use a drop of lavender mixed with skin-enriching avocado carrier oil on my face among other beautifying alchemy. (For more about youthful skin see ColorAlchemy Facials, p. 259.)

In China, the medicinal use of herbs and aromatics is recorded in medical texts dating back to 2000 BCE. Indian and Ayervedic healers have used oils for the past sixty centuries. Western Europe also has a tradition of using aromatic oils and herbs. With the Crusades, the aromatics of Arabia fragranced the West and rosewater became one of the most popular scents of the time.

During the plagues of the Middle Ages, the famous physician and prophet Nostradamus treated thousands of the afflicted with *rose pills* containing rose, aloe, cypress, iris, and cloves.

During the Renaissance, aromatics were used to combat epidemics because of their antimicrobial and antibacterial properties. Perfumery and distillation industries flourished throughout France, which to this day remains a prominent fragrance capital.

With the advent of the scientific revolution, synthetic duplicates helped launch the modern drug and perfume industry. But, to reap the benefit of liquid light, use real essential oils!

Fragrance and the Mind

Your *Mental Alchemy* is linked to fragrance. From the moment you wake up you are influenced by scents: soap and shampoo with your shower, coffee brewing in the kitchen, the ink in the morning paper, and that is just the beginning. Every smell creates a sense of familiarity and an association.

Try this, visualize:

- Smelling your soap   *Are you imagining your bathroom?*
- Taking a whiff of your coffee   *Can't you almost taste it?*
- Opening the newspaper   *What was the first thing you read?*

Scent triggers a mental movie, evoking memories and images of your surroundings. Fragrance is the catalyst that stimulates emotions and instinctive responses linked to situations surrounding the memory of the smell.

> **Exercise:**   Become aware of the link between smell and emotions:
>
> Take a white Color Breath to calm your spirit and relax your mind.
>
> Reflect on this question:
> What does your grandmother's house smell like?
>
> Did you *see or relive* an experience with your grandmother?
>
> **For every personal experience,
> each smell conjures up not only a situation
> but also an emotional response.**

The brain automatically recalls everything about a related experience when triggered by a fragrance or even thinking about the smell. Smell is a powerful tool to evoke complex visuals and feelings from the past. In fact, a memory associated with a scent is retained longer and undergoes less distortion than a visual memory. Emotions related to fragrance are subjective and based upon personal experience.

The summer between high school and college, I had the great fortune to work in Yellowstone National Park. Unlike the flat South Florida landscape I grew up with, I was taken by the park's beauty and wonder. The park is a thermal hot spot, well known for its geysers. I was enchanted by deep pools of water that swirled with the colors of the rainbow.

The wind would carry a sulphur-smelling mist and I delighted being caught in its subtle shower. (It is similar to the feeling of spraying yourself with an essential oil.) By the time it reached me, the drops were light, cool, and scented with the light fragrance of sulphur. I loved it!

Most people have a negative response to sulphur because it is linked to the smell of rotten eggs. Having never smelled a rotten egg previous to my Yellowstone experience, the smell had no negative association. Its fragrance linked wonderful memories of a magical place and a transitional time in my life.

Paying attention to the mental influence of fragrance allows you to take advantage of visual pictures painted in the mind. This shift immediately changes mood, brings memories into consciousness, and deepens awareness. Experienced in the present, smells provide reference to the past.

Combined with *Mental ColorAlchemy*, it is another key to unlocking and developing the unconscious mind. **In the same way that smell sends you into the past by triggering a memory, fragrance can be used to influence a present experience and to positively shape the future.**

The alchemy of fragrance is the ability to evoke beneficial physiological and sensory responses and code them into memory.

Even without conscious intention:

One fragrant experience can be so powerful as to lock in a memory. Whenever I smell an abundance of fresh flowers, I am transported to Giverny, Monet's home in France. I am walking though the garden and the same tears begin to flow.

Repeated smells are yours forever. By merely thinking of the smell of *Nana's house*, I am sitting at the kitchen table watching her create her culinary alchemy.

The more that fragrance is holistically anchored to a color and experience, the scent-to-brain and life-enhancing connection expands to be readily available in the present.

The good ColorAlchemy news is, you are already more than three-quarters of the way there! All you need to do is the following:

Train your consciousness with fragrant association. Create positive memories by coding the Daily Color and its life qualities with one of the related daily fragrances.

Coding Fragrance in ColorAlchemy

1. Review the daily essential oil options on each Daily Color header box.

2. Go to a store that sells essential oils.

With the popularity of aromatherapy, the beauty, cosmetic, and home-scent industries are marketing products with *natural plant essences*. Enjoy these products, but use only pure essential oils for aromatherapy and ColorAlchemy.

Essential oils come in small, dark-tinted glass bottles to protect their fragile qualities. They are usually available at health-food, new age, and natural cosmetic stores. To know whether you are buying a true essence, note that each oil is priced differently based upon its availability and ease of extraction.

For example: Orange oil is inexpensive because oranges are abundant and a relatively large quantity of oil can be extracted from its skin compared to the price of rose oil. To recover just a few precious drops of rose oil you need to distill thousands of petals.

3. Sniff out your favorites.

Your nose only lets you select several essential oils at a time. Your olfactory glands can only differentiate three or four fragrances at a time before it gets overloaded. It is said that sniffing coffee beans in-between selection helps clear your palette, but it doesn't work for me. Select a few, do your other shopping while you give your nose a 10 to 15 minute break, then select a few more.

Essential oils are more than worth the money. Take your time to build your collection. It is well worth the time and financial investment. The more you enjoy them, the more you want to learn, and the greater your mental, physical, and spiritual benefit.

4. Bless your oils in the same way that you would bless any of your materials.

Visualize the light infusing the plant with all its special energy in the first place. Then, with your energy and intention, code the bottle with its related color and its life-enhancing qualities.

5. Add fragrance to the ColorAlchemy you are already doing!

Spray the room, put a few drops on your body, and/or breathe into a scented hanky. Because the olfactory sensation of an image provides the quickest recall of an emotional response and meaning, visualize the life qualities of each color sailing on the scent as you create a fragrant, life-enhancing pause. Notice that it doesn't take any longer and that your experience deepens.

Working with Essential Oils

- **They are highly concentrated. Less is More.**
  Twelve drops per one-ounce bottle is a perfect 2% essential-oil solution.
- Most essential oils should not be used directly on the skin.
- Always test your reaction and wait a few minutes: oils migrate.

Even after working with oils for years, I still have trouble with *less is more.* To ease the congestion of a head cold through the skin and the fumes, I once put way too much eucalyptus in my bathwater. Talk about hot, hot, hot in the sensitive spots—ow!

I relearn this one several times a week. Instead of a cup-a-joe-jolt as an afternoon energizer (you do know that caffeine depletes inherent calcium that is not replaceable by supplements), I dot peppermint on my Third-Eye Chakra and temples. Usually I use too much and it migrates into my eyes.

Be careful! Always test respiratory and skin sensitivity by:

1. Breathing a drop on a hanky.

2. Diluting in a carrier oil that has little or no fragrance on its own to *morph* into the scent of the essential oil. My *heavy-hand* proportion is: 18 drops per ounce of jojoba, almond, grapeseed, or sesame oil. Sensitive-skinned people should start with 9 drops per ounce.

3. Try a small drop straight on a *tougher area of skin* before trying on delicate areas.

4. **Pregnant? Know your oils!** Oils such as clary sage, nutmeg, fennel, basil, and others can induce labor.

Learn much more about essential oils in my book

The Essence of Feng Shui:
Balancing Your Body, Home, and Life with Fragrance.

It is good scents to discover how to further integrate them with your chakras and how to use them in your Feng Shui.

Because fragrance is the catalyst of memory, conscious intention combined with repetitive fragrant experience deepens the energy and influences the memory.

Anchor scent-ual memory, so when you want to shift your *Mental ColorAlchemy* with intended purpose, just take a whiff of the coded fragrance. After coding a fragrance, benefit from essential oils throughout the day.

My Daily Aromas

Peppermint and Rosemary are *Blue, mental clarity and focus essential oils*. Because I train my mind (with a Blue Breathing ritual) before I turn the computer on to write, the air is filled with this blend, and automatically my brain kicks in. When I am blocked or mentally sluggish, a drop goes on my Third-Eye and Throat Chakras. (Be careful: mix with a carrier oil.) This blend is good for a late afternoon pick-me-up, too.

Sandalwood and Frankincense are *Violet, higher vibrational and spiritual oils*. Use sparingly, as these are expensive oils. Code your meditation time with these oils and the quiet is deepened for greater vision.

Orange and Clove are *Green, heart essential oils*. Set an automatic timer (bought at any hardware store) on a diffuser to fill the living room with *family harmony* at the time everyone comes home from work and/or school, especially on a Green day (to help code Thursday with its associated fragrance).

Tip: Notice that orange is a citrus and clove is a spice. After experimenting with basic oils, be creative with blending similar oils. My Green blend is three-quarters tangerine (citrus) and one-quarter cinnamon (spice). Experiment!

Rose, Geranium, and Ylang-Ylang are *Orange, intimacy oils*. Rose is expensive and I do not personally favor geranium, so I spray (18 drops of ylang-ylang in 1 ounce of rosewater with a light-mist bottle) on my bed linens when making the bed. Snuggle time. Yum!

Tip: Let your nose (and pocketbook) decide the essential oils that are right for you.

Here are a few more Activators I use in addition to my daily Aromatic Color Breathing:

Peppermint & Rosemary: Great to relieve a headache and jet lag.

Lavender: Helps with relaxation and getting to sleep.

Cypress & Juniper: Pulls toxins out of the body and reduces cellulite. Make a salt scrub for the bath. Scrub in a dry tub, fill tub, add bubbles, and indulge. (Shhh, secret!)

Amber & Sandalwood: Camouflages and reduces sweat at the gym. The warmer I get, the more essence is released:

Lavender & Chamomile: Cool, refresh, and hydrate the skin on-the-go or in the car. Make spray: 9 drops of each in 1 ounce of purified water. A light spray will not mess up your makeup.

Rosemary & Lavender: My husband uses them instead of cologne. He smells nice!

Are you understanding the most important fragrance tip?

You can't just read or think about fragrances, you have to experience them!

With use, their delicious, potent, and magical scents anchor in your subconscious and improve everything about YOU.

Incorporate *energy* with *Mental* or *Spiritual ColorAlchemy* reinforcement as you work with essential oils.

As I inhale this Green breath, I think about how to be kinder and more compassionate. As I smell ylang-ylang, I commit to being more tolerant and forgiving. With Healing Hands over my heart, I imagine it radiating Green light and love. I breath love, I AM LOVE, I share love.

Before journaling... *As I inhale this Blue breath, my focus and clarity to write is increased by the peppermint and rosemary that permeate my being. With Healing Hands, as I touch my Throat Chakra, it glows Blue light and its truthful inspiration radiates throughout my body.*

Discover, experience, indulge and enjoy essential oils:
- In your bath
- To enhance *Spiritual ColorAlchemy*: ritual, ceremony, and meditation
- Massage into your chakras
- Code into your hands before practicing Healing Hands.
- Massage oils into your Crown Chakra (As Above) and the bottom of your feet (So Below)
- Incorporate with your Liquid Light Meditation and add your ideas.

Practice two minutes of Color Breathing several times a day.

> Even if you are working with another color today, reinforce rainbow balance with a Green two-minute breath.
>
> With the inhalations, visualize a Green Ray filling every cell and fiber of your body. Release toxins with a Red Ray exhalation.
>
> **Take a stress-reducing, ColorAlchemy pause now and periodically during the day!**

Instead of being absorbed and toxified by thoughts of issues over which you have no control:

Practice *cultivating your Observer* and dialogue with yourself to live in the moment. Catch self-defeating or nonproductive thoughts and say to yourself, *Relax, capture a moment, and take a Color Breath. There is nothing I can do about this at the moment. I can make a conscious choice to either suffer by allowing those negative thoughts to control me, or I can choose to control my thoughts and think positively.*

I have the choice of changing toxic thoughts into positive ones and,
I AM doing it now!

Remember, journaling cuts through blockages and helps you consider alternative solutions you may have never thought of before. The process allows you to see the true side of your inner self.

If you are resistant or turned off by journaling and/or you want to explore more ways to *get to the heart of the matter,* how about two easy and fun ColorAlchemy Activators? Let's make collages and draw mandalas to cut through blockages and stimulate personal revelation.

Commit to taking a deep and invigorating Blue breath
before getting out of bed tomorrow.

wear and/or incorporate BLUE when you need to:

Balance Orange energy
Increase logic and be able to analyze conditions
Mellow frenetic energy
Trust yourself and your abilities
Communicate with others in a clear and understandable manner
Express that you are wise and serene
Have control over yourself or a situation

Energy & Antioxidant Foods:

blueberries, bramble berries, blackberries, blue corn, figs, grapes, grape juice, plums, pomegranates, prunes, currents, eggplant, purple onion, beets

Blue foods help concentration and relaxation and aid in reducing blood pressure.

Health Benefits:

Helps prevent heart disease (by inhibiting blood clots), protects brain cells against oxidative stress (a tissue-damaging process associated with Alzheimer's and neurodegeneration, keeps carcinogens from binding with DNA

Healing Stones: Aquamarine, turquoise, sapphire, lapis lazuli, sodalite, blue agate

Essential Oils: Lemon, peppermint, myrtle, pine

<<<<<<< Happy Blue-Friday >>>>>>

Today is a great day to spritz peppermint and/or rosemary essential oils and practice journaling or analyzing your doodles. You have clarity and focus in your energy field to discover something new about yourself. It is a good day to reflect on personal questions or professional problems that have been challenging. Use Blue to find answers and solutions.

Thoughtful & Holistic: Decisiveness • Clarity • Communication   185

Making ColorAlchemy Collages

Making a collage is so easy and, similar to journaling, it provides quiet *Mental ColorAlchemy* for inner thought and insight. All you need to do is:

- Go through old magazines, tear out images that *say something* to you and put them in a folder, and recycle the magazine. Make sure the color of the folder supports the vision of your collage, too. You may even want to ask friends to save their old magazines for you but go through them quickly. It is bad Feng Shui to clutter stacks of magazines.

- When you have a collection of cutouts, buy a piece of (whatever-support-color) poster board and a glue stick (which sticks more smoothly than liquid glue or paste).

- In a fragranced and quiet location with a big table, bless your materials.

- With scissors, smooth the tears by cutting the images into a design that enhances the shape of the image. As you cut each image, with conscious intention, ask yourself: *Why do I like this picture? Does the image suggest a vision that I would like to incorporate into my life? What does the picture say to me?* If it doesn't have meaning, throw it out and move on to the next cutout.

- With all the graphics spread out visually in front of you, select the image that speaks the loudest and paste it in the center. Dialogue with your Observer, *Why does it speak the loudest? Why am I drawn to this picture? Does it say the same thing as when I originally tore it out? Is this what I need? Is this what I long for? (You do know there is a huge difference between a want and a need, yes?) If my life had this would I really be satisfied? What would really satisfy me?* Keep dialoguing. *How does the image inspire me? How can I use the graphic to help clarify something? What else does my Observer need to ask?*

- Repeat this process, taking your time with each picture. Overlap them and position them as guided by your creative intuition.

- Before congratulating yourself on a job well done, do you see a theme? Is there a dominate color? What do(es) the color(s) say about the story of your collage? This is the best part...
  Discover things about yourself that you didn't know.

- Place your collage in a location that you see regularly.

I keep mine next to my morning coffee. Every time I see it, I am reminded to take a pausing breath in the Daily Color and consciously try to see what I have never seen before in my collage. You'll be amazed by the new things you learn about yourself.

I suggest you make a new collage every six months because your life is always changing and improving with ColorAlchemy. With periodic collage making, you can make them with purpose: **Fill your collage with dreams or to inspire specific desires.**

**It is up to you to create your desires.
Express Yourself to Manifest Your Dreams!**

Journal 'em, Glue 'em, and/or mandala 'em!

Even if you are working with another color today,
reinforce rainbow balance with a Blue two-minute breath.

With the inhalations, visualize a Blue Ray filling
every cell and fiber of your body.
Release toxins with an Orange Ray exhalation.

**Take a stress-reducing, ColorAlchemy pause now,
and periodically during the day!**

Drawing ColorAlchemy Mandalas

Another alternative to unlock hidden secrets and reveal insights about yourself is to draw mandalas. You have probably drawn mandalas before, but thought they were doodles. Mandalas are fancy doodles to explore the inner workings of your mind. If you started doodling with awareness and intention (the same way we talked about them on p. 97), you were drawing mandalas, as did the ancients with the mind-to-hand-to-mind connection.

Historical and Sacred Significance of Mandalas

People have drawn mandalas since the beginning of time as a method of communicating with each other and their inner spirit. "The mandala is a potent tool for a mystical, visual process of reintegration and healing. It helps us gain access to enigmatic states of consciousness in which our thoughts can be realigned and our creative imaginations infused with deep spiritual purpose: to reflect the harmonics of the divine and the beauty of the whole universal connections." [27]

The shape of the chakras are also in the sacred, symbolical shape of the universe: the circle. A mandala is a life circle; literally translated from Sanskrit, it means "circle" or "center." The center is symbolic of the eternal potential.

Life circles are tools of divination and geomancy used in the search for higher meaning and personal growth through connection to the spiritual whole. Often there are circles within circles that are symbolic of deep interconnection. Life circles are the tangible manifestation of the natural cycles represented by sacred symbolism. They are universal models in geometric proportion and progression.

Nearly all cave art drawn by ancient indigenous people includes drawings reminiscent of a spiraling galaxy, the interior of a nautilus shell, or DNA. All spirals represent the sacred geometry of the mathematical progression of phi. Spirals are symbolic of the cycles of life, man's desire to ascend to the heavens, and to be *in the light: to join God.*

Mandalas are used to bring man closer to God and to discover the inner workings of the self. Most large-scale mandalas, such as Stonehenge, the Greek Oracles, the floor of Chartres Cathedral, and all stone medicine wheels, are circles that were created for group ritual and personal ceremonies. These mandalas also marked terrestrial and astrological time. Smaller mandalas include the Aztec sunstone, the Mayan calender, Native American sand paintings, and Tibetan wheels of life.

The famous mandala by Leonardo da Vinci geometrically represents the mathematical symmetry of the Golden Section (phi) between the circle, the square, and human proportion.

This sacred mandala expresses man's physical connection to the Divine: Earth Mother and God. The circumference of the circle is mathematically the same as the perimeter of the square, thereby *squaring the circle*. The humanistic factor of this sacred geometry defines the human body as the sacred vessel that connects earth (square) and heavens (circle).

After Leonardo, our friend Sir Isaac Newton first developed the colors of visible light in the form of a mandala showing the colors correlated with musical notes and symbols for the known bodies within the solar system. Learn how color relates to music (p. 212) and astrology (p. 228), too.

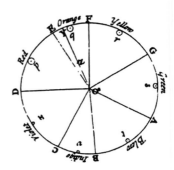

Carl Gustav Jung, the grandfather of modern psychotherapy, described the nucleus of the mandala as the unification of the universal soul or the collective unconscious. With his patients, he found that drawing mandalas or gazing at them during an open-eyed meditation was a valuable tool for self-discovery.

What do mandalas have in common in addition to their universal artistry, sacred geometry, and need for spiritual connection? They all converge in the middle. The center is defined as the bindu in Hindu spiritual art or, in Jungian language, the nucleolus of the soul. This sacred center is the space of truth. It is the light within.

Are you ready to get started with your blessed colored construction paper and colored pencils or markers?

Drawing Your Inner Light

1. Prepare a sacred space and find a quiet time.
    Set the mood with appropriate ColorAlchemy Activators:

    • Appropriate essential oils and music
    • Surround yourself with the right color(s), either alone or in combination:

    • Wear the Daily Color
    • Wear or surround yourself with any yin color (Blue, Indigo, or Violet)
    • Wear color(s) that intuitively feel right for what is on your mind.

2. Place your paper, pencils (and sharpener), markers, and whatever else you think you'll want or need in front of you. A glass of water? A sweater?

3. Get comfortable with a few white Color Breaths to absorb the energies of all colors to support your creation.

4. Commit to staying in this meditative state and holding conscious intention.

5. Intuitively:
    · Select a piece of colored construction paper.
    · Take a few more Color Breaths in needed color(s).
    · Release all fears about artistic abilities (remember, it's a doodle!)
    · Know that during this time, you are connected to the inner light within yourself, the Light of God, and are directed by all that is in your highest interest.

6. Draw your bindu in the center of your paper. Visualize the same dot in your Third-Eye Chakra for the vision to draw your mandala.

7. When comfortable, radiate your energy by drawing the shapes and patterns that come from within. Change colored pencils as often as you like.
    Turn the paper, move your body as you draw, sing, play, and have fun.

If you get stuck:
- Always come back to Color Breathing. Trust that you are the light in the center dot of your paper and try again when you are ready.
- Select another colored pencil. Draw with your eyes closed. Start drawing spirals.
- Feel like a child working with crayons. You are safe.

Celebrate the freedom.
Be free to express your inner YOU.

8.   Complete and review the image that you created.
               Reflect on what it says to you and what you were thinking during the process.

9.   Turn the paper over, date your creation, and journal your experience.

Dialogue with your Observer: *What did you learn? Was the experience easy or were there challenges? What blocked you? What did you say to release the blockages? How are those blockages influencing other aspects of your life? What colors were you drawn to? Why? Are they your favorites? Do you have too much of that color in your personality? Do you long for more attributes not included in your personality? Why? How can you incorporate more of that related color for better balance? Consider whether more complementary color be included in your life. What were the shapes of your lines? Were they smooth and fluid, or were they angled and choppy? What does the line quality say about you?* **What other thoughts, impressions, or questions does your Observer want you to answer?**

Remember, when you journal on the back of each mandala, you'll track your life progress along with having a visual record of how your life is improving. Drawing mandalas takes no longer than journaling. If time is short, just draw and reflect on the experience later. Visualize the image when doing other tasks and insights will flow.

10. As with all good ColorAlchemy habits, say a prayer of appreciation and thanks for receiving the insight or guidance.

We (you and I) have come such a long way with our ColorAlchemy, and it is becoming a part of life. We are changing negative to positive in so many ways and sourcing not only why we may be unhappy, but also outlining steps to take positive action.

This lovely stained-glass mandala is a perfect segue into Saturday. Sunlight passed through colored glass has been used for Color Toning for centuries.

Commit to taking a deep and invigorating Indigo breath before getting out of bed tomorrow.

Wear and/or incorporate INDIGO when you need to:
Balance Orange energy
Tap into your intuition or subconscious knowing
Calm a scattered mind
Have others know that you are sensitive and
receptive beyond the obvious

Energy & Antioxidant Foods:
blueberries, bramble berries, blackberries, blue corn, figs, grapes, grape juice, plums, pomegranates, prunes, currants, eggplant, purple onion, beets

Indigo foods promote stability in one's life and help grow new tissues.

Health Benefits:
Helps prevent heart disease by inhibiting blood clots, protects brain cells against oxidative stress (tissue-damaging process associated with Alzheimer's and neurodegeneration, keeps carcinogens from binding with DNA

Healing Stones: Lapis lazuli, sodalite, indigo sapphire, opal, tanzanite, dark-blue agate

Essential Oils: Lemon, juniper, peppermint, eucalyptus, rosemary, basil, myrrh, patchouli

≪≪≪≪≪ **Happy Indigo-Saturday** ≫≫≫≫≫

Do-It-Yourself Color Therapy

You have practiced ColorAlchemy through absorbing color vibration from clothes, what you eat and drink, your surroundings, through the power of the mind, and your breath. Now, with color filters, balance your chakras and enhance life qualities with the source of color: the light.

Intuition & Vision: Psychic Powers • Focus • Seeing Beyond

History

As you know, color and vibrational healing were practiced by Pythagoras and many other masterful healers from the ancient world. Modern color therapy evolved in the late 1800s with India-born Dinshah P. Ghadiali, a doctor, scientist, researcher, and inventor. After reading books on color theory, Dinshah experimented with color healing when traditional medicine failed a friend who was very sick. His friend's health dramatically improved with Dinshah's *colorized-milk elixirs*, which began his life work in what he called spectro-chrome healing. Dinshah dedicated the rest of his life to all color-healing techniques, specifically toning.

Color Toning

Dinshah described toning as projecting colored light onto the body in precise locations for healing specific ailments. There are many different ways to practice color toning. While colored lightbulbs are great for enhancing the ColorAlchemy of a room, it is best to use Dinshah's easy-to-apply formulas. Used in color healing for more than fifty years, the formulas use Roscolux color film, which is available at any theatrical supply store. This film comes in 20 x 24 sheets and is easily cut for numerous applications.

Sunlight: Similar to the effect of a stained-glass window, place the entire sheet in the window. The problem with this method is that the sun needs to be bright enough to shine through the filter to cast significant color on the body.

Flashlight: Get a flashlight with a removable top. Cut the film to size so it fits in front of the glass (in front of the bulb) toward the outside for spot healing.

Make a color-therapy lamp: This graphic, courtesy of Charles Klotsche in his book *Color Medicine,* is an excellent guide for making a color lamp.

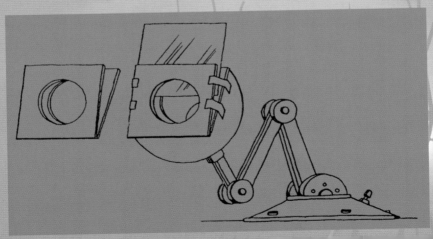

Use a 60- or 100-watt daylight or, better yet, full-spectrum bulb in your lamp. Always check and use the recommended wattage for your fixture; using a higher wattage may short-out the lamp or cause a fire.

Slide projector: Carefully open up an empty-slide casing, and insert the appropriate colored film to fit.

Per Dinshah, in *Let There Be Light*, these are the formulas for spectral and soul-spirit colors.

Matching Colors to Symptoms

Are you an expert by now?
May I assume you know the general rules?

As with all ColorAlchemy,

Balance your rainbow.

Roscolux Filter Numbers

Color	Filter #
Red	818, 828
Orange	809, 828
Yellow	809
Green	871
Blue	859, 866
Indigo	828, 859, 866
Violet	832, 859, 866
	Soul-Spirit Colors
Turquoise	861, 871
Lime	810, 871
Scarlet	810, 818, 861
Magenta	818, 828, 866

Enhance with supportive color(s) and reduce with complementary color(s).

- Determine the life qualities you'd like to enhance.
- Reduce chakra weakness
- Reduce physical pain with the chakra color closest to the location of your symptom.
- Trust your intuition and go shine the light!
- For healing specific aliments, please refer to
  - Specific human disorders in *Let There Be Light*.
  - Diagnosed disorders in *Color Medicine*.

Color Toning

Determine the color(s) you are going to use for your tonation based upon the ailment needing a remedy.

- When using several colors in one session, consider the logic of yin (Blue, Indigo, and Violet) and yang (Red, Orange, and Yellow) colors.

You'll immediately understand why it is best not to mix yin and yang colors in one session. Think about the energy basics to understand the complementary concept:

- Energies that are too active (yang), need balancing with quiet (yin) colors to calm and soothe. Adding more yang may add fuel to the fire.

- Energies that are too dreamy-yin, need balancing with active-yang colors to stimulate and motivate. Adding more yin may space you out.

- Green, as you know, is the Rainbow Bridge and is good to combine with either a yin or a yang treatment. I have found it to be an excellent color to start and end each session.

Think about the *As Above, So Below* meditation as a template for yin or yang tonation.

With yin energies and conscious intention, shine Green light on the heart and work your way up the Blue, Indigo, Violet spectrum as you move up the body. In the reverse order, complete the session at the Heart Chakra with Green.

Conversely, when yang energies are used, shine Green light on the heart and work your way down the Yellow, Orange, Red spectrum as you move down the body. In the reverse order, complete the session back with Green at the love center.

- Set the *stage* (you are using theatrical film!):
  - To maximize light penetration:
    - Colored light needs to be absorbed through your bare skin, so choose a private and temperature-controlled room.
    - Select the darkest room possible to enable color absorption at the fullest possible concentration.
  - Prepare healing music and diffuse your favorite essential oils.
  - Plan an undisturbed, relaxed hour of bathing in healing, colored light.

- Don't eat, shower, or do anything particularly physical or mentally taxing for at least one hour before or after toning to allow your aura to be receptive and return to its customary state.

- Position yourself in a chair or bed about a yard/meter from the light source. (If using a flashlight, follow the instructions but use for spot treatments.)

Dinshah suggests that lying down is best with your head facing north. From my experience, all healing is best received facing your second-best, Feng Shui direction, known as your *Doctor from Heaven*. Please help yourself to your Best Directions on JamiLin.com.

- Treat the area with Healing Hands and appropriate essential oils.

- Without external distractions, get into a relaxed frame of mind.

- As the light shines on your body, maximize the effect by simultaneously practicing Color Breathing and visualizing the colored rays being absorbed into your body.
  - Enjoy your hour of undisturbed, healing ColorAlchemy.
  - Be conscious of your experience.

It is better to undertreat rather than to overreact.

Depending on your physical sensitivities and the color that you are using, too much color may be too stimulating to a body area that may have weakness. For example, too much Red may aggravate a heart condition.

Pay attention to the rhythm of your breathing. If it remains constant, you are fine, but just like a Goldilocks prognosis, too slow or too fast, is not right.

When in doubt, stop or use less intensity and/or reduce time.

Use good judgement!

- After completion:
  - Maintain your special radiance. Stay relaxed and calm.
    It takes several hours for the light to be absorbed throughout the body.
  - Always drink plenty of purified water to flush out toxins that were shaken and stirred during the treatment. *Enjoy an after-session ColorAlchemy elixir.*

Even if you are working with another color today,
reinforce rainbow balance with an Indigo two-minute breath.

With the inhalations, visualize an Indigo Ray filling
every cell and fiber of your body.
Release toxins with an Orange Ray exhalation.

**Take a stress-reducing, ColorAlchemy pause now,
and periodically during the day!**

---

*Commit to taking a deep and invigorating Violet breath
before getting out of bed tomorrow morning.*

Feeling Color Through Skin

Spending time in nature adds enhanced nurturing and energizing capacity. This sensitivity heightens absorption of nature's color through your eyes and skin. With *Mental ColorAlchemy*, the more you practice duplicating color differences in nature and feeling colors through the skin, the more you will automatically absorb the highest benefit from the colors around you.

Collect colored construction paper or different colored fabrics in each of the seven colors. Bless them (p. 101)

1.   Select a time and place where you will not be disturbed for about 10 minutes. Set the stage with your favorite meditative ColorAlchemy Activators.

2.   Position the colored paper or fabric in front of you in spectral order. Sit in a comfortable position (on the floor or in a chair) with your back straight. Make sure that your paper or fabric is close enough to easily pick them up.

3.   With conscious intention, take a few deep breaths all the way into the belly to relax and calm your spirit. Breathe white light to not distract yourself from feeling individual colors. Fill yourself with confidence and awareness. Dismiss all negative thoughts from your mind and release any tension in your body.

4.   Hold the Red paper or fabric in your hands and visualize absorbing the color through your palms. Feel Red. *Visualize Vitality, Courage, Security, and Strength* pulsing through your body.

Journal your feelings, thoughts, and impressions.

Upon completion, thank Red and clear the energy by replacing it with a breath of while light.

5.   Pick up the Orange sample. Feel Orange. Visualize *Happiness, Desire, Creativity, Emotion, Pleasure, and Intimacy* vibrating throughout your body

6.   Practice with the remaining colors in progression.

The more you are able to feel color, the more you subconsciously benefit when you need a certain color. Once you get better at feeling color through your skin, randomly select a color and test your abilities. You will be able to feel each color and *guess* correctly.

Practice feeling color though skin as you dress in the Daily Color too.

Wear and/or incorporate VIOLET when you need to:
Balance Yellow energy
Connect to your highest mind: your inner self and God
Vibrate at the highest spiritual frequency
Wrap your body in the arms of universal intelligence

Energy & Antioxidant Foods: all "nectar of the gods"
red wine, blueberries, bramble berries, blackberries,
blue corn, figs, grapes, grape juice, plums, pomegranates,
prunes, currants, eggplant, purple onion, beets

Violet foods influence calm, balanced the mind, and initiate spiritual awareness.

Health Benefits:
Helps prevent heart disease by inhibiting blood clots,
protects brain cells against oxidative stress (tissue-damaging
process associated with Alzheimer's and neurodegeneration,
keeps carcinogens from binding to DNA

Healing Stones: Amethyst, quartz crystal, alexandrite,
opal, sapphire, tanzanite

Essential Oils: Roman chamomile, frankincense, jasmine,
sandalwood, clary sage, lotus, myrrh

<<<<<<< Happy Violet-Sunday >>>>>>

I saved my favorite Activators for last! Enjoy, ENJOY!!!!

ColorAlchemy Elixirs

They say that we all need to drink eight glasses of water a day to stay healthy. That's tough for me, but to make getting close easier I drink Red elixirs on Monday, Orange elixirs on Tuesday, Yellow elixirs on Wednesday, and so on.

Spiritual Divinity: Peace • Bliss • Inner Knowing • Inspiration   197

In ColorAlchemy, elixirs are water that you energetically charge with conscious intention with a specific color. There are many methods to beneficially charge the frequency of water. It makes the water that we are supposed to drink more enjoyable and alchemically beneficial.

While I combine all of the following methods in creating my ColorAlchemy elixirs, select one or combine any of these easy methods.

Creating Elixirs

Starting with purified water. Drink:

Solarized Energy: Remember when I suggested to keep your eyes open for ColorAlchemy accessories? If you found a set of drinking glasses or water bottles in the spectral colors, now is the time they'll come in handy. All you need to do is fill the glass or bottle with purified water and let the sunlight pass though it for three hours for a complete charge. If you do not have colored glasses or bottles, place a colored piece of theatrical film (the same kind used to make the healing-color lamp) in between the sun and a clear glass or bottle.

As you place the bottle to capture the light, speak your energetic intention. *May the pure energy of God infuse my (what color) elixir with all the nurturing energy that I need today.*

Stone Energy: Do you recall that I suggested collecting a set of small gemstones in the spectral colors? Place a small Daily Stone in purified water so you'll drink the stone's energetic properties. Charge the elixir with your personal energy and speak your conscious intention while adding the stone to the bottle.

Word Energy: Japanese researcher and humanitarian Masaru Emoto made an amazing discovery by charging water with human thought and freezing it. Photographs of the ice crystals charged with loving thoughts were in beautiful *snowflake symmetry* while ugly words produced unpleasing, even scary images.

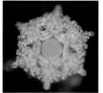

Love & gratitude

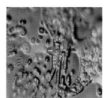

You make me sick

Dr. Emoto (who shared his photos) suggests that positive words spoken to or written on bottles of water create the same influence.

All you need to do is write the words on the bottle that you would like to be absorbed. I know you've figured it out. On your Red bottle, write the words: *Vitality, Courage, Self-Confidence, Strength, Stamina.* On your Orange bottle: *Happiness, Desire, Creativity, Emotion, Pleasure, Intimacy,* and so on.

Just imagine how our thoughts influence the sixty-five percent volume of water in our bodies.

What is the consciousness of the water in your body?
What happens to your water when watching the news?
Imagine your water during a romantic movie.

Holy Energy:

Add a few drops of holy water to your elixir. You can get holy water in several methods:

- You can get holy water from a sacred site. I add a few drops of water that I personally collected from the Ganges in India. *Did you know adding a few drops of any holy water to a larger container of water makes the entire contents holy?*

- You can get holy water from someone who blessed the water.

You are holy! Create your own holy water:

1. Find a special container and determine whether you'd like:

Yang holy water: Supports active endeavors, such as business ventures

Plan on creating your holy water in the sunlight between 11:00 a.m. and 1:00 p.m. Full-moon energy is best.

Yin holy water: Supports quiet influences, such as relationships and health

Plan on creating your holy water in the moonlight between 11:00 p.m. and 1:00 a.m.

Even though you can't see the moon, new-moon energy is the best time of the month.

2. Select a quiet time and a place when you won't be distracted.

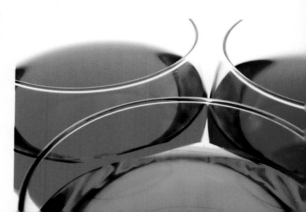

3. Create a sacred *blessing mood*.

4. Based upon what kind of holy water you want to create, go outside in the sun or moonlight.

With hands raised to the sun or moon, with conscious intention, visualize holding some of the light in your hands and say, *I hold the sacred power of light in my han*ds.

Imagine the light being absorbed throughout your body, collecting and gaining energy from all your chakras. With special focus on the Heart Chakra, add your love to the universal love of the light.

Complete your visualization and, with Healing Hands, hold the bottle to infuse your container of water with Holy Light and say, **With the power of universal love and all the love that I AM, this water is now holy.**

You created holy water!

My Elixirs

- Once a month, buy seven plastic bottles of purified drinking water. I recommend that you periodically purchase new bottles to make sure you are drinking from a healthy bottle: plastic absorbs toxins and bacteria.

- Color the tops of the bottles with a permanent marker in each of the spectral colors to easily identify the energy of each bottle.

- Matching the color of the tops, with conscious intention:
- Use Word Energy: Write the Daily Color attributes with the appropriate color marker on each bottle.
- Drop the appropriate gemstone into each bottle.

- Fill the bottles with holy water.

- Every morning, on a sunny window sill, place your Daily Elixir in the sun behind the appropriate-colored filter or in a transparent colored glass).

If you are not going to drink your elixir right away, place it in a dark and cool place. Your altar is a great place.

- Drink your elixirs all day long.

- Create a momentary pause when drinking.
    - Absorb the power of its sacred energy.
    - Feel and visualize the Daily Color inside your body as you drink.

I carry an elixir with me all the time, just like water. I even take my vitamins with the Daily Color elixir. I take elixirs to the gym, where I drink the most—haven't swallowed a rock yet! If people ask, tell them about the power of elixirs. **You'll share a gift.**

Even if you are working with another color today,
reinforce rainbow balance with a Violet two-minute breath.

With each inhalations, visualize a Violet Ray filling
every cell and fiber of your body.
Release toxins with a Yellow Ray exhalation.

**Take a stress-reducing, ColorAlchemy pause now,
and periodically during the day!**

Bathe ColorAlchemy! My favorite ColorAlchemy Activator!

Is a luxurious bath a necessity or an indulgence? It is a necessary indulgence! I am a professional bather! I encourage, if not insist, that you practice this ColorAlchemy Activator—Often!

Whether your favorite quiet place is at the ocean's shore, on a mountaintop, or nestled in the woods, your tub is as special and accessible at any time. It is the most sacred place in your home, and its healing energy is equal to any quiet place in nature. You don't need to pre-plan, make special arrangements, or delegate a lot of time—just set aside twenty minutes of time for just you.

In the tub you are alone, with your thoughts, reminiscent of, and comforted by, the warm womb from which you came.

As mentioned previously, the bath is my favorite place to journal and draw mandalas. It is the time and place where my overactive Blue mind is most relaxed and receptive. I do my best Orange creative work in the tub because my mind stops thinking about the to-do's and floats into a sea of creativity. *Did you catch the alchemical tip?* Isn't it interesting that my two least favorite colors are complementary to each other? *What "thoughtful complements" will support your ColorAlchemy?*

There are so many colorful options to expand the "event" of tub time. Surround yourself with color according to which color qualities you need or the colors that you want to be nurtured by:

1.   Surround yourself with colored candles.

2.   Fill the room with colored light: with lightbulbs, a torchere and filters, or a homemade, color-filter lamp.

3.   Lay a colored towel on your chest in the tub (very comforting).

4.   Place colored stones in the water: it's a mega elixir!

     Do you remember when I suggested collecting a set of larger stones in the spectral colors? Remember, crystals are energy transmitters and water amplifies the charge. This is a great way to absorb colored-gem energy through your entire body.

5.   Include essential oils that are coded with colorful attributes. The medicinal and nurturing properties are absorbed through your skin and your nose in the rising steam. Fantastic!

6.   Absorb color vibration through every inch of your body with opaque-colored water through *ColourEnergy.com*. Awesome!

Enjoy your energetic transformation. Whatever tensions you have, as the drain opens, paraphrase Rinpoche's wonderful words:

All stress, nonsupportive energies, and blockages are being cleansed and washed away!

You are ready for *Colors of Your Spirit*!

Commit to taking a deep and invigorating Red breath before getting out of bed tomorrow morning.

Color Alchemy

7 Days 7 Colors
7 Triumphs

Colors of Your
Spirit

Vitality Creativity Power
Love Focus Intuition Bliss

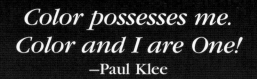

Color possesses me.
Color and I are One!
—Paul Klee

My Affirmation: _____

_____

Red Personality: The Right *To Have*

Balanced: Connected to nature and trust in the natural laws, balanced with the cycles of life, strong, brave, energetic, courageous, confident, humanistic, strong-willed, spontaneous, honest, and extroverted

Out of Balance: Cowardly, angry, irritable

Greatest Needs
• Physical contact
• Strong physical activity

Greatest Challenges
• Planning before action
• Being susceptible to feelings
• Speaking before thinking

Red's Desire: Enjoying the physical sensations: sight, touch, smell, taste, and hearing. Physical stamina and a strong, well-toned body.

Core Issues: Disappointment, rejection, obstacles that have not been conquered, tired and lack of vitality, ambitions that have not been satisfied, thoughts of success are translated into financial value: success is success in life, not a bank account, fear of financial security, feeling inadequate

Musical Note & Toning Mantra: C and Lam

Planet & Zodiac: Mars & Aries

All the ColorAlchemy you and I have experienced for the past twenty-one days is a reflection of the spirit. Your spirit is the essence of your core being and is holistically connected to your body and mind.

Applying any colorful application with conscious intention is en-Light-en-ing to your spirit. You've been absorbing the spiritual, life qualities of color by pausing your day with a Color Breath or taking a fast glance at your Daily Color shirt, spritzing with essential oils, drinking color elixirs, and indulging in color baths. These easy, quick, and feel-good enhancers alchemically transform your mind, body, and spirit being.

For the past three weeks, you have absorbed the colors of the rainbow to:

- Identify life weaknesses through spiritual, emotional, and physical habits
- Determine and apply color to support life improvement
- Receive and balance all life qualities
- Align with the light.

Are your achieving your goals?

Do you remember the formula for happiness?

Happiness = Mind + Body + Spirit

Receive the happiness energy through your:

Body: Red & Orange
Mind: Yellow, Green & Blue
Spirit: Indigo & Violet

Release the life-sabotaging energies that do not serve you. Manifest your desires through the life qualities of the spectral colors: the colors of God.

Combine and balance all the colors of your life for the totality of who you are:

A happy and balanced person!

Remember, the mind is the common denominator that connects the beneficial influence of color to the physical, emotional and spiritual parts of ourselves.

Happiness is an *inside job*: *Mental ColorAlchemy*!

You know the secret of happiness and how to create it. You also know that Monday is the best day to start projects and renew commitments, so:

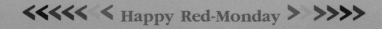

<<<<< < Happy Red-Monday > >>>>

Recommit to your *Mental ColorAlchemy*. Solidify the transformational ColorAlchemy habit you have created over the past twenty-one days. During the Colors of Your Spirit week, have fun, reevaluate the ongoing process of releasing core issues, convert habits into rituals, deepen connection to spirit, and create greater personal happiness.

As you put on a Red accessory or take a Red breath, speak a Red affirmation to further absorb and imprint today's attributes. Even though you'll write your ColorAlchemy Affirmations (in Sunday's lesson), I've included a suggestion for each Daily Color for this week to get you started:

Take a deep and nourishing Red Breath.
Place Red Healing Hands on your Root Chakra.
Feel the Red Ray filling your body.

Speak your Red ColorAlchemy Affirmation out loud.

I love, honor, and nurture my physical body. I appreciate all aspects of myself, and I am a beautiful being. I live in this physical world with my strong energy. I easily manifest everything I need into reality.

I LOVE my body. I have all that I need. I AM stable and secure. Red and my Root Chakra are automatically available for stability, power, and energy. I AM balanced with my physical self.

Amen

Having said your Red Affirmation with conviction, lets express the perfect Red Color of the Spirit and continue to follow the energetic progression of each day.

Dance Your Spirit

Dance (movement) and song (music) are expressions of the soul that connect your physical being to your spirit. They are the perfect spiritual ColorAlchemy expressions for today and Tuesday.

I just love when a toddler who can barely walk hangs onto the coffee table and with complete joy, begins to rock and roll. I grew up dancing. I *had to* go to ballet in elementary school because my mother was, and still is, a klutz. Even as a child, I knew it was too rigid for my style. In high school, I was taught by one of Martha Graham's students and had an opportunity to choreograph and perform. Throughout college, I practiced and taught karate as well as took belly dancing and yoga. These days, I am a hardcore, step-aerobics fan and love my hip-hop and salsa classes: the hour is so much fun, I happily forget that I am getting great (and essential) exercise.

Chakra Dance

Even though I try to get out of my head at the gym, often thoughts are on how to express some facet of ColorAlchemy. With a big stompy, primitive and tribal movement, I had an exciting revelation. I was waking up and tuning into my Root Chakra. Thoughts continued about other movements:

Tribal, Drums, Heart Beat, Power Dance
Salsa, Belly Dance, *Playful-Pole Dance*, Sensual, Hip Gyration, *Entice Me*
Straight, Head Up & Tall, Ballet Style, *Power-walk Dance*
Fluid *Ballroom*, Modern, Waltz
Head Music, Stretching, Free-flow, *Steven Halpern & New Age*
Yoga, Moving Meditations, Tai Chi, *Steven Halpern & New Age*
Om Vibration, Sea Shell Sound, Chi Gong, Harmonize Breath

Heat up your aura, get rid of the overindulged meal you had the night before, and/or use Chakra Dance for exercise. Have fun. *Dance like nobody's watching*, as Kathy Mattea says in her great country song.

Just as you don't have to be an artist to draw your mandala, you don't have to be a dancer to shake a tail feather. Just translate the attitudes for what each energy feels like.

There are two ways to dance your ColorAlchemy.

Dance Chakra Sequence: Start with *tribal-Red* Root Chakra movement and progressively evolve your movement into *sensual-Orange* Sacral Chakra gyrations, and so on.

Dance a Color or Chakra: By now you know which color(s) support the attribute that you'd like to improve. Put on the music that supports the color/chakra and start moving. Try rock, hip hop, or drumming for the Root Chakra, salsa for the Sacral Chakra, and so on. (Music is not my expertise so you are on your own with this one. Use your intuition and feel the music and the movement. I've recorded my audio expression of what the movements feel like on

JamiLin.com/images/stories/color_alchemy/dance.mp3

With either option, these are moving meditations so empty your mind and feel the energy vibrating in your body. Visualize the appropriate color(s) pulsing through your veins and that your body is an illuminious glow. Just put on the appropriate music, don't think, and just move!

Even though no one will ever see you, take comfort in knowing you could never possibly look like Elaine on *Seinfeld*. **Dance with reckless abandon!**

Moving Meditations

Moving Rainbow Meditation

This is a beautiful, Chinese chi gong (or subtle breathing movement) exercise that is designed to reduce backaches and strengthen the back, support kidney function and core balance, tone the arms, and, spoken in perfect Chinese, *take off fat from the belly.*

Position the heel of one foot against the instep of the other, creating a T-shape. It doesn't matter which foot you use for either position—you'll perform this exercise on both sides.

Move the front foot (leg of the T) forward while maintaining balance and the T-shape. As balance improves, progressively widen your stance.

With the back arm (on the same side of your body as the top of the T) comfortably at your side, place your front arm (on the same side as the leg of the T) on your Heart Chakra.

Raise an extended front arm, and lift it straight up to heaven. Slowly lower the arm, in an arc, creating a rainbow shape terminating at the earth's horizon (in line with your shoulder). Return to neutral with your hand on your heart with Healing Hands and repeat the move eight times. When complete, reposition your stance with the other foot in front and repeat the movement nine times on the other side.

With your arm at the zenith, visualize Violet and absorb its life qualities. As your arm slowly moves through each point of the sky downward, toward the horizon, visualize *As Above, So Below* through the spectral sequence, terminating with Red.

Practice Color Breathing at the same time. Slowly inhale as your arm extends upward to heaven. Exhale as your arm arcs down to earth and returns to nurture your heart.

Salute the Sun

This awakening-the-body-and-spirit exercise is also a chi gong. It reminds me of a simplified, and much easier version, of the sun salutation in yoga. Its purpose, as with all ColorAlchemy movement, is to move your body and fill it with the spirit of all spectral colors. This time, as you'll use the source, the light of the sun, it is best to practice outside. Just think of the vitamin D you'll absorb at the same time.

Go outside and stand comfortably with your feet shoulder-width apart. Even on a gray day, get some fresh air, and face the sun or stand in front of a window. (Remember your sunscreen and to never look directly at the sun.) With your arms resting at your sides, close your eyes, and lift your head to feel the nurturing rays of the sun on your face.

Take three slow, deep white (the combination of all spectral colors) breaths. Visualize the light filling every fiber of your body. *Ahhh, it is a gift to be alive.* Reposition your head so it sits comfortably on your shoulders and hold your hands together in reverse-prayer position in front of your Root Chakra.

Keeping both arms straight, move them simultaneously in an upward circular motion. Starting at the Root Chakra, the right arm arcs up to the right and the left arm arcs up to the left, creating a double arc that meets above your head beyond your Crown Chakra.

Lift your face to the sun as you lift your arms. Complete the process by double arcing your arms downward, Crown to Root, and returning your head to neutral.

As you move your arms upward, inhale Red to Violet. Visualize the sun's rays filling you to the brim and the light radiating out of your pores. Exhale Violet to Red as you bring your arms down.

Repeat nine times, visualizing your perfect, gold aura vibrating with the colors of the Creator. Thank the sun for sharing its life-creating, nurturing energy.

My Affirmation: _____

_____

Orange Personality: The Right *To Feel*

Personality: Considerate, kind, open, and receptive, shares emotions and feelings with others, recognizes inner beauty in people and nature, creative, passionate about life, enthusiastic, happy, sociable, energetic, sporty, self-assured, constructive

Out of Balance: Exhibitionist, untidy, dishonest

Greatest Needs
• Being respected and acknowledged by family & friends

Greatest Challenges
• Achieving deeper relationship with self
• Being oneself and giving love to others

Orange's Desire: Wanting to fit in

Core Issues: Sexually frustrated, fear of sex, history of sexual abuse or sex urge is gone, problem dealing with emotions, jealous of others who appear to be worry-free, even though you feel lonely you avoid social situations, you don't know how to be happy and have fun, you have creative blocks

Musical Note & Toning Mantra: D & Vam

Planet & Zodiac: Venus & Taurus

 ◄◄◄◄◄◄◄ Happy Orange-Tuesday! ►►►►►►

 tuesday

If you didn't take advantage of Red-Monday to jump start the week, here's your second chance to go for it and add passion to this week's projects.

Emotions & Creativity: Happiness • Desire • Pleasure • Intimacy

Get started saying Orange ColorAlchemy Affirmations out loud.

Take a deep and nourishing Orange Breath.
Place Orange Healing Hands on your Sacral Chakra.
Feel the Orange Ray filling your body.

I AM kind to myself. I create anything I desire. I AM spontaneous and present to experience joy and happiness in every moment.

I AM sensual and desirable. Orange and my Sacral Chakra are automatically available for creativity and passion when I get stuck in a routine or feel limited. I AM balanced with my emotional self.

Amen

Loving music doesn't make you an expert and I am delighted that my dear friend, Steven Halpern, has graciously offered to share his expertise. Steven is a musical genius. He began pioneering sound healing decades ago and consistently enlightens us with music.

ColorAlchemy Music by Maestro Steven Halpern

Our bodies are human instruments. Like any instrument, they play better when they are in tune. Evolution has designed your body to efficiently work with good food, sufficient sleep, proper exercise, and sound energies. Genetic programming allows you to use sound to enhance your health and well-being. For more than thirty years, I have explored the ancient and universal system that centers on the electromagnetic relationship between sound, color, and the chakras.

This is an effective and easy way to apply the healing powers of sound and color.

There is a relationship between the seven musical notes and the seven colors of the rainbow. As Jami Lin explained, Red vibrates at the lowest vibration, Hertz, or Hz, Orange vibrates at a little higher, and so on.

The sounds of music vibrate in the same way: seven frequencies, seven notes. The most common scale begins with the keynote of C, and the archetypal C note vibrates at 256 Hz.

I learned that researchers discovered C was the most common *home base note* in many, worldwide indigenous cultures. I believe ancient musicians and mystics were sensitive to subtle vibrations and could actually *hear* this sound in nature. More recently, measurements taken of the earth's atmosphere showed that the basic frequency of the Earth itself vibrates about 8 cycles per second. This is known as the Earth Resonance.

Here is the fascinating musical and mathematical relationship between 8 Hz and 256 Hz. In music, there are octaves. An octave means doubling a tonal frequency where the note is the same but with a higher, *doubled* vibration.

Chakra Suite
by Steven Halpern

Musical math: by ascending several octaves, the proportions as 8...16...32...64...128...256. Aha! The Earth vibrates in the key of C.

This explains how human beings are harmonically connected to the earth. Intuitively, the reason why human beings resonate with this sound is because the chakras also ascend with these same vibrational relationships.

Musical Notes & Traditional Sounds

Chakra	Note	Mantra
Root Chakra	C	LAM
Sacral Chakra	D	VAM
Will Chakra	E	RAM
Heart Chakra	F	YAM
Throat Chakra	G	HAM
Third-Eye Chakra	A	OM
Crown Chakra	B	AUM

When I began composing music for meditation, healing, and wellness, it was clear to me that *Chakra Suite* needed to encompass this universal relationship. Little did I know that this recording would change my life, launch a new career, and expand the horizons of contemporary instrumental music. *Chakra Suite* and subsequent recordings helped millions of people *tune their human instrument* in an effective and enjoyable manner, simply by listening.

Tune your instrument and benefit in three simple ways:

1. Active listening: Focus your attention on your thoughts and intention while following tonal frequencies. You have several options to guide you.

If you have a keyboard handy, play the middle C note.

No keyboard? Enjoy the first song on *Chakra Suite* on StevenHalpern.com.

When the C note is sounded or as you listen to my Root Chakra rendition in the key of C, focus your attention on the base of your spine.

Focus on each chakra for at least thirty seconds or the time it takes for three deep breaths. With conscious intention (as Jami says), you will feel the music resonating and vibrating in and with each chakra. Repeat the process as you climb the musical notes with your body.

Move up to the D note: Sound D with focused attention on your Sacral Chakra.

Continue moving through the musical scale focusing on each chakra.

E: Breathe deeply into your Will Chakra, and feel the vibration.
F: Experience the vibration in your Heart Chakra.
G: Breathe deeply into your Throat Chakra, and feel the vibration.
A: Experience the vibration in your Third-Eye Chakra.
B: Breathe deeply into your Crown Chakra, and feel the vibration.

Complete the sequence, close your eyes, and enter into the silence. Feel your entire body vibrating. Be aware of how different you feel than before beginning this exercise. Take a deep breath. When you're ready, return to the world relaxed, recharged, and renewed. Maximize the benefits by focusing on each center for three minutes, which is purposefully the length of each piece on the *Chakra Suite* CD.

2. Active listening and visualization: Deepen your experience of chakra tuning by visualizing the appropriate color.

(A note for folks who are not born color visualizers, like me. Research shows that even thinking of the color, without actually seeing it has a definite, positive effect. As Jami told you, energy follows thought.)

• Fill your Root Chakra with the visualization of Red and the vibration of C.
• (You may want to add Healing Hands too!)
• Fill your Sacral Chakra with Orange and the vibration of D.
• Fill your Will Chakra with Yellow and the vibration of E.

- Fill your Heart Chakra with Green and the vibration of F.
- Fill your Throat Chakra with Blue and the vibration of G.
- Fill your Third-Eye Chakra with Indigo and the vibration of A.
- Fill your Crown Chakra with Violet and the vibration of B.

3. Chakra Tuning and Vocal Toning: Using your *human instrument,* your voice, is the most interactive option. I like to focus on the vowel sounds, as you don't have to learn any new words, mantras, or chants.

Softly chant the prolonged vowel sound O with each chakra tone. Experiment with each of the five main vowel sounds too: A-E-I-O-U.

Don't worry if you're not singing exactly in tune. Getting close is good enough for starters. Once you get the hang of it, have fun with this. You can do this in the shower, in your car, while walking on the street, or while sitting in a park. Anywhere.

For extra credit, expand the O sound to the universal mantra, OM. Chanting this primordial sound is part of many spiritual traditions. You'll find that chanting OM and ascending the chakras is an even more potent combination.

Depending on your schedule, play with longer or shorter times to practice. No matter what you choose, I'm sure you'll find that working with the energies of sound adds a wonderful dimension to your ColorAlchemy and life.

Until next time, stay tuned!

Thank you Steven.

OM

I just love how science always validates what we intuitively know. Take Steven's vision for example: he *believes that the ancients could hear earth resonance.* What is the mystical sound that you hear when you listen to a shell picked up on the beach? Is the shell a transmitter that amplifies the sound of the earth? Its resonance is so soothing, almost otherworldly— could this be the sound of *OM?*

OM or Aum is the universal sound vibration and word that recreates the sound-vibration of God. It is said that when chanting the sound OM or the word God, it vibrates more than 180 billion cycles per minute. Mere mortals only vibrate at 13 to 30 billion.

God to Moslems and the more familiar, Amen, is the word of God to Egyptians, Greeks, Aum is the sacred word and symbol of the Tibetans, and similarly, Amin is the word of God to Muslims and the more familiar, Amen, is the word of God to Egyptians, Greeks, Romans, Jews, and Christians. Doesn't OM sound like Amen when you resonate it though your spirit?

Interestingly: The word amen is a declaration of faith found in the Old Testament and the Koran. Christians, Jews, and Muslims complete their prayers by affirming amen. So be it.

As science proves the earth vibrates, it vibrates a sound. It is intuitively reasonable to conceptualize the **Music of the Spheres**. Theory suggests that the energetic frequencies of color waves relate to audible sounds that emanate from all heavenly bodies. If the earth vibrates, why shouldn't each planet vibrate to its unique tone in harmony with the *universal* sound?

Because science experiences the colors of planets (through the elements of the planets as discussed in *Living ColorAlchemy*), both sound and music are transmitted through vibrational waves. Adding sound to ColorAlchemy is not only intuitive, but it is also scientifically justified, enjoyable, and a spiritual experience.

As musical masters tell us,

Color and sound are direct expressions of psychic experiences which cannot be grasped, defined, or expressed by intellect. Color reveals something that has to do with the inner nature or emotional value (energy) of form (matter).
—Lama Anagarika Govinda

And more wisdom from Steven Halpern (gathered for you from his recent articles):

Without having to analyze the science and research, just enjoy and allow it to work directly on your consciousness and on a cellular level. Music is not just the notes, it is the energy of the vibration, the spiritual essence of what comes through.

I first experienced Steven's healing music more than twenty years ago with my intellectual mind, not my feeling mind. While initially melodic and lovely on the ears, I waited for the beat, the rhythm, and/or repeating notes: they never came.

I wanted to *understand it* and didn't. I was so happy when he explained that his music enables the mind to flow in its consciousness instead of waiting for the manipulations of structure. I get it. I feel it. I love it!

Steven says:

Sound is connection to the divine, connection to the universe, and the experience of oneness. When meditating or relaxing with healing music, listen to the quiet spaces between the notes to evolve higher states of consciousness.

Healing music:

- *Percolates through your body, tickles your aura, and balances your energy.*
- *Evokes the relaxation response, shifts brain waves into alpha-theta frequency patterns, and enhances the coherence of your biometric and electric human energy fields.*
- *Speaks to the spirit and promotes a spiritually-aligned response, such as a meditative response.*

Is your mind, body, and spirit musically inspired? Try Steven's music and his exercises to feel the vibration of the colors and chakras by the way sound vibrates in and though your body.

As the relationship between sound and color becomes part of your ColorAlchemy, you can take your toning to another level. Combine traditional mantras (or sacred words) to further activate the chakras.

Chanting to Open the Chakras

There are traditional chants designed to open up the chakras with the use of specific mantras that come from Sanskrit letters. When these mantras are chanted, each creates a vibration in tune with its respective chakra. According to Steven's expertise, *the brain responds to words and mantras differently than when it only focuses on the tonal aspects of music.* So as the grandfather of healing music suggests, let's combine *some of these varied approaches to create a new synergy.*

Chanting is easy. It is the deep, resonating sound that follows the inhalation of Color Breathing. During the exhalation, while keeping your voice low and resonate, all you need to do is *exhale the mantra slooooooooooooooooowly.* Extend the word or sound though your entire exhalation.

As OM is the universal sound, rehearse with it and/or chant it whenever you feel inspired.

OooooooooooooooooooMmmmmmmmmmmmmmm

Feel the vibration in your body. Pay attention to where your body vibrates. Remember, the deeper and longer your cycle of breath, the more:

- You feel the resonance in your exhalation,
- Cells are nurtured and toxins are released,
- You cleanse and activate your aura, and
- You exercise your lung muscles.

Chanting OM, according to Buddhist tradition, is said to burn off negative karma.

Just as you start with a one-pound weight at the gym to build muscle tone and increase to a two-pounder when strong enough, start counting to ten slowly with each breath cycle, and build up to twenty or more. The deeper your breath, the younger you stay!

Experience Chakra Toning

Sequence through each chakra in a series of seven slow and rhythmic breaths while chanting the mantras.

- Inhale a Red breath, exhale Green, and chant the vibration *Lam*, while placing Healing Hands on the Root Chakra. (strength)

- Inhale an Orange breath, exhale Blue or Indigo, and chant the vibration *Vam*, while placing Healing Hands on the Sacral Chakra. (desire)

- Inhale a Yellow breath, exhale Violet, and chant the vibration *Ram*, while placing Healing Hands on the Will Chakra. (power)

- Inhale a Green breath, exhale Red, and chant the vibration *Yam*, while placing Healing Hands on the Heart Chakra. (love)

- Inhale a Blue breath, exhale Orange, and chant the vibration *Ham*, while placing Healing Hands on the Throat Chakra. (clarity)

- Inhale an Indigo breath, exhale Orange, and chant the vibration *OM* or *Aum*, while placing Healing Hands on the Third-Eye Chakra. (vision)

- Inhale a Violet breath, exhale Yellow, and chant the vibration *OM* or *Aum*, while placing Healing Hands on the Crown Chakra. (peace)

Because Indigo/Third-Eye and Violet/Crown use the same mantras, feel free to tone your favorite Crown Chakra word: peace, love, serenity, etc. With further experimentation, substitute any or all of the mantras with a one-word attribute for each related chakra, as I sampled for you in the above (parentheses).

Add chanting in the corresponding note, too. There are no rules. Feel the experience and enjoy the healing that is best for you. Share a musical healing session with a group of friends. When I do this in my classes, the room exponentially fills with vibrations and everyone experiences the healing benefits: it is fantastic! *Sing like you don't need the money*, in the words of singer/songwriter Kathy Mattea. Experiment with incorporating tuning forks, crystal bowls, and bells calibrated in each of the seven tones.

Discover the answer to what Steven is often asked, *Is it that the music is healing or is music the vehicle by which the body heals itself?*

We are surrounded by things that knock us out of tune. We need more tools that bring us into tune and support our ability to anchor the spiritual dimension in our lives. When we radiate the vibration of peace back into our world, a wonderful feedback loop cures what needs to be nurtured, continued, and expanded.

Sing, Dance, and Express Your Energy

The earth is resurgent with color and blooms of spring,
Glorying the dream and vision in the song your bring.
—William Stanley Braithwaite, educator, poet, and critic

Music is the last true voice of the human spirit.
It can go beyond language,
beyond age, and beyond color straight to the mind
and heart of all people.
—Ben Harper

Now that you felt the energy in your body on these physical days, are you ready to get back to some more Mental ColorAlchemy secrets?

Steven Halpern is a musical magician,
a healer with sound.
His music help millions experience transformative moments
that lead to greater wholeness and happiness.
—Dr. Larry Dossey

Visit www.stevenhalpern.com to enjoy his talent. Steven is approachable and friendly. He invites you to share your musical experiences with him at info@innerpeacemusic.com.

With dozens of Steven Halpern CDs to choose from, *Sound Healing* is just one of my favorites!

**The white light streams down to
be broken up by human prisms
into all the colors of the rainbow.
Take your own color in the pattern and be just that.**
—Charles R. Brown

My Affirmation: _____

_____

Yellow Personality: The Right *To Act*

Balance: Feeling of wholeness, inner calm and peace, inner tolerance and acceptance for others, balance of spiritual and material worlds, optimistic, kindhearted, good-humored, optimistic, confident, practical, intellectual

Out of Balance: Need to dominate and control, great need for material security

Greatest Needs
- Being organized and disciplined
- Understanding what is read/studied
- Being intellectual and individualistic

Greatest Challenges
- Following one's heart
- Working without personal conflicts

Yellow's Desire: To be intellectual, to be able to understand everything, as well as to be organized and disciplined

Core Issues: Spark of life is gone, the bright energy of a new day is depressing, no motivation to intellectually figure out what is creating unhappiness, lethargy, feeling of the blahs, loss of personal power and commitment, mental anguish over worldly and business matters, insecure, lack or loss of integrity or self-worth

Musical Note & Toning Mantra: E & Ram

Planet & Zodiac: Mercury & Gemini, Moon & Cancer, Sun & Leo

wednesday

Having danced like nobody's watching and sung like you don't need the money, your physical energies had a good workout! Remember, you don't have to wait for a Monday or Tuesday to express yourself whenever the spirit moves you.

Now, with Yellow's intellectual assistance, let's once again attack any core issues and the more challenging behavioral and thought patterns or *demons* that you started releasing in *Mental ColorAlchemy*. Freeing yourself from negativity leaves your spirit uncluttered and empty to fill with the colorful attributes of happiness.

Say today's Yellow Affirmations out loud to make that extra commitment!

Take a deep and nourishing Yellow Breath.
Place Yellow Healing Hands on your Will Chakra.
Feel the Yellow Ray filling your body.

I positively greet all tasks and challenges with commitment and inner strength. I maintain flexibility in decision making, am confident in the result, and take responsibility for the outcome.

Yellow and my Will Chakra are automatically available for confidence and inner strength when I feel incapable. I am capable and confident! I command my mind to change negative thoughts to positive ones. I AM balanced with my intellectual self. I like me!

Amen

 Happy Yellow-Wednesday ⟩⟩⟩⟩⟩

Affirm with commitment, *I am releasing a core issue today!*

Healing Core Issues: The Secret to Happiness

During the past twenty-one days, I hope you experienced releasing some inner demons. I shared how your mental process is used for self-realization and provided examples through dialogues with my Observer. I provided possible spiritual, emotional, and physical weaknesses to consider as you cultivate your Observer, focus your mind with journaling, and apply your favorite ColorAlchemy Activators.

On every Colors of Your Spirit day, use your preferred self-evaluation method and look at the Daily Color box. Every day, consider the qualities of each color's personality. Are the qualities of that color balanced or unbalanced within you? Do you have the color's greatest need, challenge, or desires?

Do any of the core issues define a part of you that you find unacceptable? Dialogue with your Observer or explore the questions in your journal. How do the color qualities translate into lack, limitation, or blockage? What's missing in your life? Where are your vulnerabilities?

Refocus on the color(s) to support releasing demons, healing your mind, body, and/or spirit, and manifesting your desires.

Remember, take a good look at the colors you don't particularly like as clues. Notice how unfavorable colors translate into the energies that you most need. With ColorAlchemy, there is always something new to discover about the spiritual essence of who you are. I discovered something exciting just a few days ago.

Even if you think you are proficient in a color's attributes, there is always more to learn.

It is not news that I am not fond of Blue and Orange, but:

Why do I need Blue when I am an excellent Blue communicator (with solid emotional attributes)?

Ahhh, but what about the core issue of being resentful that other people *appear* to not have to work so hard to be *successful?*

Using my skilled Blue attributes, I clearly need to journal and reevaluate what the words *appear* and *successful* mean? What is the root of my resentment? How can I add more Blue in my life? Easy! Every day, I consciously add a touch of Blue to what I wear.

How can I possibly need Orange when I am so passionate about my work and I cry during touching moving scenes?

Ahhh, but have I forgotten how to have fun and be spontaneous? No journaling necessary here, I need to get out of my head! I need to turn off my phone and computer, and go play! Sometimes I need to schedule one play day a week to relax and go with the flow. Not too spontaneous, but I commit to that day in ink on my calendar and make plans. I feel so full and refreshed after a fun outing!

Adding more Orange and Blue to my ColorAlchemy, I am happier (Orange helps that, too) and am *Light-en-ing Up*. **Are you?**

You've worked with your Observer for more than twenty-one days and hopefully it is a solid habit, so you can make adding a BETA Scan easy.

Beta Scan

BETA Scanning is an effective way to identify what facet of the personality a core issue is coming from so you can identify energies surrounding life challenges.

BETA = Belief, Emotion, Thoughts, and Actions

Every thought, emotion, or action triggered by a negative condition, such as stress, anger, frustration, or insecurity, has four components: belief, emotion, thought, and action. In other words, you cannot have a negative thought, emotion, or action without its interconnection to any component of a BETA.

Scan means engaging your Observer to identify where a condition is rooted. During an episode or memory of an event, scan the components of BETA to discover if a core issue is hidden in either a belief, a thought, an emotion, or an action. Once identified, dialogue with your Observer and/or journal the condition(s) to free yourself from the demon.

Using my *Almost-Instantaneous Example* in Metal ColorAlchemy on p. 43 to explain the components and process of a BETA Scan:

> **Action:** HELLOOOOOOOOOOO, I said in a heated tone.

I engaged my Observer:

> **Emotion:** I wasn't happy this guy didn't say hello to me when greeting him with a friendly smile and cheery hello.

> **Thought:** What is wrong with ME that he didn't say hello?

Then the work started. (This may be unpleasant, as we never want to face demons)

> **Belief:** I wasn't *worthy enough* for him to say hello.

Belief is what your self-conditioned and unconscious mind trained you to believe.

Identifying false beliefs is the key to healing core issues.

Continuing to dialogue with my Observer. But what is the truth?

Basic logic: He doesn't know anything about me!
How could he possibly pass judgement?

Judgment: So what if someone doesn't like me?
That's why there is chocolate and vanilla.
I can't be everybody's best friend—and do I want to be?

Truth: I am loving, intuitive, talented, creative, hard-working, smart, and dedicated. I am passionate for living life to capacity. I have a loving family, I am supported and nurtured by friends. I created, and continue to create, a life that I love. I AM extremely worthy.

Source the core issue to discover your belief is grossly exaggerated and/or untrue.

If you don't believe your Truth, write affirmations, and repeat them over and over again.

Write and speak them: They are true! With your talents and loving soul, YOU are worthy!

Once you have recognized a false belief that gets attached to an emotion, a thought, or an action, it is easier to identify the next time it raises its ugly head.

Each time you recognize a false belief, recondition yourself back to your real truth. Your process becomes easier, and ultimately,

Sets You Free!

From my example, notice that the BETA order is not necessarily in the sequence of the experience. Heal on the *B* component of BETA and the others will automatically follow.

Enhance BETA success with Yellow and Blue ColorAlchemy, excellent helpers to focus your intellectual and emotional mind. Surround yourself with them when journaling, too.

The most challenging part is remembering to engage your Observer and to *scan yourself* when you are stressed, angry, or frustrated. Most of us can't think clearly when upset. Recommit to getting out of your anger or frustration quickly to see beyond to the core. Remember, your mind is the only thing that you have control over. Do you need to recommit to an Oopsie strategy?

Perfecting BETA Scans also deepens relationships because:

- Getting to know yourself better improves communication skills.
- Recognizing and lovingly discussing your observations with family and friends helps grow intimacy.

Here's a great BETA and communication example that deepened mutual understanding in my marriage.

Thought: Talking around the kitchen table, I noticed Emotion and anger toward me. (My husband is usually a saint!)

I thought, *what did I do?*

Action: I sweetly asked, Why is there anger in your voice?

Belief: He replied, *Because I know what you are thinking.* Through his Action, his Thoughts telegraphed his Emotion and incorrect Belief *in thinking he knew* what I was thinking.

We easily worked it out when I asked, *How can you get mad at me by thinking what I was thinking?* Happily, we are very in sync (and often mind read each other), but how do we really know what anyone is thinking unless her or she tells us?

Once perfecting your BETA Scan abilities, lovingly share your observations with loved ones. You'll be amazed at how effectively it works!

This was a short lesson because you already learned the basis of *Mental ColorAlchemy*. Continue to cultivate your Observer, practice evolving your spirit with BETA Scans, and consciously change negative thoughts, actions, emotions, and beliefs into positive ones. These are skills that last a lifetime and make it a happy one.

Commit to skills that will last a lifetime.

Practice scanning with your Observer to create a ritual.
Greater happiness is automatic.

Get ready for some fun, less heavy, Colors of Your Spirit.

My Affirmation: _____

_____

Green Personality:
The Right *To Love and Be Loved*

Personality: Harmonious, happy, joyful, tolerant and accepting of everything, feeling of wholeness, understanding, self-controlled, adaptable, sympathetic, compassionate, generous, humble, nature loving, romantic

Out of Balance: Love is not sincere, you have ulterior motives in giving love, you cannot receive love from others, anxious, jealous, oversensitive

Greatest Needs
• Feeling protected
• Loving and being loved

Greatest Challenges
• Loving without reservation
• Controlling greed
• Controlling fear and insecurity

Green's Desire: To love and be loved, and feel protected and nurtured.

Core Issues: "Nobody loves me, everybody hates me, I think I'll eat some worms!" imbalanced outlook, withdrawn from everything and everybody, you blame others for not taking control of your happiness, you feel like a victim and you believe everybody is out to get you, feelings of rejection

Musical Note & Toning Mantra: F & Yam

Planet & Zodiac: Mercury & Virgo, Libra & Venus

After all the heavy-head stuff on Yellow-Wednesday, let's balance it with some fun on today's balancing, Green, rainbow-bridge day!

Unconditional Love: Forgiveness • Trust • Compassion • Balance   227

Please know that I am not reducing the importance of what we did yesterday. It is important soul work that supports happiness for a lifetime. But for now, relax your head and share some love by saying a Green ColorAlchemy Affirmation out loud.

Take a deep and nourishing Green Breath.
Place Green Healing Hands on your Heart Chakra.
Feel the Green Ray filling your body.

Love is the creator of harmony and balance. I am love. I freely express love without limitation, conditions, or regret. I AM capable of complete forgiveness and compassion for myself and others.

Green and my Heart Chakra are automatically available for sharing and receiving love especially when I am angry or frustrated. I AM balanced with my feeling and loving self.

Amen

<<<<<<< Happy Green-Thursday >>>>>>

Ancient alchemists looked to the stars, played with numerical sequencing, and read the symbols of the soul during the night. Over the millennium, astrology, numerology, and dream interpretation evolved into complex and effective methods of divination and tools for personal guidance. Each one is a science in itself that takes years for proficiency. If you haven't already been attracted to learn more about any or all of these, catch a glimpse into the profound revelations, specifically with their relationship to ColorAlchemy.

Astrology & ColorAlchemy

At the exact moment that you were born, each planet was in a specific location in the heavens. Since ancient times, astrologers suggest that this scientific configuration symbolically identifies your soul purpose. According to the life-quality attributes of each planet, its individual location in the heavens (zodiac signs), and its interconnectedness to the other (trines, squares, oppositions, etc.), your birth chart is a mystical window into your personality and destiny. There are two ways to use astrology in your ColorAlchemy.

1. Everybody knows his or her *sign* from *newspaper astrology*. This is your sun sign that defines the personality you share with the world.

Using the Astrology & ColorAlchemy Chart on p. 230, look at the color of your sun sign. How does that color relate to the outer expression of yourself? My sun sign is Gemini with the color Yellow. How do I express myself to the world?

Committed and confident with an intellectual mind

When the attributes of a color do not match the way you'd like to appear to the world, you are not fulfilling *your astrological destiny*. Incorporate more of that color to help inspire putting your soul purpose into action.

2. The second way to incorporate astrology in ColorAlchemy requires you to have your astrological, natal chart (get it free on astro.com, then play with free reports and free charts) and to know a little about the relationships between each planet and the sign as it sits in your chart.

Understanding the astrological interpretation and the related colors, you can discover greater ColorAlchemy depth and confirmations in your astrological interpretations.

For example: I have Venus (Green) in Cancer (Yellow):

Planet: Venus   Relationships, Love, Beauty & Style, Diplomatic
Sign: Cancer   Sensitive, Emotional, Considerate, Kind (and a homebody)

To support my design and Feng Shui work, ColorAlchemy astrology suggests that I incorporate Green and Yellow. Interestingly, to enhance my Feng Shui, my entry/living room Green and my bedroom is Yellow.

I also have Jupiter (Blue) in Leo (Yellow):

Planet: Jupiter   Philosopher, Expanded, Visionary, Optimistic, Freedom
Sign: Leo   Leader, Radiant, Personal Power, Individuality

It is amazing how both of the mental colors, Yellow (intellectual mind) and Blue (clear, communicating, and holistic mind), support communicating the work that I love so much. With Gemini's Yellow energy, it confirms my outward expression with confidence and commitment.

Have fun and discover what your astrological ColorAlchemy says about you. Incorporate more of the color(s) to support your soul purpose.

Astrology & ColorAlchemy Chart

Color	Zodiac Sign	Planet	Positive Attributes
Red	Aries	Mars	Pioneer, Assertive, Independent, Courageous
Orange	Taurus	Venus	Relationships, Love, Beauty & Style Patience
Yellow	Gemini	Mercury	Quick, Imaginative, Communication, Logical
	Cancer	Moon	Sensitive, Emotional, Considerate, Kind
	Leo	Sun	Leader, Radiant, Personal Power, Individuality
Green	Virgo	Mercury	Communication, Detailed, Precise, Analytical
	Libra	Venus	Relationships, Love, Beauty & Style, Diplomatic
Blue	Scorpio	Pluto	Intuitive, Perceptive, Intense, Penetrating, Regenerative
	Sagittarius	Jupiter	Philosopher, Expanded, Visionary, Optimistic, Freedom
Indigo	Capricorn	Saturn	Perseverance, Determined, Responsible, Disciplined
Violet	Aquarius	Uranus	Humanitarian, Equality, Futuristic, Inventive
Magenta	Pisces	Neptune	Transcendent, Universal Love, Mystical, Inspirational

Numerology & ColorAlchemy

ColorAlchemy numerology is fun and provides interesting investigation. It uses the numerical representations of your name along with your birth date. Here are the two easy steps:

Numerology & ColorAlchemy Chart

Color	Number	Letters
Red	1	A, J, S
Orange	2	B, K, T
Yellow	3	C, L, U
Green	4	D, M, V
Blue	5	E, N, W
Indigo	6	F, O, X
Violet	7	G, P, Y
Magenta	8	H, Q, Z
Gold	9	I, R

Magenta & Gold are Soul-Spirit Colors

1. Spell your name
   Write the corresponding numbers for each letter
   Add the numbers together
   Reduce to a single digit
   The color of "5" is

   Jami Lin
   1149 395
   1+1+4+9+3+9+5=32
   3+2=5
   Blue

2. What is your birthday in numbers?
   Add the numbers together
   Reduce to a single digit

   The color of "2" is

   6/2/1956
   6+2+1+9+5+6=29
   2+9=11
   1+1=2
   Orange

Orange and Blue are my ColorAlchemy numerology colors. Isn't it interesting that they are the colors that I like the least? As I explained earlier, they have attributes that I am well versed in, but I am still surrounded by Orange and Blue core issues,

Synchronistic? Coincidental? Don't think so!
What does your ColorAlchemy numerology say about you?

Dreams & ColorAlchemy

From Freud and Jung to self-help therapists and personal analysis, dreams are considered symbolic representations of the soul. Dreams are metaphoric stories written by your unconscious that, when unlocked, provide insight, clarity, and guidance considered for life experience. When I remember a dream, the story is obviously clear and parallels current events, circumstances, and/or thoughts. Pay close attention to your dreams, especially those that have repeating themes.

> For example, in recent dreams, I repeatedly get lost and can't find my way home. In my recent experience, I am moving to another city. While anxious to sell and move, all the accessories I find beautiful are already packed (with a very sad *Venus in Cancer*). With intentions to rent while building a house, I am *frustrated in finding my home*. Remember, with Venus in Cancer, *home* is very important to me, since I am not yet living where I want to live, it is in my nature to feel lost.

Adding the ColorAlchemy dimension to dream interpretation is illuminating. When a color is dominate in your dream, add the life quality of that color to your interpretation. Use the following dream interpretation chart to add to the attributes that you already know. Just like ColorAlchemy qualities, notice the yin and yang (positive and negative) associations.

Color	Dream Interpretations
Red	excitement, intense, animated, success, assertive, drive, anger, danger, illness, injury
Orange	sexual desire, satisfaction, expansion, warmth, joy, fear of failure
Yellow	optimism, bright future, intellect, possibility, opportunity, self-opinionated, self-control
Green	development, growth, needing independence, confirm personal values & esteem
Blue	truth, trust, thoughtfulness, tranquility, serene, dreamy, nervous, anxiety
Indigo	truth, trust, thoughtfulness, tranquility, serene, dreamy, nervous, anxiety
Violet	inspiration, mystical, intuitive, blockage to connection, too much fantasy

Have fun with these! Remember to journal your experience to gain additional insight. Tomorrow, we'll add more ColorAlchemy ritual to deepen your ColorAlchemy Activators and Colors of Your Spirit.

My Affirmation: _____

_____

Blue Personality:
The Right *To Talk and Live in Truth*

Balanced: Balances outer communication though inner silence and trusted intuition, open-minded, creatively expressive, thirsty for knowledge, loyal, tactful, affectionate, inspiring, inventive, caring, cautious

Out of Balance: Talks all the time without much to say, fearful of being rejected, sarcastic, overly ambitious without clear foundation, afraid of silence or not being heard

Greatest Needs
- Living an ideal life
- Surrounding yourself in beauty/peace
- Controlling your mental abilities

Greatest Challenges
- Living more spontaneously
- Taking more risks
- Finding truth in yourself instead of faulting others

Blue's Desire: To be surrounded by beauty, peace, and idealism

Core Issues: Mental conflict over psychological or spiritual concerns, shuts off feelings, in an emotional rut, stagnant thinking, suffered failed relationship, feeling blue and bored, fear of failure, worried about time wasted trying to be successful, consumed with others' success when they don't appear to have to work very hard, why did they have all the breaks?

Musical Note & Toning Mantra: G & Hum

‹‹‹‹‹‹‹ Happy Blue-Friday ›››››

Today is the clarity-of-mind day to incorporate conscious ritual in everything that you do. So far, so good. Every ColorAlchemy habit practiced so far included holistic and conscious-Blue-thoughtful energy.

Through your habits, you probably even created rituals by:

- Wearing Daily Colored clothing or accessories
- Taking a Color Breath when getting out of bed in the morning periodically during the day, and before going to sleep
- Consciously being aware of and absorbing the colors around you
- Tapping into your Observer and BETA Scanning
- Practicing your favorite ColorAlchemy Activators

The dictionary says that a ritual is a defined format or set of acts done on special occasions. But why do you have to wait for a special occasion?

Isn't every precious moment a sacred and special occasion?

Like now! Create a colorful ritual and practice saying your Blue ColorAlchemy Affirmations out loud.

Take a deep and nourishing Blue Breath.
Place Blue Healing Hands on your Throat Chakra.
Feel the Blue Ray filling your body.

I AM clear with my thoughts that define who I AM. I know the truth of how I feel and think. I freely express my inner truth and am committed to my beliefs. My "voice" is a gift to myself and others.

Blue and my Throat Chakra are accessible for communication and thoughtfulness for clarity or to release mental blocks. I AM balanced with my thoughtful self.

Amen

Ahhh, a blessed moment. You created a sacred, private ritual, reserved for the special and sacred being that you are.

Rituals are no more than habits practiced with spiritual, conscious intention. Converting habits into rituals is so easy. Just like the mental-training habit of creating positive behavior and thoughts, consciously:

1. Add the clarity of Blue:
    Decisiveness, Truth within Self, Communication, Clarity behind Illusion

2. Then, focus on life-qualities of Indigo and Violet for spiritual insight and inspiration:
    Intuition, Vision, Psychic Powers, Focus, Seeing Beyond
    Peace, Bliss, Spiritual Love, Divinity, Inspiration

All rituals start by first getting into a sacred, *blessed mood*. Create a sacred blessing mood as you have already done many times when Blessing Your Materials, Feeling Color on your Skin, Initiating Healing Hands with Colored Rays, Creating Holy Water, and Preparing for Journaling and/or Drawing Mandalas, just to name a few.

Wow! We've done a lot of great ColorAlchemy!
Be very proud of yourself!

Rituals can be performed any time and any place. Ritualistically, take a healing and nurturing breath while standing in line at the bank or grocery, filling up your car with gas, and any time you want to create a sacred moment. Absorb the sacredness of a moment by adding spiritual thoughts when drinking holy water (even to hydrate at the gym), taking a ColorAlchemy bath, toning with colored light, dancing or singing the chakras, speaking ColorAlchemy affirmations, and celebrating favorite Color Applications.

It doesn't take any longer to live in spiritual consciousness.

Awareness of Spiritual Consciousness

Spiritual ColorAlchemy is ritual awareness to enhance your personal connection to God. It is so unbelievably simple. The more you pay attention to how the colors around you are energetically supportive, the greater your universal connection will increase happiness within and throughout your life experience.

With a blast of creative energy last Saturday (maybe I was channeling Indigo and Violet energy), I worked until four in the morning. Nine a.m. came way too quickly so I purposefully wore bright pink to Sunday's exercise class. Violet would not have supported the high energy needed to maintain my stamina and Red would have burned me out (like drinking too much caffeine).

It was amazing. Seventy-five percent of the class wore variations of Red and Orange. Fifty percent were wearing bright pink (a variation of Red).

Pay attention when the world *seems to be* radiating the color that you most need in any given moment.

With ColorAlchemy support all around me, I made it though the class, showered, then enjoyed what you are supposed to do with Sunday's energy: count your blessings and regenerate your spirit.

Tap into the unconscious support of the universe that you may not have noticed before.

Take ColorAlchemy moments and appreciate connection to spiritual wholeness.

Fire Rituals

From the Native American tradition of smoking peace pipes with sacred tobacco, to lighting Sabbath candles, to burning incense in Buddhist temples and Catholic churches, fire ceremonies are used in spiritual rituals the world over. Fire rituals are universally popular because of the symbol of sending prayers to heaven on the smoke. To bring your consciousness energy (or prayers) into manifestation (matter), make wishes physical and as detailed as possible.

Write down your:

• Demons: to release and set them free
• Prayers: for the universe to help you create them

The Fire Ritual:

• Use blessed colored papers and pens based upon need
• Select a special, fireproof container used only for fire rituals. It is best to only use special, ritual objects for sacred purposes to not dilute the powerful energy that radiates from them. (I have a well-charred, brass planter that has served me for years.)
• Position your container in a safe location outdoors
• In a sacred-blessing mood, speak your affirmations out loud, and burn your written prayers
• Visualize your prayers on the smoke rising to the light, God, Great Spirit, or the Universal Energy you hold most sacred in your heart

And most important:

- With sincerity and the purist of intentions, thank the energy for receiving and listening.
- Release any attachments to your desires.
  Continue to work on balancing your life qualities.
- Know that you are spiritually in good hands. Trust the outcome.
- **Allow the manifestation to surprise you!**

New Moon Rituals

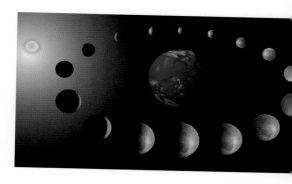

Universal ritualists have used cycles of the moon for rituals since the beginning of time. Consider the phases of the moon symbolized as a growing plant for connecting to heaven's assistance in creating your desires.

I do thirteen new moon ceremonies a year. Timing is everything, and like you, *I want it now!* Every month, in addition to practicing my monthly Flying Star Feng Shui ritual (details on JamiLin.com), I burn wishes to *plant the seeds* for what I want to create during each monthly cycle. Time your cycles according to the earth and moon's harmonic rhythm (that's the reason why Flying Star Feng Shui consistently works, too!).

Moon Phase	Plant Cycle	Manifestation	Concept
New	Seed	Thoughts & Ideas	Beginnings in the Quiet & Still Darkness
Crescent	Sprout	Concept/Nurture	Peeking Through
First Quarter	Growth	Action	Action
Gibbous	Bud	Progress	Coming Together
Full	Flower	Materialize	Achievement
Disseminating	Fruit	Give Back	Release/Detach
Last Quarter	Harvest	Reward	Reap
Balsamic	Compost	Momentum & Readiness for New Creation	Ease Satisfaction

If your calendar does not indicate the new moon, I recommend that you get one or get new moon dates off the Web. Write your prayers, and burn them on each new moon. Track the results in your journal to monitor your success.

Candle Rituals

I've included some ColorAlchemy candle-burning rituals because we all have them and they are so easy to use.

Suggestions: By now you probably have one or more sets of seven colored candles or colored-candleholders. Make sure you bless them (the same way you bless any of your materials on p. 101).

If using colored candleholders, use white candles or the same color candle. I just bought a set of seven-juice glasses in the spectral colors—I can never resist! With holders like this, tea lights in disposal metal cups are the most convenient. They are inexpensive enough to ritually use for each Daily Color.

If you are using colored candles, place them in clear glass or neutral-colored holders. Please make sure to use a candleholder—I wouldn't want you to stain your furniture with dripping wax or oils seeping from the bottom.

Daily Candle Ritual: Every day, light a Daily Color candle. Determine the best place to locate your Daily Candle depending on where it will be of greatest benefit. The Daily Color holder is on my desk (the rest are in a drawer) for ColorAlchemy motivation, and I allow the tea light to burn itself out.

Create a ColorAlchemy ritual. Get into a blessing mood and speak the appropriate affirmation as you light the candle. On the smoke, visualize the Daily-Colored ray carrying all the attributes in through your nose as you take a deep and nurturing Color Breath.

Candle Ritual for Meditation

This is a ritual that uses colored candles and/or colored candleholders in all seven spectral colors. I have a set of seven on my altar, on my bathtub sill, and on the dresser in my bedroom.

With all the candles and holders blessed, line them up in spectral order and select the ritual most appropriate to your needs.

1. **One-color ritual/meditation** with intention of:

   • Absorbing one color's attributes
   • Reinforcing one chakra
   • Strengthening a weakness in the related body location
   • Integrating all three energies: attribute, chakra, and related-body location

The one-color ritual

- Light your chosen candle with a Colored Breath.
- Speak your related ColorAlchemy Affirmation.
- Practice slow, rhythmic Color Breathing either with closed eyes or focusing in the flame.
- Visualize the color's attributes riding on a Colored Ray filling every cell and fiber of your body.
- Imagine the related chakra saturated with pure color.
- With Healing Hands, rub the color (with the appropriate essential oil) as you would a healing salve on a sore body area.
- Visualize the color on any other tense area until all uncomfortable sensation is gone.
- Exhale any toxicity with the complementary color until your exhalation is free of any negativity.
- If your mind wanders in the process, gently bring it back and refocus on Color Breathing.
- Open your eyes and focus on the candle as needed.

- Repeat this process until there is no longer any tension in your body.
- Feel your body glowing a healthy-colored aura in your chosen color.

Upon completion, ritualistically extinguish the candle with your wet fingers or a candle snuffer. Many spiritual traditions suggest it is inappropriate to blow out a ceremonial candle, as the spiritual energies get blown away.

Meditate in this state for as long as you have the time. Practicing for at least five minutes trains the mind and deepens your periodic two-colorful-minute breathing. Try it every day for one week. Journal the difference in your experience. I bet your week will be exceptionally good!

2. **Spectral-color ritual/meditation** with intention of:

- Balancing your rainbow: all attributes, chakras, and related-body locations

  This meditation is exactly the same as the previous meditation except you spend equal time with each colored energy. You can light the candles in whichever order. Consider the options:

  - **Spectral progression:** Intuitively start with either the Red or Violet candle

  - In *As Above, So Below* **order:** Start with Green (as the supreme balancer) then intuitively choose the *As Above's* (drawing energy down to the heart: Violet, Indigo, Blue) and then the *So Below's* (pulling energy up to the heart: Red, Orange, Yellow) or vice versa.

- **Intuitive order** - As your spirit suggests

As you light each candle, spend as much time as needed breathing and meditating on each color. When all candles are burning, visualize that every chakra is full and radiating its liquid light throughout your body. You can even integrate your favorite Colors of Your Spirit ritual, such as the Cosmic Orbit (which you'll learn tomorrow).

Regardless of the order in which you light the candles, complete the circle by extinguishing them in the reverse order that they were lit. For example, if candles were lit in sequential order starting with Red, snuff them out in rainbow order beginning with Violet.

Incorporate a candle ritual with any Colorful Application to get you in a blessing mood. And of course, remember, never leave a candle unattended. Personalize them to fit your individual needs.

Personalizing Rituals.

Regardless of whether I am doing a chi-clearing ceremony, or house-protection blessing, a new-moon ritual or lighting a Daily Color candle, I always modify the ritual according to who I am doing it for and its purpose.

Components of Rituals

In *The Feng Shui Anthology* there is brilliant article for helping you create personalized ceremonies. See it at JamiLin.com/images/stories/anthology/David.pdf. While the article details the *Components of a Feng Shui Cure*, I know you are clever enough to translate his detailed suggestions into ColorAlchemy rituals. You might even learn some Feng Shui in the process, too.

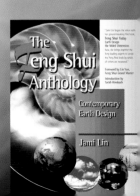

My Affirmation: _____

_____

Indigo Personality: The Right *To See*

Balanced: Intuitive, fearless, practical, idealistic, wise, a truth seeker, idealistic, psychically sensitive, awareness of spiritual nature, invites intuition and inner awareness in daily experience, connects to universal consciousness

Out of Balance: Rejects spirituality, total reliance on science and intellect, only sees on-the-surface meaning, remote, fears intuition and insight, depressed, undisciplined

Greatest Needs
• Trusting intuition
• Inspiring human development

Greatest Challenges
• Turning vision into reality
• Developing the five senses

Indigo's Desire: Being part of humanitarian evolution and being connected with the universe

Core Issues: Loss of faith, dwelling upon disloyal and dishonest people, lack of trust, resistant to things you don't understand, limited thinking, critical, passes judgment according to unrealistic standards and (mis)conceptions, and feelings of inadequacy in education, ability, intelligence, competency

Musical Note & Toning Mantra: A & OM

Planet & Zodiac: Saturn & Capricorn

≪≪≪≪≪ Happy Indigo-Saturday ≫≫≫≫≫

Precious Time

Practice all the ColorAlchemy Activators that I shared since you took your first two-minute Color Breath more than three weeks ago. Transforming your life takes so little time and effort. Benefit by living ColorAlchemy every day. Immediately!

No Time:
- Change negative emotion, thoughts, or actions into positive
- Hydrate with your ColorAlchemy elixir
- Spritz your favorite ColorAlchemy aromatherapy
- Say your ColorAlchemy Affirmation

Twenty Seconds: Every few hours for a sacred, stress-free momentary pause

Savor your Indigo ColorAlchemy Affirmations out loud.

Take a deep and nourishing Indigo Breath.
Place Indigo Healing Hands on your Third-Eye Chakra.
Feel the Indigo Ray filling your body.

I AM receptive to my innate talents of seeing the unseen. My sixth sense is awake and continually improving. I trust and act in accordance with my inner vision as it comes from Universal knowledge, understanding and truth.

Indigo and my Third-Eye Chakra are unlimited in intuition and inspiration. I AM balanced with my intuitive self.

Amen

Two to Ten Minutes: Color-Breath meditation and cultivate your Observer, using your chakras, with a short version of most meditations. Ten-minute journaling session or a refreshing color bath/shower with frozen-light crystal

Thirty to Sixty Minutes: Color-tone light therapy, draw mandalas, chakra dance, longer meditations, burn ritual, and all quick ColorAlchemy Activators

And if all these Colors of Your Spirit weren't enough, on this spiritual Indigo day, enjoy my five favorite ColorAlchemy meditations for greater ColorAlchemy insight.

ColorAlchemy Meditations

As with all meditations, select an area where you will not be disturbed and create a blessing mood. Calm your heart and mind with any Color Breathing or preliminary ritual of your choosing.

As you get comfortable (sitting, standing or lying down), there are two tips to magnify, harness, and channel the energy created through your meditations:

1. Place your tongue on the roof of your mouth to complete the channel of energy.

2. Position your hands in the Anjali mudra (or prayer hands position).

   This universal-hand position contains the cycle of energy in the body and influences inward reflection, gratitude, compassion, and prayer. There are physical benefits of this mudra too. It reduces stress, calms the brain, creates flexibility in the hands, wrists, and arms, and opens the channel to the heart.

Buddha's Mind, Body, and Speech Color Meditation

According to Sogyal Rinpoche in *The Tibetan Book of Living and Dying*, this traditional color meditation is *purifying, empowering, and sows the seeds of enlightenment*. This meditation is perfect for ColorAlchemy because it incorporates color and most important, it focuses on your spiritual power to change negative thought and behavior into positive manifestation.

As you take your time with each of these three distinct phases, visualize:

1. White diamond light streaming out of Buddha's (or your vision of God's) forehead and beaming into your Third-Eye Chakra. The white light represents the *Body* of blessings of all Buddhas and cleanses negative karma (repercussions from inappropriate thoughts or behavior). This light opens a channel for compassion and self-realization.

2. Red ruby light streaming from the Throat of the Buddha and into your Throat Chakra. This is the blessing of *Speech* and cleanses karma from negative communication. The Red light opens the channel for all prayers and affirmations to be heard and manifested.

3. Blue, lapis lazuli light streaming out of the master's heart and bursting into your Heart Chakra. This is the light of Buddha's *Mind* and it releases karma of all negative thoughts. The Blue light opens of the channel for heart-full thought, realization, and purity.

Upon completion, know you are empowered through the Buddha's blessing with unwavering body, speech, and mind. Thank the Buddhas and Sogyal Rinpoche for sharing this meditation with you and for all the blessing received from its practice.

Crystal Rainbow Meditation

This special meditation came from my first Feng Shui teacher, Lin Yun Rinpoche. With sincerest gratitude and appreciation, I modify it for ColorAlchemy.

Calm your mind and spirit with your favorite ritual. Visualize that all is quiet and everything is dissolved into the universal void (the emptiness in your mind).

Visualize thousands of Buddhas appearing in the darkness (or images of everything that is sacred to you such as unlimited blessings).

Visualize the brightest light that you ever saw sparking three inches below your belly button (Sacral Chakra, also known as the Tan Tein, Hara, or Triple-Burner) with a buzzing sound as if coming from a welding machine. The sparks fill your body and explode out of the top of your head.

Allow the buzzing sound to fade away and watch the sparks fall. As the sparks fall on you, your body vanishes and turns into a Red Crystal Body.

Visualize the light below your belly, hear the buzz, watch the sparks fly from your head and back onto your body. See your body turn into an Orange Crystal Body.

Repeat this process five more times for your Yellow, Green, Blue, Indigo, and Violet Crystal Bodies.

Visualize your entire Rainbow Body as a vibrant, transparent crystal radiating all the colors of Buddha (or God).

Visualize the image of your Crystal Rainbow Body in an instant disappearing into thin air. Your Red Body disappears first, then your Orange body, and so on. The faster the better. Poof! Poof! Poof!

Visualize your physical body (back to normal) and visualize a lotus blossom (we talked about this throughout *Colors of the Body*) blooming in your heart. As the lotus opens, Buddha energy (or love, compassion, and peace) fills your body and you become the Buddha (or your vision of God), and the Buddha is you.

You now hold all the wisdom, great compassion, and infinite power of the loving Buddha.

Cosmic Orbit

I learned the Cosmic Orbit at least three times while traveling all over the world: At a goddess weekend in my own backyard, by a Buddhist master in China, and from a Yogi in India. I wish I could remember their names, as I would love to credit them for providing me the opportunity to add ColorAlchemy to this universal and powerful meditation.

It is almost the same as the *As Above, So Below* meditation (p. 136) but with several differences.

Start with Orange at the Sacral Chakra, your powerful, inner burner.

Morphing and moving the colors of liquid light up or down the chakras, circle the rainbow energy around the front and back of your body.

 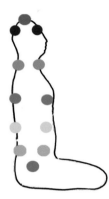

- Women, start the rotation counterclockwise. Men, start clockwise.
- Depending on which way you are circling, as you reach the Violet Crown Chakra, move either down the front or back of the body, morphing the colors of liquid light in spectral color progression.
- Reaching the Red Root Chakra, move either up the front of the body or the back of the body, morphing the colors of liquid light in spectral-color progression.
- Depending on which direction you are moving, after circling in that direction for nine or more rotations, circle in the opposite direction for the same number of cycles.
- Complete the rotation at the Sacral Chakra, your Tan Tein burner, where it is healthy and safe to store the excess energy.

This meditation is called the Small Heavenly Cycle of the Cosmic Orbit. It completes the circuit of energy in your *smaller body* or torso.

Extend the energy through your legs and feet to practice the entire Great Heavenly Cycle. Follow the small sequence and add:

• At the Root Chakra, draw the energy down your legs and through the bottom of your feet to connect with the earth.

• At the Crown Chakra, visualize connecting to heaven.

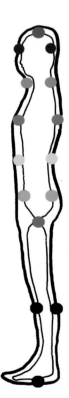

Inner Smile Meditation

During the fragrant, liquid light section (p. 176), I talked about how memory is stored in the unconscious mind. Recalling a memory immediately triggers emotion that directs how you feel. Obviously, happy thoughts and experiences combine into a happy life. The inner smile meditation trains the mind (like all *Mental ColorAlchemy*) by producing happy feelings generated by the emotional experience of a smile.

Just as you feel warmth when someone smiles at you, the Inner Smile Meditation is an opportunity to smile at yourself and bring that happy, health-generating emotion throughout your body.

Prepare for meditation and get into a happy frame of mind. (Remember, you control your mind to think as you want it to. The more meditation you practice, the better you become at training your mind.) If you are having trouble getting into a happy mood, smile and recall a happy memory.

SMILE BIG and follow the sequence of the Cosmic Orbit meditation. Allow your face to relax in the beautiful Buddha smile (as seen on every depiction of him) and hold the smiling energy in your mind and spirit. Smile completely through the process and feel happiness radiating, smiling, and being absorbed by every cell in your body.

By training with this meditation and converting it into a memory, you can call upon this emotional state whenever you need friendly and loving comfort.

Jami Lin's Simplest Meditation

It is a good idea to tape these meditations in your own voice on a recorder. Make them easy to experience whenever the spirit moves you. If there is ever a time when you do not have access to them or you can't remember the details, enjoy my quick and favorite meditation.

Get into a meditative mood. Close your eyes and practice Color Breathing. When reaching the quiet of your empty mind, just watch the colors on the back of your eyelids. Focus on how the colors and shapes keep changing like a subtle kaleidoscope. If your mind wanders, just bring your consciousness back to the beautiful colors. I love this one and, going back to the simplicity of *Spiritual ColorAlchemy*, the two minutes are wonderfully calming and refreshing. Ahhh...

My meditations keep getting better and better and they will do the same for you the more you practice.

Get ready for tomorrow, it is the day of your ColorAlchemy INITIATION.
Plan a special day to celebrate.

My Affirmation: _____

_____

Violet Personality: The Right *To Know*

Balanced: Inspirational leader, kind and just, humanitarian, self-sacrificing, visionary, creative, strong mentally, artistic, living with divine knowledge, reduced connection to ego, lives in harmony and grace

Out of Balance: Unable to let go of anxiety and fear, arrogant, fanatical, daydreamer, depressed and unsatisfied, unable to connect with cosmic divinity

Greatest Needs
- Feeling at one with the universe
- Knowing that everything in life is purposeful

Greatest Challenges
- Relaying the *big* inspiration to other people
- Not acting like an authority

Violet's Desire: Maintain universal connection and understand one's purpose in life

Core Issues: Overpowered by the enormity of life, lack of inspiration, feels threatened by people's political, spiritual views

Musical Note & Toning Mantra: B & Aum

Planet & Zodiac: Uranus & Aquarius
Neptune & Pisces

 ≪≪≪≪≪≪ Happy Violet-Sunday ≫≫≫≫≫≫

Your ColorAlchemy INITIATION!

Connecting to the Light of God

With consistent Daily Color consciousness, by the end of each week you:

- Benefit from each color on its respective day
- Balance all holistic attributes of Mind, Body, and Spirit
- **Create, absorb, and connect to the white light of God**

So simple. So easy.

**You are living a ColorAlchemy meditation.
You are living the colors of spirit!**

*Take a deep and nourishing Violet Breath.
Place Violet Healing Hands on your Crown Chakra.
Feel the Violet Ray filling your body.*

I AM part of the universal whole. I AM linked to all cosmic energies and to the Divine. I AM peace. I AM bliss.

Violet and my Crown Chakra are limitless in my connection to God and peace. I welcome my soul purpose and spiritual guidance. I AM balanced with my spiritual self.

Amen

Affirmations

You've said Colors of Your Spirit affirmations all week. Affirmations are powerful *manifestation declarations*. The more you declare a statement as fact, the more you affirm it as fact.

Affirmations program the mind to create a positive-feedback loops and fulfil your desires. As discussed in *Mental ColorAlchemy*, positive thoughts create grooves in the mind according to the power of will. Engage Yellow and your Will Chakra. Blue clarity and your Throat Chakra support repetition to penetrate the mind and to transform thought into reality.

You are the creator of your reality.

Speaking Affirmations

Add greater power to positive manifestations.

- Speak affirmations out loud in the past tense as if you have already created your reality.
- Use your visualization skills. As if watching a movie, see yourself on the screen in your mind's eye, already living your affirmation. For example, if you want to find a life partner, visualize yourself being with him or her, doing all the things that you enjoy together.
- Believe the words as you repeatedly hear them in your mind, heart, and soul. The more you KNOW the affirmation is true, the faster the affirmations manifest into reality.
- Repeat affirmations often.
- Set a ritualistic schedule to create a positive habit.

Writing Affirmations

While I provided daily affirmations to get you started, when inspired, write your own with blessed pens and paper.

- Use the powerful words *I AM* to accept the truth of your affirmation. I AM defines self-worth, individuality, and personal commitment.
- Figure out the perfect between detailed but brief affirmations for the greatest possibility for all aspects to come true and to make them easy to remember.
- Use *amen* at the end of your affirmations.
- Remember, amen holds the energy of universal vibration, and it evolved into the powerful affirmation of divine truth: ***So be it.***

Having come this far, you passed your initial ColorAlchemy Initiation.

ColorAlchemy Initiations & Triumphs

Initiation implies a beginning. Its verb, initiate, means to begin a process. Your ColorAlchemy Initiation is an alchemical life-transforming event. It is a rite of passage.

ColorAlchemy secrets were revealed and your Initiation and your Triumphs brought you to higher levels of understanding through personal evolution. Your Initiations create fundamental and powerful transformation.

You did the work, but you are a work in progress.

Continue your ever-challenging process.

Every time you encounter a stressful situation, you are tested.
Did you change negative to a positive?

How did you handle yourself?

Make this final, and most important, concept present in your conscious thought. **Add *Initiation dialogues* to conversations with your Observer.**

Did you pass the Initiation? Were you Triumphant?

Most likely you will be tested daily, perhaps several times a day.

Here are a few examples of Initiations:

- In the car, a neighboring driver is irresponsible. Instead of raging, send a blessing to him and those around him to stay safe.

   Why fester over that which you have no control?
   How do you respond?

Did you pass your initiation?

- The grocery, post office, or bank line is excruciatingly slow. Instead of getting frustrated and releasing inpatient toxins (which you and everyone around you absorbs), practice Color Breathing.

   How do you respond?
   Experience the positive difference.

Did you pass your Initiation?

· Your boss hollers at you.

Perhaps he is taking his lousy day out on you (and he is out of control).
Maybe he is just lousy! (It is his choice to be lousy.
Lousy is a reflection of unhappiness.)
It is not about you! Don't be a mirror or pass judgement.

Don't lose your cool. Be grand!

• Screaming children in a restaurant or movie theater is clearly unpleasant.

Internalizing anger does not serve you.

Did you pass your Initiation?

How many times a day are you put to the test?
How many times are you Triumphant?

Seemingly insignificant events are not about the other guy.

**Initiations are about controlling your thoughts and reactions.
Passing Initiations is vital to mental, physical, and spiritual
health as well as to happiness. Control positive thoughts to:**

• Diminish negative moments
• Minimize stress
• Reduce toxic buildup in the body that can lead to disease
• **Provide training for the big Initiations**

Little moments monumentally add up to create happiness.

A happy moment —a happy hour—a happy day
a happy week—a happy month—a happy year
A happy life!

I pass and I fall short on Initiations every day. The keys are to:

- Remember to consciously be aware of daily *little* Initiations
- Progressively pass more than you falter
- Learn from challenges
- Commit to passing next time

Recognizing Initiations

Initiations are BETA experiences that *push your buttons,* leading to a negative response.

Did you:

- Recognize the test?
- Apply ColorAlchemy skills?
- Pass the Initiation, even if subtle and seemingly insignificant?
- Acknowledge if you:

  - Falter
    - Be proud that you recognized an Oopsie!
    - **Commit to *pass* the next time!**
  - Pass
    - Be very proud of yourself!
    - **Commit to *pass* again the next time!**

Every experience is an Initiation to celebrate your wholeness of being. This is clarity of personal wisdom and the truth in knowing your inner self.

**This truth provides sincerity, integrity, and love
in everything you think, do, and say.**

**Passing Initiations grows character of spirit that
reflects light and illuminates those around you.**

*A man's character always takes its hue from
the form and color of things around him.*
—Frederick Douglass, abolitionist and author

**Be conscious of your Initiations. Honor and respect them.
Journal your process and personal progress.**

And because you are human, a work in progress, and a seeker in the perfection of God, remember:

The light, the colors of the rainbow, and the energy of God are the inexhaustible source of transformational energy.

Self-discovery happens in places that are the most familiar when you least expect them.

Colors of your mind, body, and spirit release negativity and fear, which keeps you separated from the light. Dark energies and negativity are returned to the source and are recycled into positive rainbows of mental, physical, and emotional abundance available to everyone.

Just because our month of ColorAlchemy is complete, it doesn't mean you are finished. Continue evolving good ColorAlchemy habits and pursuing personal growth. Recommit as needed; pick up your favorite week of *ColorAlchemy Triumphs*: everything is right here.

Life's goal is being in touch with one's most personal themes: the values, ideas, styles, and colors that are the touchstones of one's individual life, its real texture and substance.
–Gloria Vanderbilt, fashion designer

Personal Initiation Celebration

In celebration of your Initiation, create a block of time alone today for a private celebration and reflection. Take a quiet walk in the park, meditate next to your favorite stream, soak in the tub with celebration candles, or bake yourself a cake. Enjoy the colorful presence of you.

During your Initiation celebration, reflect on these twenty-eight glorious days:

- What you have learned?
- How you have grown?
- How easily has ColorAlchemy become a part of your life?

Celebrate the Initiation of YOU, the ColorAlchemy of YOU!

Coming Full Circle

Let's come full circle to the place you and I started, and move into new beginnings.

- You have all the transformational *soul-purpose* ColorAlchemy tools.
- The endless supply of color is available at your command.
- The mental, physical, and spiritual benefits are immediately accessible and ready to be harnessed.

All ColorAlchemy serves you in your moment-to-moment ability to be happy in the attributes of color.

Support your individuality and enhance your personal desires.

Being a Color Alchemist is:
- **Awareness of the subtle nuances of thought and circumstances.**
- **Realizing hidden secrets with your Observer's assistance.**

You are a Color Alchemist! Be proud of yourself!

You've come so far. Imagine where you are going.

Your easiest day is always *yesterday*.
With practice, and love, pass your Initiations.
Celebrate your Daily ColorAlchemy Triumphs.

Begin where you started.

Life is a precious treasure. Colors are the jewels.

Celebrate your colors within and throughout.

May the light shine in you and be expressed through you.

As always, it is an honor and privilege...

Amen. So Be It!

And your transformation continues ...

Acknowledgments

My beloved treasures, whose love and gifts extend beyond words, space, and time.
I am forever grateful.

Joel Levy
Ardis & Burton Jacknow

Roberta Binder, James Moser, and Denny Fairchild

Pamela Ihlbrock, Besty Lampe (master publisher, who shares everything about creating first-class books), Dr. Darren Starwynn (who offers his light and genius to create beautiful skin and wellness), Oscar Perez (who edited my audio in the 4-hour ColorAlchemy Training DVD), Maryann Karinch (my agent, who loves ColorAlchemy), Peter Morrisette & Scott Booth (computer and webmaster wizards), Melanie & Robert Sacks, Susanne Murphy, Sam Holland, Steven Halpern, Steven Skinner, Paul Kane, Marion Bodner & Stefanie Taddeo (who taught me so much about professional skin care), Renae Jensen & Deana Schimmenti (who shares conscious design with the world), Karen Levy, Stephanie Roberts, Holly Ziegler, Rossy Cortes, and Carole Becker (precious editors).

End Notes:

1. Joel Achenbach, "At the Heart of All Matter: The Hunt for the God Particle," *National Geographic* (March 2008): 98.
2. Dan Campbell, *Edgar Cayce on the Power of Color, Stones, and Crystals* (New York: Warner Books, 1989), 24.
3. Ibid., 25.
4. Ibid., xiv.
5. F. Lanier, *The Rainbow Book* (San Francisco: The Fine Arts Museum of San Francisco, 1975), 103.
6. Campbell, *Edgar Cayce,* 34.
7. Sogyal Rinpoche, *The Tibetan Book of Living and Dying* (New York: Harper Collins, 1992), 168.
8. Campbell, *Edgar Cayce,* 100.
9. Ibid.
10. Plato, *Republic: Book X* (Roslyn, NY: Walter J. Black, Inc., 1942)
11. Rinpoche, *Tibetan Book,* 109.
12. Giuseppe Tucci, *The Theory and Practice of the Mandala* (Mineola, NY: Dover Publications, 1992)
13. Judith Cornell, *Mandala* (Wheaton, IL: Quest Books, 1994), 48.
14. Campbell, *Edgar Cayce,* 11.
15. Ibid.
16. Rinpoche, *Tibetan Book,* 104.
17. Ibid.
18. http://www.webcom.com/gnosis/library/marygosp.htm
19. Rinpoche, *Tibetan Book,* 101.
20. Manly P. Hall, *The Secret Teachings of All Ages* (New York: Jeremy P. Tarcher/Penguin, 2003), 302.
21. Ibid.
22. Ibid.
23. Hall, *The Secret Teachings,* 305.
24. Campbell, *Edgar Cayce,* xv.
25. Hall, *The Secret Teachings,* 311.
26. Terry Clifford, *Tibetan Buddhist Medicine and Psychiatry* (Newburyport, MA: Weiser Books, 1984), 81.
27. Cornell, *Mandala,* 103.

Graphic Credits

The artwork from Dreamstime.com and Ardis Jacknow (my mother) helped me create this beautiful book that I am so proud to share with you. They were edited to fit my design. I created the charts. All graphics from Dreamstimes artists unless noted by *.

Thank you all!

cover/title Denise Fortado, *Jami Lin
iii Vernon Wiley
iv/v Robyn Glover
vi Elen
vii Yurok Aleksandrovich
viii/ix Stasys Eidiejus
x Linda & Colin Mckie
1 William Attard Mccarthy
3 Robert Mizerek
4 Eric Gevaert
5 Roberto Anguita
6 William Attard Mccarthy,
   Roman Krochuk, Oksanaphoto,
   Socrates, Wolfgang Amri
7 Oksanaphoto
8 Trout55, Groza,
   Anette Linnea Rasmussen
9 Groza
10 Anita Nowack
11 Yanik Chauvin, Jose Manuel Diaz,
   Geoffrey Kuchera,
   Philip Sigin-lavdanski, Tommy Schultz
12-13 Cornelia Togea
14 Roxana González
15 Scott Rothstein
16 Inger Naess and ColourEnergy.com
17 Paul Van Eykelen, Petrol
18 Sergey Cherkashin, Appler
19 Ng Yin Chern
20 Scott Rothstein
21 William Attard Mccarthy
22 Sebastian Kaulitzki
24 Wd2007, Nikhil Gangavane
25 Bram Janssens
26 Rolffimages
27 Anette Linnea Rasmussen
28 Nikhil Gangavane
29 Laura Stone
30 Lynn Gladwell: boxes throughout
31 Madartists
32-33 Solarseven
34 Stephen Coburn, Solarseven,
   Tatiana nikolaevna Kalashnikova,
   Rolffimages
35 Andres Rodriguez
36 Steven Neil
36 Andrejs Pidjass
38 Scott Maxwell
39 Idrutu
40 Rewat Wannasuk: boxes throughout
42 Stasys Eidiejus
44 Nikolay Okhitin
47 Alexandr Derischin
48 Saeid Shahin Kiya
50-51 imagination
52 *Ardis Jacknow
53 Trout55
54 Dean Pennala
55 Youssouf Cader
56 *Ardis Jacknow
57 *Ardis Jacknow, Danijel Micka
58 Yanik Chauvin
60 Charon, Rodferris
61 Solarseven

63 Pixel-pizzazz
64 Assignments
65 Andres Rodriguez, Dawn Hudson
66-67 Tommy Schultz
68 Rolffimages
69 Anette Linnea Rasmussen
70-71 Roberto Zeleny
72 Vitaly Titov
73 Charles Shapiro, Thinkart
74 Nikhil Gangavane, Falk Kienas,
   Vova Pomortzeff
75 Nikhil Gangavane
76 Lucretia
77 Andrey Sobolev
78-79 Solarseven, Orlando Florin Rosu
80-81 Ramzi Hachicho
82 Sveta Gucalo
83 Cammeraydave, Dmitry Maslov,
   Saustoni, Ti_to_tito, Anette Linnea
   Rasmussen, Peter Holmqvist,
   Nikhil Gangavane, Jackson Gee
84 Solarseven
86 Florin Tirlea
87 Cammeraydave,
   Donald Sawvel: wave throughout
89 Daniela Spyropoulou
90 Robyn Glover
92 Lubov Ostrovsky, Dmitry Maslov
94 Paul Moore, Saustoni
96 Netris, Dmitry Mordolff
98 Olga Zinatova
100 Beth Ponticello , Ti_to_tito
101 Iloveotto, Stephan Zabel
103 Mayangsari
104-105 Ginesvalera
106 Rolffimages, Anette Linnea
Rasmussen
108 Fabrice Gallou, Peter Holmqvist,
Nikhil Gangavane
110 Ralf Kraft, Jackson Gee
111 stained glass by trabaz.com
112 Pixel-pizzazz
113 *Beautiful body illustrations,
   Ardis Jacknow, my mom!
114 Nasaruddin Bin abdul muttalib
115 Rolffimages
116 Aron Brand
117 Kristina Castagnola
118 Constantin Opris
122-123 Maigi
128 Yakobchuk
129 Pixel-pizzazz
130 Olga Mishyna
132-133 Shhaase
137 Alexander Fediachov
140-141 Galdzer
146 William Attard Mccarthy
152 Elen
155 Anthony Villalon, Kajetan Stozek,
   Holly Kuchera, Larisa Lofitskaya,
   Alejandro Duran, Anikasalsera,
   Guilu
158 Bryan Busovicki

159 Dzianis Kazlouski, Axel Drosta,
   Beata Jancsik
160 Feng Hui, Baloncici, Lein De Leon,
   Mario Lopes
161 Feng Hui
162 Eric Gevaert
165 Putnik, Donald Erickson, Brenda
   A. Smith, Monika Adamczyk
166 Ruta Saulyte-laurinaviciene,
   Dušanzidar, Hartemink
167 Dmitry Kutlayev, Dušan Zidar,
   Jaimie Duplass
168 Rewat Wannasuk
170 Idrutu
171 Norma Cornes
172 Elenaborodynkina
174 Gvictoria
176 Michele Perbellini
177 Irochka
179 Geoffrey Kuchera
180-181 Olga Shelego
183 Yanik Chauvin
184 Lynn Gladwell
186 Jacques Kloppers
188 Olessya Laskova
189 Stephanie Connell, Abdone
190 Joan Kerrigan
192 Terrance Emerson,
   *Charles Klotsche
193 Tibor Fazakas
194 Laura Gajewski
196 Grosa
198 Nikhil Gangavane,
   *Masaru Emoto
199 Oleg Kozlov
200 Anca Cocota
201 Dreamstime.com Agency
202 Andrey Popov
203 Shailesh Nanal, Madartists,
   schoolgirl, Shhaase, Jgroup,
   Rolffimages, Desiree Walstra
204 Rui Vale De Sousa
208 Solarseven
209-210 *yogini Andrea Pallen (model)
214 Nejron
215 Shailesh Nanal
216-217 Marek Chalupník
218-219 Micspix
220 Paul Moore
222 Madartists
224-225 Lev Dolgachov
226 Brooke Lewis
229 Jitka Saniova
235 Rolffimages
236 Yurok Aleksandrovich
237 Dannyphoto80
238-239 *Jami Lin
240 pdtnc
245 *Jami Lin
246 Jitka Saniova, Andrew Kerr
249 Fantasista
250-251 Yuri Arcurs
253 Himel

About Jami Lin

Influenced by her mother's artistic talents, Jami Lin fell in love with finger paint and color when she was three years old. Her artistry grew into a Bachelor of Design from the University of Florida, School of Architecture.

Jami has practiced interior design for more than thirty years and her special talent for color has become her trademark.

Naturally drawn to Feng Shui in 1990, Jami has written six best-selling Feng Shui books and an online home-study certification program that integrates her color expertise.

Her ColorAlchemy work helps people further unlock their greatest potential by mastering the colors of the body, mind, and spirit. Jami also specializes in technologically advanced, youth-enhancing ColorAlchemy skin care to help people look and feel their best.

Through Jami Lin's Feng Shui mastery, evolutionary ColorAlchemy program, and innovative youth-enhancing skin care, she is invited to teach internationally, and she continues to experience the colors of the world.

International conventions
Training & certification
Intimate groups
Personal coaching
Site & phone consultations

Jami loves sharing what she loves and Enhancing Your Life!

Call TODAY!
941-276-8689

Visit JamiLin.com for many complementary programs and offerings from her life-transforming and colorful passions.

much more
Color Alchemy

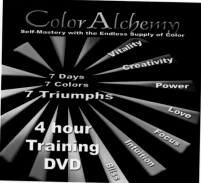

28-day online Triumphs

4-hour training DVD
Listen to Jami teach you
with more than 180 slides

Oracle Cards

Color Alchemy Facials

Youth-Enhancing Skin Care
LookYoungerOasis.com

In just one pampered hour, experience reduced and softened wrinkles along with firmer, more radiant skin. Holistic bonus benefits: often, people lose weight, pain is reduced, and energy is increased, further optimizing facial vitality.

Rejuvenating, technologically advanced treatments are customized and include:

LED Light/Photo Regeneration increases collagen and elastin, validated by NASA and Harvard Medical School clinical studies. **MicroCurrent** mimics the body's natural electrical system. "Exercising" facial muscles strengthens, contours, and tones. University of Washington, School of Medicine studies confirm increased circulation, collagen, and elastin. **Colored-Light Therapy** stimulates and renews the skin's natural-healing process. Quantum science supports the healing benefits practiced since ancient Egypt. **Acupressure**, integrated with specific healing colors, activates youth-enhancing facial points. Organs and functions connected by sage-old, body-energy meridians also benefit. **Advanced Restorative Cremes** penetrate deeply with Color Energy & Mircocurrent accelerating superior cellular regeneration.

Relax! Renew!
Revitalize!

Transform YOUR Life from

Immediate access

Personal Success Map
Includes do-it-yourself Feng Shui guide

Only ONE (of 2048) Bagua Maps is correct for YOU and your Home!

S	SW	
8. Great Professional Success, Fame & Wealth. Enhance with Water.	1. Intelligence, Academic, Scholarly, Professional Advancement. Enhance with Water or Metal.	SW
8. Great Honor & Integrity, Social Status, Spiritual Growth. Enhance with Earth.	6. Personal Ease, Graciousness, Inner Strength. Enhance with Earth. Healing Energy & Good Fortune. 2nd Best Marriage Relationships & Intimacies	
	6. Personal Power & Leadership, Distinction, and Success. Enhance with Water and/or Earth.	W
	1. Inner Knowledge, Spirituality, Self-Cultivation, Wisdom & Philosophy. Enhance with Water and/or quiet Metal. Comfort, Peace & Stability. 4th best Children Your Creations, Creativity & Spontaneity	

Face Best Directions

Activate Life Desires

Enhance Flying Stars

Your Success Map is a must-have to achieve your Feng Shui goals.
—About.com

Essential Feng Shui Advice Customized to YOU & YOUR Home!

Same personalized at-a-glance solutions that Jami provides during consultations for every room in your home

Jami Lin's books & DVDs

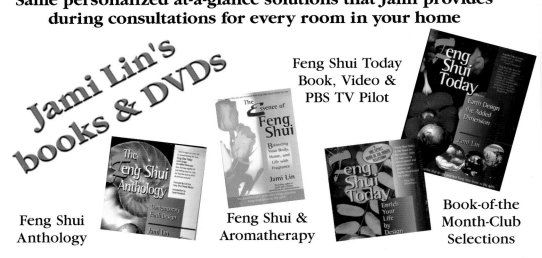

Feng Shui Today Book, Video & PBS TV Pilot

Feng Shui Anthology

Feng Shui & Aromatherapy

Book-of-the Month-Club Selections